Thanks for all you do for
the Lincoln Heritage Council
High Adventure program.

Yours in Scouting,

William F. Cass

Return to the
Summit of Scouting

Dick Fellows Photography, Philadelphia

About the Author

William F. Cass is a suburban Philadelphia business executive who spent his college summer vacations as a member of the Philmont Scout Ranch staff. His wife, Sarah, teaches history in the West Chester (PA) Area School District. They are both graduates of Washington College in Maryland. Their daughter, Holly, is a journalism major at the University of Maryland. Will, their son, is a high school student and Eagle Scout.

Mr. Cass is an active Scouter in the Chester County Council, B.S.A. He has served as a Scoutmaster and Jamboree Director, and is currently High Adventure Chairman in his council.

Return to the Summit of Scouting

William F. Cass

Wilderness Adventure Books

Library of Congress Catalog Card Number: 93-12448

ISBN: 0-923568-29-8

First Printing, April, 1993
Second Printing, December, 1993

All photographs, unless otherwise specified, from the collection of William F. Cass

Illustrations by William F. Cass

Cartography by Marjorie Nash Klein

Wilderness Adventure Books
Post Office Box 17
Davisburg, Michigan 48350

Cass, William F., 1942-
    Return to the summit of scouting : a mid-life journey back to Philmont / William F. Cass.
    p. cm.
Includes bibliographical references.
    ISBN 0-923568-29-8 : $12.95
    1. Philmont Scout Ranch. 2. Wilderness survival--New Mexico.
[1. Philmont Scout Ranch. 2. Boy Scouts. 3. Outdoor life--New Mexico.] I. Title
HS3313.Z65C37   1993
796.54'22--dc20   93-12448

Manufactured in the United States of America

For those "lean, green, hikin' machines" and the rest of the Philmont Staff—past, present, and future. But, especially for my "Scouting widow" wife, Sarah and our daughter and son, Holly and Will.

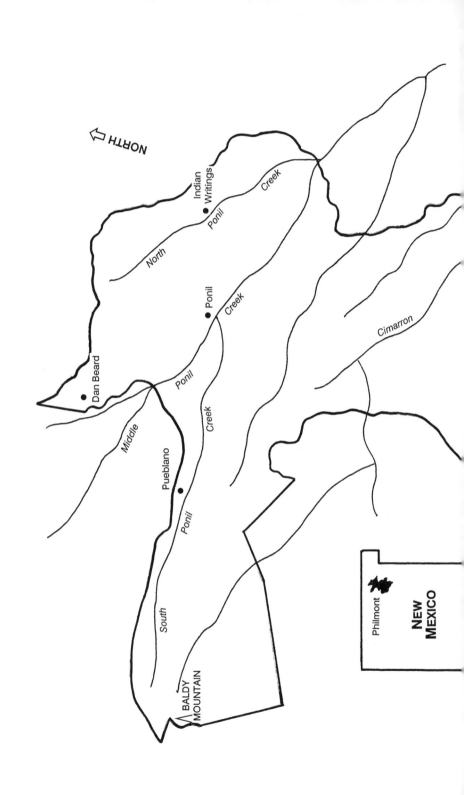

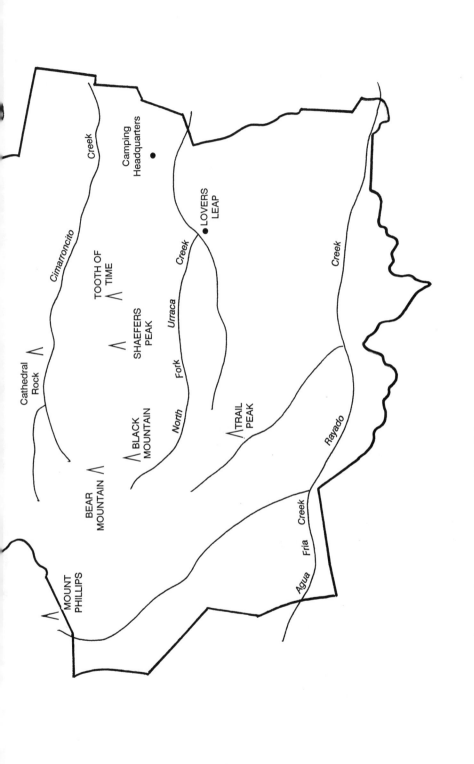

Contents

Part II   **The Upward Trail**

Part III   **The Return**

Epilogue
Suggested Reading

About Philmont Scout Ranch

Philmont Scout Ranch, located in the Sangre de Cristo Range of the Rockies, is the crown jewel of the Boy Scout High Adventure Program. With one hundred, thirty-seven thousand acres and a summer attendance nearing twenty thousand Scouts, Explorers, and their adult leaders, Philmont is the largest youth camp in the world. "Camp" is not an adequate description, since Philmont is a working ranch, and consists of hundreds of miles of trails and a series of back country, staffed and unstaffed camps. These camps offer a variety of programs emphasizing the southwest and its history. These programs include logging, mining, rock climbing, conservation, Indian lore, trapping, archeology, homesteading, etc.

Philmont is a challenging experience for youth and adult alike. Each expedition crew, consisting of seven to twelve persons including at least two adults, typically spends eleven days backpacking through Philmont's mountains, canyons, and foothills.

In the course of their expedition, crews backpack from fifty to over one hundred miles, and climb to heights nearing thirteen thousand feet. All of the skills acquired during a Scout's early training are utilized to the fullest extent at Philmont. A young person has every right to be proud of completing a Philmont expedition, which is as challenging mentally as it is physically.

Philmont Scout Ranch was given to the Boy Scouts of America as two separate gifts in 1938 and 1941 by Waite Phillips, a wealthy Oklahoma oilman.

Foreword

What is the magic of Philmont that draws and attracts an overflowing capacity of campers year after year—and motivates America's finest young and older adults to serve on the summer staff?

Is it the beauty and majesty of the land—those lofty peaks, lush mountain parks, and crystal clear streams?

Is it being a real honest-to-goodness ranch with cowboys, cattle, and horses?

Is it "Where the buffalo roam, and the deer and antelope play?"

Is it the exciting programs in the mountain camps that have been honed and fine-tuned over the years?

Is it being part of an elite staff—the finest in the United States of America, that provides the logistical support and the delivery of the program?

And what is that magic of Philmont that motivated William "Bill" Cass to write this delightful and heartwarming book, *Return to the Summit of Scouting?*

Bill Cass was a part of that dedicated Philmont staff for three summers. He served as program counselor at Beaubien, as one of Mr. Dunn's rangers, and finally as director of Abreu. He thoroughly enjoyed these rich and varied experiences.

A quarter century later Bill Cass returned to Philmont as an advisor with a crew from his adopted hometown, West Chester, Pennsylvania. His son, Will, was in that crew. This rounded out the "continuum" that he describes in his book:

"...most people view Philmont as a camping experience for Scouting youth, which it certainly is. The longer view is that the Ranch is a continuum, a pyramidal, three-tiered experience with the camper stage as the foundation. I had enjoyed the second stage, that of staffer, and now was experiencing what was probably the most rewarding experience, that of being along for the ride as a crew advisor."

Although Bill Cass did not have the Philmont experience as a Scout, he received an understanding and appreciation vicariously through the reactions of his son, Will, and the other members of the crew. This was, as he said, the most rewarding experience and one that is shared by many dads who come to Philmont as advisors. This is a mountain-top experience where mutual respect and pride are developed between father and son.

Bill Cass writes with clarity and enthusiasm. He relates the events, emotions, and reactions not as past events, but as occurring now, today, and tomorrow. *Return to the Summit of Scouting* is a book that will have widespread appeal among staffers, advisors, and campers—past, present, and future. It is a good companion piece to *Magic Mountains* by the late Minor Huffman.

This book could well be dedicated to Elliott "Chope" Phillips, the sole survivor of Philmont's donors, Waite and Genevieve. How proud they would have been to know that the half million mark in attendance was reached on the golden anniversary in 1988.

Thank you, Waite and Genevieve Phillips, for your gift of Philmont, and thank you, Bill Cass, for sharing your beautiful memories in *Return to the Summit of Scouting*.

Joe Davis
Director of Camping,
Philmont Scout Ranch
1965-1975

Acknowledgments

Any successful Scouting experience invariably involves parental support and the leadership provided by a devoted Scoutmaster. My parents were always there when needed. They provided everything from equipment and encouragement to the countless car rides to troop meetings and sessions with merit badge counselors when I was a young Boy Scout.

Mr. Kenneth W. Derr, former Scoutmaster of Troop 40 in the old Lancaster County Council, provided the leadership and opportunities to grow in Scouting. Without the foundation provided by parents and Scoutmaster, the Philmont experience documented in the following pages would probably never have happened.

This narrative also would not have been possible without the confidence of my superiors at the Ranch—the Directors of Camping; their Assistant, Buzz Clemmons; and Chief Ranger Mr. Clarence Dunn. They placed me in very rewarding positions and in the company of as fine a staff as could be assembled in any Scouting endeavor.

Joe Davis and Ned Gold read the manuscript, and made valuable suggestions for its improvement.

My wife, Sarah, and our daughter and son, Holly and Will, were most encouraging during the writing of the manuscript. They were also tolerant of an absentee husband and father who would disappear to his den for hours on end when there were other matters that probably required more immediate attention than being glued to a word processor.

Nor would this chronicle of high adventure have been possible without the principals at Wilderness Adventure Books, Clayton Klein and Erin Sims Howarth. Their interest in the manuscript, suggestions, and professional editing are deeply appreciated.

Introduction

This memoir is about high adventure at Philmont Scout Ranch where I spent several wonderful summers on staff. This story did not occur last year. It happens every summer and will always happen at "The Ranch" as it is known by those of us who have been lucky enough to serve there.

This journal is a story of young men growing up and bridging that gap from late adolescence into manhood. It describes some of the adventure that helps guide the next generation into paths that will lead to good citizenship and parenthood. This book's pages are also a tribute to the many professional Scouters who have devoted their lives to the ideals and traditions of Boy Scouting.

I was always taught to avoid the first person singular in writing. But, to a large extent, this is *my* journal, so the use of "I" is unavoidable. These were my experiences—those I would later draw upon to fight fear in troubled skies, to build a family with the young lady of my dreams, to pursue business goals, and to eventually keep the faith by returning to Scouting. In another sense, this is not my journal. It is *our* journal—the alumni of Philmont's staff. My story is not unique; I am sure there were many others who served longer and had more exciting assignments.

This is also a story of renewal, about going back, not just to Philmont's trails, but also to what those trails represent. They say it is better the second time around. They also say that nothing endures. The truth is that you will never know until you journey back to whatever your special summit is. May your trail be as rewarding as mine was.

Part I

South Country

South

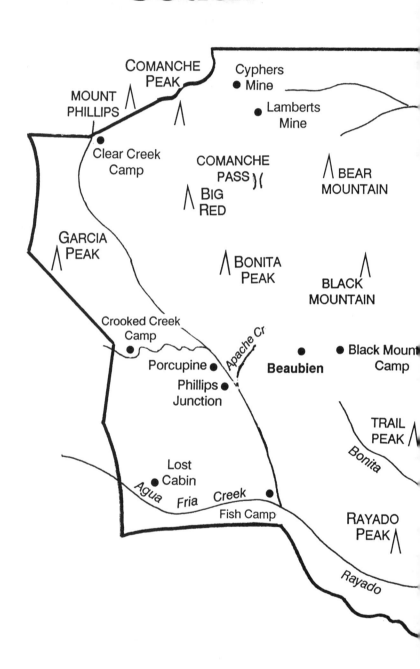

Country

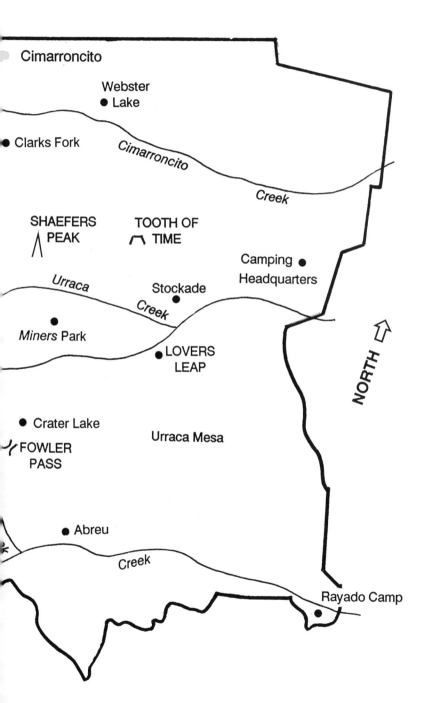

Cimarroncito

Webster
● Lake

● Clarks Fork

Cimarroncito

Creek

SHAEFERS
∧ PEAK

TOOTH OF
⌢ TIME

Camping ●
Headquarters

Urraca

Stockade
●

● *Creek*

●
Miners Park

●LOVERS
LEAP

NORTH ⇧

● Crater Lake

Urraca Mesa

⋊⃮FOWLER
PASS

● Abreu

Creek

Rayado Camp
●

Scatter

As dawn broke above the campsite on the sixth morning of backpacking, sky conditions brought little reason for enthusiasm. This day was to be one of our busiest, so we needed a good one. I shuddered to think how our Trail Peak climb, horseback ride, conservation project, and chuck wagon dinner would go if we had the previous day's rain. The sky was completely overcast. It was reminiscent of a dreary, late November morning back east. Where was the deep blue sky and pine-scented breeze that heralded the onset of another sunny, Philmont day? Well, at least it wasn't raining—yet.

We had to get an early start since the horseback ride was at one P.M. and the climb up to the old Army bomber wreck on top of Trail Peak and back was billed as a four-hour show, including lunch.

By now, we were "old hands," wise in the ways of Philmont camping, thanks in large part to the excellent job our ranger had done. Our crew chief had a penchant for snoozing, so I shook his tent vigorously. He soon had the bear bag crew heading up the hill to get breakfast. By 8:30 we had the campsite buttoned up, and were walking past Trappers Lodge on our way down the Bonita Valley for the first serious climb of our expedition.

Our crew had been formed only about five months before as one of eleven groups from Chester County Council in southeastern Pennsylvania. It is a small council in terms of total numbers, but a very active one, as the total of eleven crews implies. We were the last crew to form, and the only one containing Scouts from two different troops. The other ten crews were of the single troop variety. Excepting the occasional minor squabble over setting the hiking pace on the trail, our two groups had meshed nicely. I had wondered if we would have any difficulties over camp duties, but there had been none.

Our hopes were lifting as the cloud base was rising. The top of Trail Peak had been obscured by clouds when we left Beaubien, but after rounding a bend in the jeep trail, its crest was just visible. Below the crest was a clearing from which dull silver portions of the bomber wreckage were visible. It looked like a long way up there. On paper though, it seemed like an easy climb. The base was about nine thousand feet, and the top of the peak was around 10,200 feet. What would seem to be a piece of cake was not, since we were only six days removed from suburban Philadelphia, where the elevation was barely four hundred feet above sea level.

It was warmer than the previous day, but we still needed jackets. Within a half hour of leaving Beaubien we came to a great curve in the jeep road where several of Philmont's finest cattle were grazing. A cow and her calf were blocking our way. This was initially perplexing to some of our boys whose only

contact with the bovine world was the dairy case at a suburban
supermarket. Having grown up on a farm, I gave old bosse a pat
on the flank. She turned and gazed at me with one great, placid
brown eye, batted at the flies with her tail, and ambled on to the
greener side of the road. She was a good-looking specimen. Not
taller than the Holsteins I helped milk as a kid while living on my
grandparent's dairy farm, but much wider. This Hereford bore the
unmistakable sign of the Philmont cattle brand—something that
had just appeared on several of our hikers' boots the day before.

Within a few minutes, we came to a well-weathered sign that
said "Trail Peak." Appropriately, the sign was angled up at thirty
degrees. In starting the trail, it seemed more like forty-five
degrees. Although it was still cool, the absence of switchbacks
hastened the removal of our jackets. This was much more like
hiking back east where the humidity prevented perspiration from
evaporating. After about forty-five minutes of climbing through
dense woods, we encountered the first signs of wreckage—a bent
access door, mangled filter, and then a dented wingtip. Although
the trail was becoming much more rocky, we still encountered a
variety of flowers and some striking, fire-engine red mushrooms.
While sighting pieces of wreckage stimulated our desire to get to
the top, our lack of altitude acclimation was catching up with us.
Even with the few switchbacks that had started to appear, we
were taking more breathers as we stopped to look at the widely
scattered pieces of wreckage.

As we came across one of the three-bladed propellers, we
knew we were getting close. My son, Will, and one of the boys
from the other troop, Jeff Mann, were aviation-minded, and
paused upon the rusting metal. The prop still had the hub
attached, but was badly bent. We were nearing the top, or at least
the ridge line since much more sky was visible. During one of the
breathers, I paused near what appeared to be part of a hatch door.
Most of the debris was bare aluminum in color, but here and
there were patches of badly faded olive drab. Usually, it was a

dull yellow. Had the wartime camouflage paint faded and been weathered away or were we looking at the primer? After a minute or so, I caught my breath and pushed on. Almost immediately, we came out onto a clearing that held one of the great wings. It turned out to be the only main member of the bomber that remained intact. After examining the starboard wing closely, several of us sat above it, and looked at what scenery was available.

The view to the east and north was obscured by a solid wall of cloud that was threatening to envelop us at any moment. To the west was the Mount Phillips massif. Black and Bear Mountains were intermittently visible as the clouds billowed and shifted back and forth. The view to the south was striking in an eerie sort of way. Directly below us was Bonita Cow Camp, and snaking westward was the grassy valley that we had descended earlier that morning. Looking down at Bonita Cow Camp brought back a line from Bill Mauldin's *Up Front*. His characters, Willie and Joe, are on top of a mountain looking out on the vista below. Willie was saying something to the effect of, "Gee! There we wuz, and now here we are." We really had covered some territory that morning since the cabin at Bonita Cow was nothing more than a dot at the edge of a distant meadow. Above the flanks of Burn Peak was La Grulla Ridge, which occasionally was bathed in bright sunlight. We read the memorial to one of the bomber's crew members, a Kansas City lieutenant who had been very active in Scouting. After taking the inevitable pictures of our crew, we broke out the squeeze-cheese, crackers, and beef sticks. This was not our favorite lunch, but considering how quickly we had ascended the peak, anything would have hit the spot.

The view to the west was holding me spellbound. Big Red and Comanche Peak would be in sight one minute, and gone the next. The army crew that had flown to their deaths on Trail Peak had certainly never seen those mountains. In fact, they had missed hitting several peaks around here since Trail Peak is a couple of thousand feet below the highest peaks. Renewed after our lunch, most of us walked up to the summit, which is only a few minutes away from the wreckage. The view was much the same. Unfortunately, a foggy curtain hovered just below us, eliminating what must have been a spectacular view of the Tooth of Time and Camping Headquarters. Although we were disappointed, at least we weren't getting rained upon. Also, we had seen some of Philmont's greatest peaks from a vantage point not seen by many campers.

"Whoa! Freeze," I whispered with my right hand extended behind me as we descended the trail from the crest. Just a few feet from us was a bird that looked like a small cousin of our eastern grouse. This bird was different though, since it was gray all over. It had to be a rock ptarmigan, and had we been here a few months earlier, it probably would have been colored white to blend in with the snow. We filed past, and the partridge-like bird seemed totally unconcerned with our presence.

We had been taking our time, and a glance at my watch suggested that we had best pick up the pace. We were due for a horseback ride in less than an hour.

"How much farther is it?"

It was the perennial question of groups ascending. One bunch of Buckeyes was relieved to know that they were less than fifteen minutes from the wreck. The Virginians we met at the base were dismayed to learn that it was "rough, real rough, and you've got a good hour to go." It was perhaps not quite that bad, but all mountains assumed a more rugged dimension once they had been climbed. The one dimension we were running out of was time, since we had an appointment with Beaubien's equestrian experts in less than a half hour. I wasn't in a hurry since I wasn't planning on riding, so I told the crew to head back at their own pace. This let several of us get back to Beaubien at a more leisurely stride.

We came across some turkeys down in the Valley, and then

there were the ubiquitous ground squirrels. I wondered what their average life span was, since their pace of life was so frenetic. As we passed the Bonita corral, Will and I had fallen behind our little group. This would be one of the great treats of a Philmont expedition—a little "father-son bonding." Will and I had the usual disagreements as he had been growing up, but we also had shared some really great times together. Beyond Scouting we had enjoyed lacrosse, hunting, fishing, aviation, and several other activities. But we had never shared "adversity" quite on the Philmont scale. Adversity is part of the Philmont mystique. It comes in many guises, and for us, it had been the weather for the past twenty-four hours. The weather a Philmont crew will experience is very much the luck of the draw. Some crews, especially our brethren who headed north, got far worse than we experienced. We had been soaked the day before, but Will was holding up. In many ways he and his fellows were beating his old man at this game. I never saw him seriously out of breath. After adjusting his pack straps on the second day, he seemed to have no problems at all in carrying his cargo. I was immensely proud of him as we rounded the last bend by the Beaubien horse corral.

Although I had grown up on a farm, I had lost any enthusiasm for riding horses. Besides, I was our crew's official photographer. I busied myself taking pictures of the pre-trot lecture, donning of the helmets, and the muddy departure of two crews worth of suburban horsemen.

Beaubien was our layover camp. If we had to have poor weather, this was the place to have it. At least there were hot showers, and opportunities to relax. Relaxation was definitely in order considering the morning's exertions. One curse of my life has been a near total inability to catnap during daylight hours even when exhausted. So, unlike some of my compatriot advisors who were snoozing, I opted for a leisurely walk around Beaubien. It was such an idyllic place. The only item that seemed out of context was the set of solar panels way up in the meadow. They struck me as an unpleasant intrusion of modern technology in a place that should have retained a more rustic air. The antenna on the cabin seemed out of place as well. However, I wouldn't complain if we needed an emergency radio transmission for medical help. I also wasn't grumbling as I showered away some grime in Beaubien's nice, warm showers made possible by the skyward-gaping panels.

It was easy to lose track of time as I wandered around Beaubien's meadow edges, its chapel, and the trails that lead to secluded campsites. The look on young faces returning from the horseback ride seemed to say that they were ready to turn in early once the chuckwagon dinner was over. They were all looking forward to the dinner after a chilly afternoon in the saddle. The chuckwagon promised a ranger style cobbler, a stew complete with chewable meat, and something hot to drink. Our contribution to the cooking crew headed for the chuckwagon program area around four in the afternoon. The rest of us—cups, spoons, and plates in hand—followed an hour and a half later. Everybody had a poncho tucked into his back pocket. Experience had taught us well.

As we formed the dinner line, the rains started. This was a mountain rain, and not the dishwater-temperature pitter patter easterners might be used to in the summer. Fortunately, our crew had arrived early, and managed to find shelter among the trees before the worst of it hit. The food was enjoyable, but with its warmth came the realization that my boots, which were finally showing signs of drying out, were now taking giant steps backward into a new, soggier age.

We finished the remaining pieces of cobbler, and headed back to our campsite where there was some respite from the rain. At least our tents were high and dry. Before long, I donned my poncho again, and headed down to the porch of Trappers Lodge for the advisors coffee hour. It was only 7:30 P.M. but most of Crew 11 was tucked in behind tent flaps talking about their mothers' cooking or what they were going to do once they got back to civilization. The rain was slackening as I brushed past the tall spruce trees that guarded the porch of Trappers Lodge. By force of habit, I had brought my camera along thinking I might get some casual shots of other poorly shaven, chilled Scouters on the porch. Quite unpredictably, the clouds were parting. Lo and behold, the sun was breaking through here and there. As I was watching a couple of kids come back from cleanup duty at the chuckwagon, I was the first to see something quite unexpected.

It was a spectacular rainbow whose left arc was descending into the horizon just above the horse corral. Then another segment appeared touching down along the ridge line above the chapel. Finally, we saw the entire arc itself. People were dashing for cameras everywhere. Even my wide angle couldn't catch the entire rainbow, which was now turning into a full *double* rainbow. What a treat! I hadn't seen one in eons.

The horizon to the east was clearing, and the clouds to the west were breaking so quickly that I thought we might be in for a nice sunset, or at least whatever the ridges surrounding Beaubien's high meadow setting would allow.

The rainbow proved to be the good omen we needed. The campfire had been cancelled the night before, but tonight the Beaubien staff would put on its show for us. The coffee hour broke up, and advisors wended their way back to campsites to have crew leaders alert everyone to the campfire. By the time I got back to the campfire area, a respectable fire was starting to blaze. Paul Ebner, who had also put on the chuckwagon dinner, bore a striking resemblance to the country singer Johnny Cash. They shared a deep, rich voice and commanding presence. Paul welcomed us and broke into an opening song. Then there was some joking and story-telling by other members of the staff.

There was a scary story about the disappearance of a Philmont Horse Department Manager, Boss Sanchez. Then Paul sang what we were learning was a staff favorite, "Running with the Wind." During the Sanchez story and Paul's singing, my mind was drifting into reverse gear—a backward daydreaming that took me to a different Philmont and another summer long, long ago.

Paul continued to sing, but the music I was listening to was not his. The voice in my mind was that of Jim Talley, and the song was "The Master's Call." Boss Sanchez may have been the stuff of ghost tales to Vern Fails who was telling the story, but the Boss was a real, live person to me. I knew that he had retired to Raton only a few years ago, and had not disappeared somewhere on the upper reaches of Burn Peak. As the story was being told, it was easy to picture myself in front of the fire, telling older stories about Cimarron's raw, frontier days, or of settlers crossing Palo Flechado Pass in the middle of a blizzard.

Beaubien revisited. Black Mountain Camp is below the end of the rainbow on the other side of Bonita Ridge

The campfire in my mind's eye was not opened by our current host, but by Paul Dinsmore, who presided over a much younger Beaubien. In many it was the same Beaubien though—Trappers Lodge was essentially unchanged, the corral bunkhouse looked identical, and the old commissary still stood, albeit for a different use. The staff was almost double in size, but they too had come from Scout troops and Explorer posts from all over America. The campfire would wind down as "The Philmont Hymn" was sung against a backdrop of glowing embers. The song affected everybody as it had stirred me and my fellow Beaubien staffers from a past Philmont era.

These reveries had been occurring constantly over the past few days. Their images were incredibly fresh. So intense is a Philmont staff experience that even the smallest details become locked into memory banks forever.

As the campfire broke up, I thought about the college kids who were running Beaubien. They were majoring in engineering, environmental science, and business administration among other pursuits. They had come from big cities and small towns. They were probably not that much different from the eight of us who passed a wonderful summer bringing high adventure to thousands of Scouts. What brought this new generation of staffers to Beaubien? The same thing that brought me to the Ranch, I suppose. That set me off on another journey into the past—the trail I followed to Philmont.

◆ ◆ ◆

I had decided that there was a better way to spend the summer than working for the Pennsylvania state roads commission or at Camp Chiquetan, the Lancaster County (PA) Council camp. It suddenly struck me that I might apply to Philmont for a summer job. I happened to be in Lancaster one day during Christmas break, and stopped into the council office to ask about it.

Surprisingly, they actually had some applications. It was almost a spur-of-the-moment decision. I didn't know much about Philmont beyond what I had seen in brochures or *Boys' Life*, since I had never been there as a camper. Assessing my capabilities, I figured that teaching marksmanship or working as a nature counselor made the most sense.

I had enjoyed Scouting immensely when I was in elementary school and later in high school, and had gotten a lot out of the experience. Our troop setting was ideal: a small town, tremendous support from the community, and a devoted Scoutmaster, Mr. Kenneth Derr. In troop meetings we had talked about Philmont, but our focus was directed toward our own council camp or the troop's lodge. It was situated on an acre of land owned by our sponsor, the local American Legion post.

I didn't have the foggiest idea what rangers were, and starting as a camp director wasn't realistic. It would be a couple of years before I would even be old enough for a director's job, so I checked off rifle range, wilderness survival, and nature. I mailed the application after getting the Council Executive's recommendation, and forgot the whole matter until an official-looking envelope arrived just before spring break. I could see through the envelope, and figured I had the job because there was a line that said "signature" and "date signed."

Inside was a contract calling for me to be Program Counselor in "Riflery-Archery" at Carson-Maxwell. Pay was $165 per month, including room, board, and ground squirrels. So I signed on, and by mid-May a staff roster arrived along with a revised contract saying that I was to teach Hunter Safety at a place called Beaubien. As it turned out, the last minute switch was an extraordinary piece of good fortune that became the foundation of a wonderful, three year staff experience.

The school year was winding down. It was late spring on Maryland's Eastern Shore where I was an Economics major at Washington College in Chestertown. Lacrosse, fraternity activities, and late night studying would be giving way to a decidedly different routine.

I had not yet learned to appreciate the Eastern Shore with its lazy, wide rivers, pine woods and flat horizons. It was home country in one respect though: farming was big business. While the Shore agriculture was dominated by corn, soybeans, and wheat, my roots were in the dairy country of northern Pennsylvania. It would be several more years before the sailing and waterfowling offered by the Shore became passions. Nor would I develop an appreciation for the architecture and colonial heritage of places such as Easton or Chestertown. Like most of my fraternity brothers, I was interested in having a good time, and studying enough to keep parents, the academic dean, and my major advisor reasonably content.

I finished my last exam, said goodbye to friends, and headed home hoping that the decision to work so far away was a wise move. I would not be disappointed, and the spur-of-the-moment idea of working at Philmont ultimately proved to be one of the brightest thoughts I have ever had.

The train seemed the best way to get out there, so I sent my steamer trunk by rail to a dot on the map named Raton. A few days later, I caught the night train to Chicago from the railroad station in Lancaster. While the Pennsylvania railroad would be passing into history in the future, I was then passing through some of Pennsylvania's finest scenery as we sped into the darkness. After stopping in Harrisburg, we crossed the broad Susquehanna River, and headed on toward the towns that coal and steel built: Altoona, Johnstown, and Pittsburgh.

After a night of not so deep sleep, I woke not to see the jagged horizon of the Alleghenies limned in the moonlight, but instead fields of Buckeye wheat. This was later followed by Hoosier corn and lastly by the industrial suburbs of Chicago. By early evening, we were pulling into center city Chicago.

I had to catch a cab from Union Station to Dearborn Station

to ride the Santa Fe. In later years I would often think about Dearborn Station as I waited for flights at O'Hare. The two places were similar in the sense that they were the crossroads of America. At one point, I was flying to Chicago once a week, and caught up in the inevitable delays and cancellations that provided me with every opportunity for "people watching." Observing the travelers, I would try to guess where they might be from, where they were going, and what they did for a living. They were all there: buttoned down businessmen from Boston, Texans in their hats and boots, vacationers returning from the south, and sales managers. There were computer engineers with beards and glasses, and college students on their way to jobs in Yellowstone, Yosemite, and—Philmont.

I was looking up at the departure information display when I became aware of somebody else looking over my shoulder. I looked around to find a faceful of miniature poodle.

"Where ya goin' kid?"

"Raton."

"Great place, we go down there for the races all the time. You go to the races?"

"Uh, well no, actually. Never even been to a race. What do they race there, cars?"

"Naw, horses. Santa Anita it ain't, but we like it anyway."

"Well, hope your luck holds up, Mister."

With that, I excused myself from this rather odd encounter. The speaker was instantly recognizable as one of television's supporting actors. He had a gravelly voice with a hint of a New York accent. He usually played lesser roles in comedies or was cast a gangster's sidekick. He was dressed in a black suit, charcoal shirt, and an outrageous pink tie. The carnation in his lapel was the final touch. He looked as though he had just stepped off an "Untouchables" shooting set without having changed his costume. His "associate" (friend, valet, or bodyguard) was holding the pooch at shoulder level, and was wearing similar attire. The bodyguard was well over six feet tall, and looked like he had just come from Muscle Beach. And this bizarre pair wondered if Joe College in a Scout uniform was a regular at the two-dollar window!

Dearborn Station was indeed the rally point for every Philmont staffer in the Midwest. There was no question about who was headed for Philmont: Scout uniforms were everywhere. Here and there, a few clusters of veteran staffers were getting reacquainted, but most of us were first timers. But as part of the Scouting brotherhood, we weren't strangers. The long socks and green shirts might draw ridicule from young people of another age, but then we were the focus of approving glances. However, some observers, with an occasional double take, probably were thinking we were a bit old to be in the "Good Turn Daily" and "Be Prepared" circuit.

Soon we were getting acquainted with our fellow staffers. Jim Phipps, from Mattoon, Illinois, was on his way to a program job at Olympia. This would be his first and last Philmont season before heading onto the Army Corps of Engineers. Tom Sothard was headed for Indian Writings after having left Benton Harbor, Michigan, that afternoon. Stu Heberg would be teaching program at Abreu. His was a short ride from the suburbs, as was John Lussenhop's. John was a nature specialist, and had come prepared for the job. He was carrying a small glass case full of some ferocious looking little bugs. They would pale in comparison to some of Philmont's beetles. Before long, we were getting aboard the El Cap, which would take us into the setting sun. We congregated in the lounge car, where it seemed we couldn't find any two guys assigned to the same camp. We continued our getting acquainted session until midnight, when most of us drifted back to our seats to catch some sleep. The night owls stayed up to see the Mississippi crossing, but for me, sleep beckoned. It came easily due to the lack of sleep the night before.

We awoke to more flatlands, but they were different. In

contrast to the verdant East and Midwest, we were now in land that looked almost parched. Gone were the many little whistle-stops of Ohio and Indiana. We were traveling for long stretches at a time without stopping or even seeing towns. One landmark came and went. It was Dodge City, but Mr. Dillon and Miss Kitty weren't on the main drag, and the Long Branch Saloon had long since passed into history. Dodge looked like a small modern city complete with paved sidewalks, gas stations, and grain elevators. We were all straining to see the livery stable or Doc Adams' shingle, but like Chester Good and Festus, they were just another part of commercial television's fantasy. As it would turn out, most of Philmont's back country staffers would find that the return to a pre-electronic age, even for a few months, would be both refreshing and reassuring.

With our newly found friends, we went in small groups to the dining car for breakfast, and saw more views of the broad prairie. The monotony of the prairie was getting to me. I missed the reassurance of hills on the horizon. It also occurred to me that the people who lived on the great plains probably liked the feeling of freedom, and would feel hemmed in if they had grown up where I did. I had lived in small towns in northern Pennsylvania as a kid. Waking up in the morning, I could look out my bedroom window and see the high cliffs on the other side of the Susquehanna River. I spent time with my grandparents in the small hamlet of Rome, named because it was in the same latitude as its Italian namesake, and it too was surrounded by seven hills.

"Look, there they are, the Rockies."

It was Tom Sothard who saw them first. Look as I might, I couldn't see anything. I thought Tom was seeing a mirage. When I finally saw them, they looked like they had a layer of cloud on top. It couldn't have been snow, I naively thought, because it was early June. In the next couple of hours, I learned what distance and altitude were all about, since it took several hours of "clackety-clacking" before we were in the mountains.

The Santa Fe was speedy in the flats, but not in the mountains. We came up over Raton Pass, which I learned was more properly pronounced "ruh-tone," and in short order we descended into the town of Raton. Not many people got on the train, but plenty got off.

Philmont was prepared for the onslaught, and had both trucks and buses ready for us. There were a few moments of panic when nobody could find the previously shipped steamer trunks and duffel bags. The unlocking of a storage room door revealed a small mountain of personal gear that we quickly muscled onto a waiting truck. Then we were off on the fifty-two-mile road down to Cimarron, and the beginning of a landmark summer.

First impressions of Cimarron were a bit underwhelming. There were the main drag, a lumber mill, and a few retail establishments. They were dominated by what appeared to be a general store called "Lambert's." How well we would come to know the place and its soda fountain in the years ahead. After passing a few more commercial establishments, we turned left on the Philmont road and went past "Villa Philmonte," which was definitely not underwhelming. The other striking sight was the buffalo herd in the buffalo "pasture." I was used to a pasture of several acres, but here it was several *thousand* acres. It was full of those great hunchbacked, shaggy beasts that most of us had only seen in books or cowboy movies.

The other sure sign that we were in different territory was the magpies hanging around on the fences of the buffalo pasture. The magpie looks like a small crow with the tail of a kite and prominent white splotches on its wings. Its personality, hybrid for sure, combines the neurotic aspects of that southerner, the mockingbird, and the chronic scolding of the catbird. To top it off, the magpie is every bit the showman that the bluejay is.

Then the bus turned right, and went beneath the Philmont gateway. That first sight of the Ranch is burned into the minds of every staffer. The Tooth of Time, or as we called it, "the solar molar of contiguous movement," dominates the scene in an oblique way. Only the east side and its ridge are visible from camping headquarters. Urraca Mesa, in all of its flat-topped glory, was in headquarters' southwestern quadrant. Looming in the background were Trail Peak and Black Mountain, which served to remind us of higher peaks out of sight. On a clear day, which was nearly every day early in the season, we could make out a fort snuggled in the foothills between the Mesa and the far reaches of the Tooth Ridge. It was Philmont's Stockade camp, the reconstruction of a frontier army fort.

After checking in, we received our staff packets with their instructions and training timetables. We then went through the health lodge and headed for Tent City. "City" was the right word for it. I had never seen so many tents in one place—not even in pictures of World War II Army training bases.

Philmont had the training routine pretty well nailed down, although I still didn't know who I would be working with. I had their names from the roster, but had not yet connected the names with faces. That would all be taken care of that evening, at the opening dinner. We got more briefings after dinner when introductions were made. Paul Dinsmore was introduced as Beaubien's director along with the other camp directors and department heads. After leaving the dining hall, we met in small groups to get acquainted. Paul turned out to be a real Philmont veteran with a commanding voice, a noticeable limp, and steel blue eyes that let you know immediately he was in charge. His assistant, John Dimalanta, was an ebullient Californian from Santa Barbara. Already a politician, John was the captain of his football team and president of his college class. Paul and "Dimalanty" were no strangers, and had demonstrated their capacity for teamwork as the Black Mountain staff of the previous summer. It was a quantum leap to go from a two-man camp to an important center like Beaubien in just one year.

In addition to the Hunter Safety program, Beaubien offered western lore, including a formal campfire. This dual rating was carried by Jim Talley. Tall, dark, and eminently urbane for a young man, he looked the part of cowboy and troubadour combined.

Our other "Jim" was Jimmy Money, the commissary man. Built like a bear, Jimmy was a linebacker on his football team, and hailed from Portales, New Mexico. He was a gentle giant, and would give you the shirt right off his back. What we really needed was a true Southerner to counterbalance all these territorials and the lone Yankee on the staff.

That southerner emerged from the crowd, sauntered up and said, "Ah'm Freddy Blair. Pleased ta meetch'yall." Central casting couldn't have done a better job. Beaubien's quartermaster was the rough-edged essence of the young Volunteer. Freddy, another football player, was a student at Middle Tennessee State College. His most prominent feature was an extraordinary jaw that had "determination" written all over it. That mandible, the freckles, red hair, and thumbs stuck in belt loops suggested that Freddy knew what he was talking about when he declared that he missed his "chittlins," black-eyed peas, and fatback.

Oddly enough, two of the Beaubien staffers were missing. Our cook and packer couldn't be accounted for. Paul mentioned that unlike us, they were regular, year-round staff. We would meet them later.

Meanwhile, the first couple of days zipped by in a series of briefings and orientation sessions. We became more closely acquainted with other members of our immediate staff group. *Everybody* got trained in the ways of the Ranch, and in one's own specialty. In my case, that meant getting together with all of the other range officers. Our instructor was an NRA professional for whom pronunciation of "Beaubien" seemed nearly impossible. It came out like "Bow-Bane." He had one of those Smokey Bear type field hats on, and had the neck string drawn tightly around his throat. Maybe that's why anything beyond two syllables was difficult. However, we got along famously, and most of this group would serve Philmont for several years to come. Carter Rilla was as round as Ron Price was tall. Iuka, MS gave us the soft-spoken Wayne Woods, who, with Ron, would head to the northern sector to work at Pueblano. Wayne's path and mine would cross again in several years, but for then he was just one more face and voice in a stream of new acquaintances.

On our third morning, all of the Hunter Safety instructors piled into the back of a truck, and headed for Cimarroncito's rifle and shotgun ranges. They were more extensive than the usual Scout camp ranges to which I was accustomed. We all qualified as instructors, but my score with the .22 was only average. I was clearly in fast company. I had never really done any trap or skeet shooting, and my introduction to this game was not promising. My new associates were regularly breaking twenty or more out of twenty-five while I was struggling to do better than fifteen.

The trip to Cito provided us with a close-up glimpse of Philmont's wild creatures. For most easterners, the first jackrabbit is an interesting experience. It looked like a dwarf mutant burro with huge ears and haunches. It hardly looked related to the little eastern cottontail rabbit. Pronghorn antelope were prancing out in the fields to the west of camping headquarters. The nervousness of these flighty creatures prevented any close up looks. We all had to take a brief session on Philmont's natural history, flora, and fauna, whatever our program specialty. The curiosity of campers and advisors alike would mark the nature lectures as having been very worthwhile. We learned that the second wave of astronauts had done their geology training at Philmont, due largely to the tremendous variety in geomorphology within the Ranch boundaries.

For the geologist, Philmont is a goldmine. Mountains have come and gone and come back again. The area has been under the ocean, has experienced volcanic activity, and has seen both swamps and plains. Campers would be thunderstruck to know that if they looked hard enough, finding fossilized shark's teeth in Philmont's earth was quite possible.

I was particularly impressed with the quality of instruction in each program discipline. Quite clearly, the talent available to the Boy Scouts of America was of world class caliber. The summer staff wasn't exactly bush league either. I had never seen so many Eagle Scouts at once—not even at a jamboree. To see so much achievement under one roof would probably require attending a National Eagle Scout Association (NESA) convention.

In conversations with these new acquaintances, I was becoming aware of something else. "Where ya from?" "What's your job?" and "Where ya workin?" were typical questions. From their comments and the looks on their faces when I said I was working at Beaubien, I knew I was headed for a special place on Philmont's landscape.

Just as we were really getting into our instruction, we broke up abruptly for something called "Operation Scatter." "Scatter" meant exactly that. All four hundred of us scattered to the four corners of Philmont. The headquarters staff, cooks, trading post, commissary, and administrative staff didn't have to scatter very far. Rangers scattered off for their week on bivouac, and commissary trucks took the camp staffs out to their new homes for the summer. The purpose of "scatter" was to open the camps, sweep out the cobwebs, identify problems early, and turn each camp into a well-oiled machine. The thirty of us on the trucks watched camping headquarters fade as we headed out to our first landmark on the bumpy road to the south country.

Miners Park, the first stop, was a typically small operation with tents for staff quarters. It looked like a great place to camp: a broad meadow, tall pines, and a forest floor softened with pine needles. Our next stop, Crater Lake, was set on the side of Fowler Mesa, and was an original Phillips Lodge. Its walls were of stone, and the view to the east was breathtaking. The "Lake" was more of a pond, but at least it was consistent with the western practice of calling a creek a "river." Crater had served as a hunting lodge and halfway house on the trail to Fish Camp, which was Waite Phillips' exquisite fishing complex at the confluence of the Rayado and Agua Fria. Crater's sweeping vista made it the home of Philmont's astronomy program. The small staff was headed by Frank Estes, an Ivy Leaguer with sky blue eyes and considerable musical talent. Tom Whiting was the assistant, and ran the astronomy program. We helped them unload their gear, and were off again.

Up the switchbacks we went until we rounded the last one to emerge on top of Fowler Pass. Ahead of us swept the Bonita Valley, which climbed gently all the way to Beaubien. We rounded the base of Trail Peak, and passed one of the herds of cattle that summered in the highland pastures.

All that beef on the hoof put the "Ranch" into Philmont. These were actually not raised for beef, we were told, although Philmont butchered a few head each year for steaks. Instead, they were for breeding. Only indirectly did Philmont's finest beef ever make an acquaintance with Armour or Hormel.

Within a few minutes, we reached Beaubien, where the convoy split up. The trucks carrying the Fish Camp and Porcupine staffs kept on going. My first impression was that Beaubien had to be one of the most beautiful camps on the Ranch. The road to Trappers Lodge swung past the bunkhouse, which contained more than just the two cots for our cook and packer. It was a granary, barn, and smithy all in one. Inside were many trappings of farming that I was already familiar with. The odors—kerosene, binder twine, oats and old canvas—told me that I really wasn't so far from home after all.

Surprisingly, we didn't stop at Trappers Lodge first. Instead we parked by the newly expanded Commissary building, and moved our food for the next few days into the walk-in reefer at one end of the building. It was here that the guys from Black

Mountain and Red Hills got out and met our "packer," Bobby
Maldonado, a Cimarron native. The confusion of duffel bags, wall
tents, pictures of girlfriends, and steamer trunks all got sorted out,
and we started moving gear into Trappers Lodge. There was the
usual scramble for a bunk. As soon as we secured our gear, Paul
called us together, and was promptly interrupted by the arrival of
an International Harvester Scout.

Emerging from the Scout was the chunky, cheery-voiced gent
who was our cook, Dick Gertler. He was a year-round employee
of the ranch. He had been a professional cook before signing on
at Philmont several seasons before. I was the last to be introduced
to Dick, and while I was waiting, something was becoming more
obvious with his every word. His accent was pure Pennsylvania
Dutch.

"My name's Bill Cass, and I'm from Lancaster County
Council, just like you," I announced.

Dick was pleasantly surprised, but already nodding his head
in agreement. Although we had never met, we did have many
mutual acquaintances.

We never hurt for nutrition since Dick fed us well. Beyond
the "bug juice" kool-aid, we each averaged a quart and a half of
milk a day.

Paul told us that we would have lunch, and then take a walk
around the Beaubien area to get oriented. We were to list things
that had to be done over the next few days. While the camp had
been left in good condition the previous year, nearly nine months
of dormancy meant that there was cleaning to do. Paul was light
years ahead of his time when he asked us to get rid of all totem
poles, gateways, rails, and hitching posts. He believed that these
were more appropriate for council camps or camporees, but not
for Philmont and Beaubien in particular. This was hard work—we
did not just cut them off at the base, we dug them out and then
cut them up for firewood. Over the years, it would be interesting
to watch the rise and fall of these tacky trappings. Some directors

felt that no camp was complete without these impediments, and the grounds promptly sprouted the unsightly improvements. Others would follow Paul's example and take great pleasure in turning the misdirected hard work into firewood.

Winter had taken its toll, especially on the aspens. The trees that looked like they were about to fall got the crosscut saw treatment. The woodyard was well-stocked by the end of the day. We brushed away cobwebs in the bunkhouse, reconditioned Dutch ovens, rebuilt the campfire circle, repaired the benches at the chapel in the woods, and brought Beaubien to a state of readiness in just a few days. Freddy quickly mastered the intricacies of the water pump's engine. It was located up at the head of the meadow and may have been Philmont's only engine that was not malicious. Freddy was also responsible for getting the wood-stoked hot water shower up and running. Jimmy Money had a mass of inventory to sort through since Beaubien, in those days, dispensed trail food, and even had a modest trading post.

Probably the most enjoyable aspect of Scatter was the bull sessions that happened in front of our fireplace. That's where we really got to know one another. Jim Talley and I were becoming good friends. We shared many of the same interests and outlooks. Of the eight of us on the staff, we would have the most contact with the thousands of campers that would come through Beaubien. As the close of Scatter approached, we all helped Freddy finish repairing several latrines that hadn't fared too well over the winter. Jim and I creosoted one latrine and then painted its floor. Our conversation ranged from the meaning of life to El Greco's art and the music of Berlioz. Where else but the Ranch?

We returned to headquarters one afternoon for a final peptalk and campfire. The "Git along little dogie" lyrics of some old western song came alive as we headed down the jeep road in the commissary truck. Rounding the great curve below Trail Peak, we found a Hereford calf running full tilt toward its mama. The reason for the speed was a large coyote about twenty yards behind the calf. It was a real treat for the easterners in the truck, and a sure reminder that we were indeed in the west. The evening in headquarters was inspirational, and we all returned to our camp with a burning desire to excel. It would take a few more days before the first campers reached our high country camp, so we continued making Beaubien ready for our first arrivals.

Under Paul's keen eye, we were becoming an efficient, high-spirited team. We had to—our expertise and enthusiasm would be tested by thousands of Scouts in the next ten weeks. Jim Talley spent most of those shakedown days at the corral running through his western lore programs and practicing his campfire routines. At the same time, I was making some progress on the shotgun range. Most of my time was not spent breaking birds, although I was now improving. I spent more time practicing my instruction technique by lecturing to the weeds and flowers in the meadow.

At Trappers Lodge

Teaching Hunter Safety was fun and rewarding. I was, hopefully, imparting some basic skills that would ensure campers' safety around firearms. Philmont had two permanent centers for hunter safety and marksmanship. There was a running deer range at Pueblano. Here Scouts got an introduction to high power, 30:06 rifles while shooting at a moving, simulated deer target. Cito had shotgun and .22 ranges.

Rarely would any Scout complete the four-hour course at one camp. Typically, I would teach sessions one and three and sign their cards. When they got to Cito, they would complete the course with sessions two and four. Or they might start at Cito and finish at Beaubien or Pueblano. Over the years, the program evolved. Beaubien eventually dropped it after taking over from

Rayado. Then it shifted to Olympia. Finally, Abreu became the south country center for Hunter Safety. Eventually, the program was improved by converting many of the ranges to black powder rifles, which were much more in keeping with Philmont's frontier heritage.

Meanwhile, we blew up thousands of clay pigeons. I was not a natural with a shotgun, however. Bringing down the occasional pheasant was no problem for me, but batting more than .600 on the ceramic birds certainly was. Now and then, an advisor would come close to getting all twenty-five clay pigeons, but it was a goal that eluded me. It would always prove maddening, especially in later years when I could drop fast flying teal ducks over blinds on Maryland rivers, but not hit simple clay pigeons that flew such predictable courses.

Occasionally, we would get a smart-aleck kid who would want to show off once he got a shotgun in his hands. All staffers were in the public relations business, but it never deterred me from dismissing the occasional boys who wanted to clown around, even after participating in safety demonstrations. The crestfallen kids would appeal to their adult advisors for reinstatement. The adults would remain stonefaced, and send their errant charges back to the campsites while the rest of the course resumed. We hated to disappoint anybody, but safety was paramount. The Hunter Safety Course was well designed, but we modified it to include more interaction with the demonstration. Once the instructional aspects were over, there was free shooting, and after that, campers could pay for extra shooting.

The session ran from ten A.M. to noon, and again from two P.M. through five P.M. The staff was given no discount when it came to ammunition or clay pigeons. This proved to be no obstacle for the well-connected Dimalanty. Surprisingly, he received several large, very heavy packages in early July. How his father had shipped several cases of clay pigeons without them being shattered in transit remains a mystery. He was one of the better wing shots on the Beaubien staff, and thus became the range officer on my days off. With his gift of gab, it was a task he fulfilled with great gusto and success.

My attempt to teach lacrosse to the Beaubien staff was a dismal failure. Lacrosse had always been popular in upstate New York and in the Chesapeake Tidewater, but was not common in the west. The game consumed a large share of my energies at college, and I was anxious to stay in practice. I hadn't brought my stick, and since we didn't have time to make lacrosse sticks, we tried using shovels instead. This proved to be cumbersome and dangerous. Predictably, Beaubien lacrosse was a very short-lived adventure.

Paul introduced another Indian game however, and we played it several times a week, usually in the evenings before the campfire. It required only two sticks. A short stick, about an inch in diameter with blunted, beveled ends was used with another stick slightly under two feet in length. We laid the smaller stick on the ground. The object was to strike one of its ends with the larger stick causing the small stick to pop several feet into the air. The batter then attempted to hit the small stick, much as a baseball player hits balls for fielding practice.

The other players, standing away from the batter for obvious reasons, attempted to catch the smaller stick in its flight. If they failed (usually the case), the batter scored points based on the distance between the smaller stick's takeoff and landing position. When a player caught the stick, it was his turn to be the batter. My hours spent on squash courts proved to be quite an asset, but were no match for Dimalanty's talent.

Paul, whose childhood injury precluded covering much ground in a hurry, was actually the best player. Quite observant, he carefully studied the batting styles of each player, and predicted the arc of the small stick. He would usually position himself at the right place where he could easily catch the stick. The rest of us weren't quick enough to notice the subtleties. We had to dash, leap, or crash land to even get close to the flying stick.

Paul was not a regular player at this game, and when he did play, he usually arrived late. His practice after dinner was to collect one or two of us, and make the rounds of our various campsites. He would introduce himself to every advisor, and let it be known that he and the staff were there to serve. The invitation to the advisors' coffee hour was a personal one; we always had a full house.

While most of us had some spare time for games in the evening, there was little during the day. Beyond the demands of our specific jobs, there was always camp work to do. Checking groups in and out didn't take very long unless there were many groups in camp. Rounding up logs for the evening campfire is what consumed the time.

We never solicited the help of campers in preparing wood for the fire since it involved felling dead trees. We took out plenty of aspens which were losing their war with Beaubien's pines, but we felled the occasional Ponderosa pine as well. These logs had to be cut up and then split for the campfire. Tree cutting was physically exhausting labor. The duty fell to Dimalanty, Jim Talley, Freddy Blair, and me, although we usually worked in teams of three.

We used the granddaddy of all saws, the crosscut. Heavy, sharp, and about seven feet long, the saw commanded respect. Two of us would sit on opposite sides of the tree, and cut nearly halfway through the tree close to the base. The cut would be made at right angles to the direction in which we wanted the tree to fall. From the same direction, we would cut down at a fifteen to twenty degree angle, which would result in the removal of a wedge from the tree. The rest was simple. We cut in from the other side to meet the first cut. What wasn't simple was staying on the same end of the saw for the entire procedure.

That's why we worked in teams of three. When one of us became exhausted from pulling the saw (and it didn't take long at an elevation of nearly 9,400 feet), another would take his place. The rotation continued until the tree was down and cut into sections. Then, using sledge and wedge, the sections were split. While there were no injuries, there were frequent cases of flying wedges. This proved the point of separating campers from this activity. Cutting wood in the thin mountain air did wonders to develop muscles and boost our pulmonary capabilities. Freddy and Dimalanty returned to their low altitude football teams at the peak of fitness. I played a lot of golf in the autumn, but felling those many trees added only to the distance of my slice, and did nothing to improve my handicap. Still, those of us who chopped wood added noticeable definition to our shoulder muscles within weeks of starting the Paul Bunyon program.

The larger logs found their way to the evening campfire, which was part of the Beaubien program. The campfire started fairly early by council camp standards, but at Philmont, darkness came quickly, and staffer and camper alike were usually very tired. With his deep and commanding voice, Paul would open the campfire with words of wisdom and inspiration. Dimalanty and I would come on next, and usually tell some tall tales. Freddy followed with what theater professionals call the "warmup."

Freddy's act was entitled the "Bumble Bee." Freddy, wearing a large hat, would stand between two volunteer scouts. Freddy would announce that he was going to make buzzing sounds, and gently tap one Scout on the back of the head. Upon that signal, the Scout was invited to take a swipe from the rear to knock the hat off. Freddy would dip and roll while holding cupped hands to his mouth all the while making buzzing sounds. He sounded like a blend of Texas hornets, model airplane engines, and bits and snatches of Rimsky-Korsakov's "Flight of the Bumblebee."

Freddy would buzz threateningly for eight to ten seconds, and then gently, but quickly, slap one of the lads on the back of the neck. Freddy had already set the record for the world's fastest squat before the camper's open hand swung over his head in a fruitless attempt to knock the hat into the audience. Freddy consistently embarrassed the two campers, whose swings never met with success. He would go through another two or three sets of campers before the act showed first signs of wearing thin. At that point, the campfire moved to the main act, Jim Talley's western music.

Jim's music consisted of western ballads, theme songs from the TV westerns that were then popular, and most of the songs typically sung at Scouting campfires. His version of "The Master's Call" was one of our favorites, and his "Ghost Riders" would easily have turned Vaughn Monroe's head. The staff usually attended every campfire, and we never tired of Jim's music. He could belt out the Frankie Lane "Rawhide" type of music, and then quickly switch gears to become a Crosby crooner. He was frequently asked for encores, and, invariably, the "Ghost Riders" would ride again, much to our pleasure.

Unlike most of the western lore/campfire program staff, Jim's musical ability extended beyond playing the guitar. He was equally gifted with the banjo, which added variety to our campfire, and gladdened many a southern heart. Even then, Jim was a budding song writer, but we were unaware in those days just how far he would develop his talent in the years ahead.

We were encouraged to learn each others' trades. This created the backup so essential to running a camp while some fellow staffer got his two days off per month. The only disagreeable part of backup was cranking the electrical generator, a job normally performed by Freddy. This beast of a machine, probably military surplus, was the size of a truck engine and was very much in contrast to the compact, modern generator possessed by the Fish Camp staff. Theirs had a gentle, little lawn mower sized engine that purred along. Our monster had the nasty habit of backfiring from time to time which meant that we had to be prepared to suffer the consequences when cranking to get the beast roaring. It was a backup task that Freddy was delighted to pass along, although the effort required must have helped him prepare for the football season.

The backup ended at the campfire since nobody could match the mellow voice of Jim Talley when it came to running the campfire. Jim was a double threat artistically. A fine arts major at the University of New Mexico, Jim was best known for his talent in the performing arts. What was less obvious was his capability in the visual arts. Several years later, Jim would send me a present recalling the Beaubien of summers past. It was a water color of Black and Bear Mountains, and it remains a prized memento of Philmont service to this day.

◆ ◆ ◆

Black Mountain is one of the steeper peaks in the south country, so is less frequently climbed. The camp itself is among the Ranch's most picturesque. We rarely saw the Black Mountain staff, although we had become well-acquainted with them during Operation Scatter. The Director, Johnny Montgomery, was a classmate of Jim's at the University of New Mexico, and headed for a dental career. DeWitt Blamer III, better known as "Skip," was the extraordinary Assistant Director/Program Counselor at Black Mountain. He was, in the most literal sense of the word, a whitecap in the rolling sea of green Explorer uniforms, which was the common denominator of staff dress. Skip's uniform was the white of a Sea Scout. The only black and white square knots on the Ranch were those of Skip's Quartermaster Award (worn with his Eagle knots).

Black Mountain never got the volume of traffic that Beaubien did. We suspected that the lack of company might explain why Johnny and Skip were always such cordial hosts on our infrequent trips over the ridge to their camp. While Black Mountain was not far away as the crow flies, the ridge that separates the two camps is steep enough to get the blood circulating quickly.

At Beaubien, all signs point to high adventure

It would become a familiar trail, and the one I used on my first day off. Normally we would get one day off every two weeks. In effect, that meant leaving after lunch, having the rest of the day off, and being back by noon the next day. I was always the maverick, since I never accepted a ride in the jeeps or trucks that returned to headquarters from Beaubien. I was very conscious about never having attended the Ranch as a camper, so I decided to see as much of Philmont as I could on days off. When the first opportunity came, I went over the ridge to Black Mountain, and took the North Fork of Urraca Creek down past the Miners Park cutoff. I had left at two P.M., and after passing by the Stockade, arrived at Camping Headquarters by 5:30. It was a lovely hike. The creek was clear, and small trout could easily be seen in its pools. I thought it odd to see trout here, since I had been led to believe that the only good fishing was to be found in the fabled Agua Fria and Rayado. But here were trout in the

North Fork Urraca. I would later find that Cimarroncito Creek held fine little trout, and if they fit in a pan, they made a delightful meal.

I ran into Tom Sothard and a couple of his north country friends along with Steve Radford, a program counselor at Porcupine, so we decided to have a big night on the town. This usually consisted of doing laundry, and going into Cimarron for either a Mexican dinner or, better yet, a steak. We would take in a movie and wind up the evening at Lambert's with a milkshake or ice cream soda. Guys with wheels might head to Raton or range as far as Taos, but without connections, we were content to hitchhike into Cimarron.

Nearly every staffer had grown up with parents' warnings about hitchhiking and getting into strangers' cars. It was good advice, but around Cimarron it wasn't especially valid. Several local families owed their livelihood to the Ranch, and were glad to show some out-of-town lad what hospitality was all about. We only needed one ticket—our red jackets. It worked every time, whether we went to Raton or Taos.

Red and green were always the colors of the day, but those colors took on special meaning around July 25 when the Philmont staff celebrated Christmas. The mountain man rendezvous origins of this practice were lost upon us, but the opportunity to party was not. The staffer version completely missed the religious meaning of the original holiday. For that reason it was replaced with "Fiesta," a midsummer festival more in keeping with a southwestern atmosphere. Most camps had their own banquet, so the tradition was maintained. Nobody tried to push their luck with any suggestions of New Year's parties, however.

Dick Gertler had spoiled us with his regular cooking, but was more than up to the celebration when he produced our Beaubien feast. It didn't occur to me then, but some wood badge patrol would have lucked out had Dick become a member of their group.

Steak, sweet corn, and some of Gertler's homemade pies were the fare that evening. Just before dessert, Freddy started becoming nostalgic about the absence of some of his Tennessee home cookin'. I knew what was coming next, and it had to do with chittlins, black-eyed peas, and fatback. It was more than I could resist.

"Now Freddy," I intoned, "they're more properly pronounced *chitterlings.* We do pronounce our Rs and Gs."

"Shut up y'damnyankee!"

I had already decided not to press the issue since the mincemeat pie was being passed around. We actually had very little in the way of regional rivalry. Freddy and I were the only ones who would spark on the Billy Yank and Johnny Reb business. I figured not to do so might be upsetting to my 141st Pennsylvania Volunteer Infantry ancestors. Dick Gertler was from North of the Mason Dixon, but above such regional bickering. As Pennsylvania Dutch as he was, he probably looked upon any confessed Yankee as just as foreign as any rebel. In reality, the rest of the staffers were territorials. While Paul was from Texas, he was an Illinois transplant. The two Jims were real territorials along with Dimalanty. Talley, an Oklahoman by birth, was the real outlander. His family had moved to Albuquerque from Washington State.

Although Freddy and I had a lot of respect for each other, it hardly prevented the steady flow of good-natured humor between us. Most of the banter was based on perceived shortcomings in our respective regional heritages. Freddy would lubricate the generator with "ole" whereas I might use "oil" (pronounced with nearly two syllables). Freddy would rear up and say, "Well, it sure isn't 'oy-ull,' is it, yew scrawny Yankee?" These confrontations would go on and on until the rest of the staff would threaten to have the two of us "boled in ole."

♦ ♦ ♦

Other than at campfires, our campers usually stayed together in their own crews. Only the occasional game of pickup football or gathering at the commissary would cause them to mingle. The commissary was also the one place most of the staff seemed to congregate in the very late afternoon while Dick was cooking dinner. After the range was shut down, and Jim Talley had closed shop at the corral, we all wound up at Jimmy Money's trading post. Of all of us at Beaubien, Jimmy probably had the best rapport with campers. His was the most ready smile, and there was always plenty of conversation over the Dutch door at the trading post when Jimmy was selling flashlight batteries or dispensing trail food. But it was the candy bars Jimmy sold that made the trading post so popular with campers.

We always knew when campers were coming. Just a few minutes before they would heave into view, we would hear the telltale clanking of cook kit pots banging against the metal pack frames.

One day just after lunch, I was hanging around the commissary talking to Jimmy when the metallic chorus of an approaching crew became audible. Sure enough, a small group rounded the little stand of aspens down trail, and headed toward us.

"Hey, Sho-Man! How's it goin'?" There, before me, was an advisor wearing a Washington College sweatshirt. Yes, he had been a lacrosse player. Our teams were known as "Sho-Men," a contraction for Shore Man (Eastern Shore of Maryland). As it turned out, he was a school teacher from New Jersey, and had graduated from "WC" nearly twenty years before. I thought it odd for such an "old" man to be on the trail, but this guy was still trim and fit. This was a major event for me. We had seen our share of Penn State University, Rutgers, Ohio State, and other big school T-shirts, but nothing from Washington College.

That crew got a choice campsite for the evening. They stayed with us the next day in order to side hike Trail Peak. It was my pleasure to check them out the following morning.

We usually had a pretty hearty breakfast, before which our hard core staffers would be out at the wash basin brushing teeth and shaving in ice cold water. The more genteel among the Beaubien staffers would wait for the leftover hot rinse water from the breakfast dishes. It is odd how some habits stick—ever since that summer, I've never minded shaving with even the coldest water. Temperatures got pretty cold at Beaubien; had there been a sprinkle of rain late the night before, there would be a thin sheet of ice on the porch in the morning. Trappers Lodge had been planned well, and the southern exposure quickly melted the ice. With coffee consumed, we were busy checking groups out and doing our morning chores. We rotated on the housekeeping and dishwashing chores, which rarely consumed more than fifteen minutes.

One Sunday morning I was on garbage duty. It wasn't difficult; we created a small amount of garbage because we burned all of the paper and crushed the cans. Philmont was very ecology and conservation minded then, but not as environmentally conscious as it is today. Then, crews camping in unstaffed trail camps were expected to pack out their garbage, but staffed camps did not have regular garbage removal service by truck. We did have a modest garbage dump which was little more than a scrape in the meadow. It was discretely obscured by a small hummock, and hardly visible from any of the trails leading into Beaubien. We chucked crushed cans into the hole in the ground, and covered with a couple of shovels full of loose dirt—a far cry from today's policy of removing one hundred percent of the garbage.

At the end of the season, a layer of earth thoroughly covered the little landfill. By the following summer, it would be growing flowers. Incredibly, we never had a single bear hanging around the dump. We burned the wet garbage in a fifty gallon drum by tossing some gasoline on it, letting the gas soak through, and then throwing a match into the mess. Occasionally we would dump the burned remains onto the garbage dump.

On this particular day, the garbage was unusually wet. I tossed the match in. There was a flare up, and some short-lived burning. As a rule, one Crisco can full of juice was enough to do the job. This fire was a disappointment, and seemed to go out too quickly. I was reluctant to throw more gas onto it, since there was still smoke, and where there was smoke, there had to be fire. I thought if I stood upwind, and chucked the can into the fire, it would start up again, and burn right. It proved to be a bad idea in the most pyrotechnic sense of the word.

Returning from the generator, where the gas was kept, I stood upwind, and flipped the blue and white can at the fire. Unfortunately, there was a spectacular "whhoooosh" and flare-up right in front of my face. I couldn't understand how quickly the flame could have gotten back to me, but it had. Apparently, there had been a secondary explosion, since my right hand and forearm were a mass of flames. Within a fraction of a second, I was rolling on the ground with my right arm tucked beneath me. The entire affair had consumed less than three seconds from toss to my horizontal dance in the dirt. I jumped to my feet and looked at my arm, which was now hairless. Oddly, it didn't hurt at all, but there was the slightest hint of tingling. I rubbed my arm and the tingling went away. All that ever came of it was a slight flaking of skin on my wrist.

I had flaky skin twice earlier that summer. I acquired the first case simply because I was not sufficiently tanned when I arrived at the Ranch, and got a moderate sunburn as a result. The second case was a rather bizarre mechanical accident. We pumped water from a well in the upper Bonita Meadow to a tall water tower. It was well shielded from view among the tall pines behind Trappers Lodge. This was Freddy's job, and he usually had it well timed. If he blew it, we all knew since the water tank would be overflowing. There was also a small feed tank from which the water purification chemicals were introduced into the system.

As a rule, we took our showers late in the evening, after the campers had stoked up the woodfire under a holding tank. Most of the staff was down showering when we became aware of a strong chlorine odor. It wasn't overpowering, but it definitely pinched the nostrils. We all knew immediately what it was, and Freddy dried off quickly, and went to see what malfunction had overdosed us with chlorine additive. We didn't think about it too much until the next morning when half of us looked like we had been bleached. We had dry, flaky skin that was several shades lighter than it had been the previous day. Fortunately nobody had consumed any of the water, and Freddy refilled the entire water tank. None of the campers suspected anything, but for the next several days, a few of us looked as though we had just seen a ghost.

At least the bleaching was less frightening than the scene I had just experienced. Deciding that perhaps the warm sun might dry the garbage over the rest of that day, I looked about to see if anyone had observed my lunacy. My reacquiring a respect for gasoline's explosive qualities had to have been a ridiculous sight. I was hoping that all eyes were elsewhere. Nobody was about, and the only observers had been the placid horses over in the corral, so my secret was assured.

3

Man and Beast

When it came to horses, I had dropped the ball long before arriving at the Ranch. It is hard to understand why, and I am sure my ancestors must have been rotating in their crypts at this serious shortcoming. The Cass, Parks, and Allen clans were all excellent horsemen, but I was clearly the broken link in the chain. It was doubly hard to explain since I had been a farm boy and was very familiar with horses. While I had ridden horseback, I gained most of my experience with the creatures from my Grandfather Parks' draught horses.

Tom and Ted were his great Belgians who hauled the manure spreader and cultivated rows of corn. Gramp had long since mechanized, but used the giant beasts largely out of his farmer's respect for traditional ways. Granted, he used John Deere and

Massey Fergusson for the heavy duty jobs, but Tom and Ted had tenure. I rode on their backs when he "hay'd it" in the smaller fields near the barn and granary.

Around Trappers Lodge, I had no use for the dozen horses in our corral. We had several good-looking horses that served many purposes, including Jim Talley's western lore program. The others were used by members of the horse and cattle departments, although these staffers usually brought their own horses.

It was trout fishing that signalled my reintroduction to riding horses. I had always been something of a pragmatist, if not a conservative, especially in later business-world years. Paradoxically, I was a wild-eyed, egomaniacal, holy-rolling optimist when it came to my fishing talents. If I didn't come home with a creelful, it was because there were no fish in the creek—pure and simple. If there were fish in the water, I would get them. After all, I had been taught by my mother, who had forgotten more about fishing than the average Isaac Walton Leaguer learns in a lifetime.

Mom fished for the table. When she was a girl, she would persevere at the edges of Bradford County's Wysox Creek, and bring home the brookies for the evening dinner. That was in a day when the trout were native, and the Great Depression permitted only slim fare on many a table.

Jim Talley and I were the only Beaubien staffers who were really keen on fishing. The problem was getting time off to go fishing, although the Rayado and Agua Fria weren't that far away. The die was cast when some campers tied into some trout down at the Crags, and gave the staff what they couldn't use. Dick Gertler sauteed those beauties, and Paul melted like hot butter when Jim and I proposed an occasional fishing trip to supplement our regular dining fare. The horse was our ticket to this diversion since we could cover the distance to the Crags or the upper Agua Fria in only a fraction of the time it would take on foot.

Paul laid down the ground rules. We had to get somebody to take our morning programs, and we had to be back by noon. Night fishing was ruled out because Jim was the *sine qua non* of our campfire. There was one other rule—bring back dinner or the next fishing trip would be on our vacation time. It was therefore a simple matter: we would get up well before dawn, saddle up, and ride. Jim and I decided to have a go at the upper Agua Fria on the first trip mainly because it was infrequently traveled that year. Therefore, it promised better fishing, if not in big trout, at least in quantity. We would save the Crags for another day, although I was anxious to see that location. The palisades on the north side of the Rayado Canyon added to the beauty of one of Waite Phillips' favorite fishing holes. We didn't set any records getting started. After a quick breakfast, we got our rods and flies, and made our way to the corral.

"You know, Jim, I haven't been on a horse in ten years."

"Don't worry about it, I'll show you what to do."

We led two horses over to the corral and tied them up so we could saddle them. Jim got the palomino, a fine looking steed, and I got a nameless plug. I had already learned that a "plug" was a senior beast who owed each drawn breath to Philmont's generosity and the fact that business was slow at the glue factories.

I had seen enough of Jim doing his western lore program to do a workmanlike job of getting the saddle on right. It was cold. I was surprised at how icy the metal rings on the saddle and straps felt. On the other hand, I wasn't too surprised since it regularly got down into the forties and occasionally the thirties at night. Soon, we headed up toward Apache Creek with me hanging in there wondering why the saddle was constantly slapping my butt. Surely, this "slap-slap-slap" wasn't going to go on for the rest of the trip. We turned south onto the trail at the head of Bonita Valley toward Fish Camp, but then dropped down into the Apache Creek Trail to save a little time. It was a mistake.

For most expeditions, Apache Creek was a wise choice. Granted, it was a bit steeper than the switchbacked jeep trail, but it also shaved time off the trip down to Porky or Fish Camp. The creek was really just a rivulet in a gully. The gully walls were narrow, steep, and in some places, lined with sharp outcroppings. We were nearly at Porky-Ado Junction when something spooked Jim's horse. His horse, one of Beaubien's better specimens, reared up and started to turn. The Lone Ranger's "Silver" couldn't have been more dramatic. The popular misconception is that horses are only spooked by bears or rattlesnakes, but in truth a defiant ground squirrel can do the job. In a matter of seconds, Jim's horse completed a couple of pirouettes, and bolted down the creek. At least Jim hadn't been scraped off the saddle by the outcroppings.

My situation was much less desperate. This old gelding I was riding probably wanted to join the horse ballet as well, but if his mind was willing, his flesh wasn't. He reared up, couldn't keep it going, lost it, and then dropped back onto his front feet. When he first started to rear up, I was dumbstruck about what to do. If I didn't do something quickly, I wasn't going to be in the saddle for much longer. Not knowing if I should grab one of his ears, his mane or what, I just leaned forward, and held onto the saddle horn for dear life. This old plug didn't have the energy of Jim's horse, and he dropped back onto all fours, broke wind, and then hung his head. He took a few slurps of water from the creek, and stood there, awaiting further instructions. After regaining my composure, I got old Dobbin underway, and caught up with Jim at Porky-Ado Junction (site of Phillips Junction today).

We were no longer in confining surroundings, and quickly cantered down to the Buck Creek turnoff. I liked cantering—my rump didn't get slapped to pieces, and we made excellent time. After about a mile, we turned South at Buck Creek Camp, and bushwhacked toward Bear and Turkey Creeks. This was Philmont at its pristine best, and new territory for both Jim and myself. We had planned our trip the night before, and brought a map and compass to be on the safe side. I was glad to be on horseback. None of what we were negotiating was difficult, but it was definitely enough to put somebody out of breath and eat up a lot of time. Although it was still early morning, the horses were sweating.

This southwest corner of the Ranch was undeveloped then. Buck Creek, Agua Fria, and Lost Cabin were listed on the map, but unstaffed. We rode through lush meadows, dense woods, and aspen stands. We caught a passing glimpse of a mountain lion while we were resting the horses by Turkey Creek. The big cat crossed the edge of a meadow on the eastern side of Apache Peak, and was out of sight in several seconds. It was a rare treat, especially in broad daylight.

This was clearly elk country. We never saw them, but we did find their antlers. We headed south on the trail to Lost Cabin, but if there had been a real cabin there, we missed it. Then we descended the ridge down to the Agua Fria. We tied up the horses and fished a promising stretch that produced a few small trout. Then we moved down the creek, picking up a few more trout as we went. They weren't big fish, but what they lacked in size, they made up in aggressiveness. Most of these were little trout which we understood to be native fish. We had heard that the New Mexico state game authorities occasionally stocked rainbows and the wily browns. Rumor had it that Agua Fria Lake was also stocked. When water was high, some monster trout were supposed to escape and populate the Agua Fria. This may have been the case because time would tell that the upper Agua Fria held some truly huge trout. The sun climbed over La Grulla Ridge, and when its rays struck the water directly, the fishing slowed almost to a standstill. Even my favorite fly, a black gnat, wasn't working. I was tempted to start digging for worms but figured that wouldn't be in keeping with the local tradition of using flies.

We had caught only a couple more when we ran into some

campers between Agua Fria and Fish Camp. We had an even dozen trout, which would feed the staff well, and guarantee another trip in a few weeks. These little trout were not trophy class since the largest was only nine inches long. But they were "pan sized," and Dick Gertler would turn them into a great meal for the Beaubien staff. The sun had climbed to the point where it was getting warm, and with thoughts about getting the fish cleaned and refrigerated, we headed back to Beaubien. There was no question about the route; we would take the main drag and leave Apache Creek to campers.

We made it back to Beaubien well before lunch. Bobby Maldonado, our packer, had taken Jim's ten A.M. program while Dimalanty had assumed range duties for the morning. As we were cleaning the fish, I became increasingly aware of a dull ache in my pelvis and knee joints. I wondered if my behind was blistered or maybe calloused as a result of all that trotting. I got through my afternoon program all right, but was really sore by dusk. The trout dinner offered some diversion from my aches and pains.

"Just wait until tomorrow. You won't be fit to feed the horses let alone ride one," Jim said. Boy, was he right. My rear was extraordinarily tender—blistered in several spots—and I had burned out a new pair of BVDs while acquiring that agony. I was a basket case for the next several days, but as I gimped around Beaubien, I resolved that I wasn't going to get "stove up" like that again. So, I made my peace with the horse world. I decided that a brief ride every evening would break in my bones so that our next fishing trip wouldn't end in such orthopedic disaster. I also decided that some instruction was in order. Bobby and Jim taught me the basics, which began with letting the horse know who is in charge. My view of how to get on a horse had been shaped by the movie westerns. That was quickly remedied. Over the next few weeks, I would pick a horse, often Jim's palomino, and go for a ten minute jaunt around the jeep trail above Beaubien.

Returning on the commissary truck from a vacation day

The regimen worked. When Jim and I next set out, the riding went smoothly, although we didn't bring home as many fish. My interest in an evening ride spread, and soon Jimmy Money and Dimalanty started riding. Since I was the one who saddled the horse, I claimed the first ride. I had an ulterior motive: to see the badger whose den was just below the Black Mountain trail. The badger was usually out for his evening constitutional, and engaged in grounds maintenance at his front door. I started off at a canter, and then slowed to a trot when I approached the den. I'd stop and wait for a couple of minutes for the badger, who usually showed up with a contemptuous look on his face. He would go about his digging, stealing an occasional, furtive glance back at me. The dirt would fly, and after observing his disapproving looks in my direction, I'd tickle the horse's flanks, and we'd be off.

Occasionally, the horse tried to show me who was master by cantering off the jeep trail and into the meadow. If I were in his place, I'd probably do the same. In contrast to the hard packed and stony jeep road, the meadow was soft and inviting. A couple of firm reminders to his cheeks usually got the message through, and then he would follow the rein.

I never did get to the point where I was a fervent fancier of horse flesh. For me it was a simple matter of transportation. Horses might be unintelligent, foul smelling, and frequently obnoxious, but at least they could cover ground a lot faster than I could. If there were some serious obstacles to negotiate between points A and B in order to catch some fish, I'd rather the horse arrive in a sweat than I. I never could understand people like my friend Jim who was a great admirer of horses, but then he probably never understood what beauty I could see in some old biplane from the thirties.

While most of Beaubien's horses were tired bays and sorrels, we did have several good-looking stallions. Jim's palomino could have been mistaken for Roy Rogers' "Trigger." This was undoubtedly the reason the Horse Department made this particular horse the star of the Beaubien western lore program. Bobby Maldonado, who packed supplies to back-country camps, usually rode the big pinto. We had "guest" horses that were left in our corral by members of the Ranch and Cattle Departments. Hubert Powell, an assistant Ranch superintendent, was a frequent visitor.

Powell's prize horse, "Peanuts," was a buckskin. The term buckskin was as unknown to me as his horse was beautiful (I was by then picking up a modest appreciation for horses). As I learned, a buckskin was essentially a palomino in body color, but instead of a blond mane, buckskins had the dark mane of a bay. The effect was striking; no wonder it was one of Powell's favorite mounts. Powell was a very compact man, and had sky blue eyes and crows' feet like a veteran airline pilot. He visited Beaubien once or twice a week, occasionally accompanied by his wife, and would disappear down the valley where several of Philmont's cattle herds summered. Philmont had nearly six hundred head of cattle that year. Come October, they would all be herded to winter pasture down near Rayado. That would be something to experience, but it was not to be for the summer staffer.

We were charged with the care of Peanuts in Powell's absence, but forbidden to ride his pride and joy. This was eminently understandable and caused no hard feelings. Late one afternoon in mid-July, Powell returned to the corral about the same time Bobby Maldonado got back from packing in supplies to the back country camps. Jim Talley had wound up his program for the day, and there was a lot of activity in the corral with the unsaddling of horses and removing of packs from the plugs. My range duties were over, so I crossed the road to help remove saddles, and tie on the food bags full of oats. This procedure usually went without a hitch, but not on this day.

We had close to a dozen horses in the corral, all of them still saddled, when something spooked Jim's palomino. This was the same horse that had bolted in Apache Creek only recently. It was probably the scurrying ground squirrels that set off the stampede. The little rodents seemed to surface all at once and dash madly from one end of the corral to the other, or from beneath the bunkhouse to nearby trees. The spilled grain was a bonanza for the little critters. A dozen or more of them, zigging and zagging all at once, was probably more than some of the horses could stand. In no time, we had wide-eyed horses whinnying, flaring their nostrils, and running in a frenzy toward fenceposts and barbed wire. Hubert Powell kept his cool, but clearly saw the damage barbed wire would do to Peanuts, his prized horse. It was all over within thirty seconds, and astonishingly, not one horse was bleeding.

The damage, which was extensive, was confined to several ripped out fenceposts. Peanuts had already had his saddle removed, so there was little left with which to catch the wire. The plugs did all of the damage. The packing bags on their backs, what Bobby Maldonado called "kayaks," caught the barbs, and the horses pulled wire and rotten fenceposts apart. The situation remained quite tense since we had three plugs milling around, still festooned with coils of wire and pieces of fencepost. This was no place for amateurs, so I promptly got out of the way. Powell and Bobby sweet-talked the horses into separate corners of the corral, and turned the pinto, Trigger, and Peanuts out. Jim Talley, already thinking ahead, had ducked into the bunkhouse, and emerged with a pair of wire cutters. Within five minutes, the three of them had the wire off, although two pairs of the kayaks were definitely the worse for wear and needed replacing before Bob's next packing run.

Horses never ceased to amaze me. Here they were, terrified of a platoon of ground squirrels. I wondered what they would do if we ever got any bears at Beaubien. Even with the liberal garbage disposal policy of those days, we never had a single bear. Bears had been through earlier in the year, though; their claw marks on trees were obvious, especially in some the upper campsites just above the showers.

We came to the conclusion that the lack of bears had something to do with the horses, and the fact that they were turned out at night. Other camps like Clarks Fork had bears and horses, but their horses didn't have the run of the place to the extent that Beaubien's did. And our horses did run, especially on the few cool, drizzling evenings we experienced at the end of the season. There must have been something in the air, for the descending darkness and chilly, wet breeze even got the plugs pumped up. They were like a bunch of felines with catnip. Maybe the sight of these energized chargers kept the bears at bay. What kept the horses at bay was "Bob Dog," our resident shepherd.

Bob Dog was Bobby Maldonado's Australian sheepdog. Bob Dog was a bundle of energy, and with one brown eye and one blue eye, he was the personification of mischief. He was not to be taken lightly though, since he was definitely a one-owner dog. His allegiance to Bobby Maldonado was complete, although Bobby made a point of proving that the members of the Beaubien staff were his friends. He did this by relaxing with us, shaking hands, putting an arm around us. Bob Dog understood this, and eventually thawed enough to be petted. Anybody coming back to the lodge after dark made sure he called to Bob Dog in friendly tones. Bob Dog liked to lay beneath the kitchen porch steps in the evening, and his treatment of strangers was usually harsh.

Fortunately, we had no bites that summer, but more than a few close calls. Occasionally, we would have a visitor with a dog in his truck. When Bob Dog was in residence, we tried to inform our guest that it would be a good idea if his pooch stayed in the vehicle. A forestry department official came up one day with a male German shepherd that Bob Dog nearly took apart. Bobby broke up the scrap shortly after it started. He managed to get the two separated, although it was at considerable risk to hands and legs to wade into that melee.

Bob Dog was raised to herd cattle, but he made the transition to horses very easily. It was bigger sport for this small package of dynamite who looked like a border collie that had been slightly compressed from both ends. His technique for driving our horses back to the corral was fascinating to watch. Bob Dog became the grass level, hot rock fighter jock of Beaubien's high alpine meadows. He would charge and swerve, head back, and race from flank to flank behind the horses, barking all the time. Now and then, one of the more dominant horses, usually Bobby's pinto, would break away, and try to head off on his own. Bob Dog would not bark, but would shear in from the rear quarter at high speed, and gently nip one of the horse's rear legs. The horse would try to kick the offender. Bob, like the champion he was, saw the punch coming, and broke off the engagement long enough to set up another pass.

Bob Dog never showed much interest in the deer that were plentiful at Beaubien. The only deer we saw in the middle of the day was a fawn, a little orphan that had been brought in by a Michigan group. The doe had probably fallen to a mountain lion or other predator, so we sent "Bambi" down to the nature exhibit at headquarters.

Most of the deer emerged from the woods in the early evening, and grazed contentedly near the campfire circle. One buck, "Charles" as we called him, was either the tamest, most trusting deer we had encountered, or he was not in full possession of his faculties. He wouldn't attempt to get out of the way when we walked back to the lodge after the campfire. On the darkest of nights, it was not unusual to bump into Charles. For advisors on their way to the coffee hour, suddenly walking into a deer and getting arms tangled in antlers was a rude shock.

But, Bob Dog probably regarded horses as bigger game, especially since they didn't vanish into the woods when frightened. Bob Dog's owner, Bobby Maldonado, worked for Philmont's Horse Department, and was assigned as Beaubien's packer. His job was to pack supplies in twice a week to those camps not served by the commissary truck. Bobby was a Cimarron native. He had never left Colfax County except for being stationed in California during service with the Coast Guard. Bobby was "old;" he was twenty-six. He was also a real cowboy—the genuine article. Lanky, with a ready smile, he used expressions like "old boy" and "over yonder." He was the only smoker on the Beaubien staff, and rolled his own cigarettes (Bull Durhams).

Bobby had a very droll sense of humor, and occasionally took part in our evening campfires. His favorite stories were about city slickers coming up hilariously short in attempts to take advantage of good ole country boys. The reactions to his campfire stories were predictable: about half were howls of laughter and the rest groans of despair.

Bobby always enlisted help when he was packing supplies out to other camps. We would help saddle up the plugs with Bobby's kayaks. The kayaks were similar to the small boat in that they were wooden frames covered with canvas, but they were not intended for white water use. Our kayaks carried milk and meat chilled almost to freezing, canned fruits and vegetables, trail food, and letters from loved ones.

Bobby usually got off to an early start because he had "many miles to go." He looked the part. The wide-brimmed hat served a real purpose, and so did his black leather chaps. He wore a perennial grin and occasionally an old jacket, but he also had a yellow rubber rainsuit in his saddle bags.

On the surface, his job may have been glamorous to the campers. However, the glamour must have paled in the downpours that occasionally accompanied Bobby's return from the high country. Perhaps the real glamour of his job was the unique opportunity to know Philmont like none of us ever could. Paul, Jimmy Money, Dick Gertler, or I could tell most expeditions how to get to Brownsea Camp, but we had never been there. Bobby could tell an advisor where the best campsite was, and where the nearest spring was as well. We shared an interest in getting off the beaten trail, but the mobility of packing put him in a position to see some of Philmont's most inaccessible treasures.

Bobby was also a goodwill ambassador when he was on the trail. He had never been a Scout, but he never failed to stop and talk to the Scouts he would meet on his travels or in the Beaubien corral. The Scouts could pick out the real McCoy, and Bobby would perch tall in the saddle, and answer their questions with the utmost of patience.

One day, he showed up with a rather brutish looking colt. It had an odd-looking nose, and its hair was much shaggier than most of the ponies I had seen. It was without horseshoes. We had often heard Bobby talking about wild horses, but I never put much stock in the talk. Yet, Bobby was not one to tell tall tales, and wasn't there a place called "Wild Horse Park" just beyond Crooked Creek? Sure enough, Bobby had caught a young mustang. Bobby may have thought it routine, but it was something those of us in the camping department never could have pulled off.

Bobby probably forgot more about the Ranch than most of us could learn in years of working on the summer staff. When I left Philmont two years later, I only had a few regrets. One was the fact that I was too stupid to get a really good camera and take plenty of pictures. Another was that I never went packing with Bobby, but, there just wasn't time for it. Bobby Maldonado was the lifeline for places like Black Mountain and Red Hills, but he was also an essential element in making Beaubien the special place it was. Bobby's performance transcended his "packer" job description. On those days when Bobby took the western lore program, the look in the campers' eyes said, "Here is a true cowboy. This is the real thing." They were right. He *was* a cowboy. His rich brown eyes, that dusty ten-gallon hat, the chaps, and brown curly hair along with the ready smile and quick wit were part of our claim to being a "western" camp. More important was Bobby's oneness with the land, his partnership with Bob Dog, and his devotion to duty, not just to packing out of Beaubien, but to his true western heritage.

◆ ◆ ◆

Beaubien was the crossroads of the high south country. Our visitors included cattle and horse department professionals, like Lawrence "Boss" Sanchez. Boss Sanchez visited our corral now and then, and occasionally brought his daughters with him. The word *hombre* came to mind when we saw Boss Sanchez. He was a long-term and highly respected Philmont employee who was solidly built. He was the type who might have wrestled steers and broken broncos, and would do the same to us if we looked at his daughters, Bella and Gloria, the wrong way.

Beaubien was a place where forestry department specialists and the occasional ranger showed up. Rangers were always looking for a ride back to camping headquarters, and Beaubien was the best place to find a returning commissary truck or jeep. Rangers Paul Felty and Doug Trevett came though Beaubien several times that summer, and I made a point of picking their brains on their rangering business. While I was more than content to be on the Beaubien staff, rangering seemed like a possibility for the following summer. Those guys saw the Ranch like few other staffers ever could. They played the pivotal role in getting the green expeditions ready for the rigors of a mountain back-packing experience.

Rangers weren't the only visitors. We got visiting VIPs as well. One Wednesday in mid-July, we got word that the Chief Scout Executive of the BSA would be having dinner with the Beaubien staff that Friday. The place was quickly spruced up, new blades were put into razors, and the special uniforms came out of steamer trunks. The Beaubien staff would not be found wanting in any respect. The Commissary Department complied with our emergency request for special provisioning. We were ready for the big day.

"You look kind of shaggy, Cass."

"I don't want to hear it. Especially from you. Even Bob Dog looks better than you do. In fact, I bet you've got more fleas than he does."

Exchanging insults with Freddy was nothing new, but it did prompt each of us to take a serious look in the mirror. We hadn't wasted our few days off in barber shops, and more than just two of us needed to have our ears lowered. It was time for some frontier trimming, so justice was administered on the front porch. We took turns cutting each other's hair. Considering Jim Talley's deft touch with brush and palette, it was an easy decision to let him cut my locks, which were getting a bit unruly. The collective net result was probably positive in that our ears were indeed lowered, but the edges were on the ragged side.

On the morning of the great day, the radio crackled to life with the message that the Chief Scout Executive was forced to change his itinerary. We would, however, be visited for lunch by the Assistant Chief Scout Executive, Bob Billington. He had most recently been the Council Executive in New York City, and was obviously no lightweight. Accompanied by other dignitaries, Bob Billington turned out to be a very genial fellow. He had a faint southern accent that had been dulled by years of professional service north of the Mason-Dixon.

While we were making small talk with other members of the entourage, we noticed that Billington and our own Freddy Blair were engaged in animated conversation. It turned out that Freddy's hometown of Columbia, Tennessee was also the birthplace of Bob Billington. The two were deep in conversation about their hometown, country music, and mutual acquaintances while the rest of us stood by, thunderstruck. It even impressed the unflappable Dimalanty. By two P.M., our visitors had made their apologies, and were on their way. We wondered about the entire deal. Had Phil McGarr (a.k.a. "McGoo"), Cito Camp Director, lured our dinner guest away? In any case, we buried our sorrows in some really fine steaks that Dick Gertler prepared to perfection. We expecially savored the extra portions of sirloin.

The initial selection of Beaubien for VIP visits was important in one respect—*esprit de corps.* We had plenty of that—maybe a little too much. We knew we were playing in Scouting's big leagues, but we were also very much aware of how lucky we were to be employed at this national Scouting treasure. If we hadn't gotten a sense of how important our jobs were when we read our contracts, it certainly came across in the eyes of the advisors and campers. We saw it not only during program instruction or at the campfire, but all the time. If anything, it was most intense when we checked groups in.

We were all hometown boys. We watched the expedition sheets to see when our own council would arrive. I knew when Lancaster County Council was coming, and my anticipation had been heightened by neighboring councils passing through. Lebanon County had come to Beaubien with York-Adams. Crews from Chester County spent two days with us, and I enjoyed the conversation of their advisors at the evening coffee hour. Little did I know then how significant this council would become to me in future years. Nor did I know how high this small council consistently ranked in terms of Philmont attendance. We had Valley Forge in Camp, and the unmistakable dropped "Ds" and purred "Os" marked the arrival of a raft of Philadelphians. There was no sign of Lancaster County, though. Even if they had come our way, I probably would not have known many of them. Our Order of the Arrow (OA) lodge, Minqua #519, was not large, and it was my only avenue to meeting Scouters outside the southern district of the council.

We had groups from northern Pennsylvania and upstate New York councils, but not Lancaster County. They must have started at Cito and gone North or vice versa. There was always a certain amount of disappointment in not seeing the home council. We couldn't help but see ourselves as "local boy makes good" types. We weren't braggarts, but still, here was an opportunity to portray the Ranch in a unique way. Maybe some of those up-and-coming kids back home would get bitten by the Philmont staff bug, and come west the way we had.

Teaching program to an increasing number of campers each day seemed to make the days run together. There was one day about which there was no mistake, and that was Sunday. Within our staff, religious persuasions were pretty much split between Protestant and Catholic. Dick Gertler had been a recent convert to Catholicism, and had an excellent handle on the various religious holidays. Regardless of preference, we all befriended the pastors, priests, and rabbi on the staff. Not only were they all interesting conversationalists, they were dedicated Scouters. These chaplains were a great source of comfort to the occasional homesick camper or the youngster who was having a hard time coping with the rigors of the trail.

Our church services were held in a chapel below Trappers Lodge. It was in a serene little amphitheater at the edge of the woods. The setting perfectly captured the spirit of the "Philmont Hymn," with its lyrics about "wind in whispering pines and eagles soaring high."

4

Wings Over Beaubien

Beaubien was not a hotbed of aerial activity other than the occasional golden eagles that soared over nearby ridges. It was, however, the jumping off point for side hikes to Trail Peak. Trail Peak's western ridge was marked by an air disaster that subsequently became a Philmont landmark. The details of the 1942 crash of an Army Air Force B-24 Liberator have never been widely known. With the passage of years, the story's repetition by rangers and camp staffs has muddied the facts surrounding the accident.

We know that an Army B-24D Liberator crashed just below the crest of Trail Peak at approximately 8:30 P.M. on the evening of April 22, 1942. This "Lib" was practically brand new. Based at the Combat Crew Training School (CCTS) at Kirtland Field in

Albuquerque, Liberator 41-1133 had been accepted from Consolidated Aircraft only two months before the crash. It had been flown less than one hundred twenty hours. The mission of the CCTS was to provide crews with the final, advanced training before assignment to operational units. The purpose of the April 22 flight was navigational training. The pilot, co-pilot, and flight engineer were not Army Air Force personnel. They were a contract crew provided to the Advanced Four Engine Flying School by Trans World Airlines. The aircraft commander was a veteran pilot with over four thousand hours and an Airline Transport Rating obtained in 1930.

They took off from Albuquerque shortly after eight A.M. local time, and landed at Kansas City about three and a half hours later. They began the return flight to Albuquerque shortly after four P.M., estimating four hours en route, although they had enough fuel for eight hours of flying. Two of the crew, the TWA flight engineer and 2nd. Lt. R.E. Jeffries, one of two navigators, were from Kansas City. In less than an hour, the crew reported in over Newton, Kansas. Three and a half hours into the flight, they requested an instrument clearance. In their next transmission, they reported climbing to fourteen thousand, but part of the report was garbled. The crew indicated their position as being seventy-five miles northeast of Las Vegas, New Mexico. Because the radio transmission was garbled, it was unclear whether they said "northeast" or "northwest." Seventy-five miles northwest of Las Vegas is high country, and would have explained the climb to fourteen thousand. They called in again at 8:05 when the weather was decent at Wichita and Albuquerque. The weather at Philmont was another matter. Ceilings were limited to less than six hundred feet in rain.

The big bomber plowed into the mountain, leaving five small craters where the fuselage and engines hit. The plane sheared off tree tops for sixty feet before the impact, after which the wings separated. The fuselage continued for another two hundred fifty feet. Lt. Jeffries, who had been an active Scout in his Kansas City Area Council, flew clear of the wreckage with the other officers. The nose section was completely demolished back to the flight deck, and the fuselage broke into two pieces aft of the wings. The aft section of the fuselage, complete with the tail section, rolled inverted but was left intact. With their momentum, the engines punched great indentations in the ground, and flew on for many feet before stopping. One of the four engines came to rest on top of the ridge just below the mountain's crest, while another fell below the ridge on the north side.

The wreckage would go undiscovered for another week, until it was spotted by another B-24 from Kirtland. On May 2, a party consisting of local police, representatives from the Four Engine School, and people from TWA reached the peak in poor weather conditions. They had brought horses to carry out the crew's remains that were found in the snowfield surrounding the plane. The investigation added to the mystery of the crash.

Altimeter analysis indicated that they had been at 10,050 feet at the time of the crash (about two hundred feet too low to miss the crest). They were on a heading of eighty degrees, with the port wing slightly low, and had been going two hundred miles per hour at impact. They had also lost an engine before the crash since number four had been feathered and the fuel to it was shut off. Every member of the crew was on oxygen, and had his parachute on, fastened, and adjusted. This suggested that they were prepared for the worst. Under normal circumstances, 'chutes were not worn, but stowed near one's station. Their radio direction finder had been set on a bearing of 256 degrees or roughly the course one would expect for an Albuquerque-bound ship.

The crash raises many questions. The winds were southerly. Had they been blown much further north than they had imagined? But, at fourteen thousand feet they could have cleared anything in the area. Why the heading of eighty degrees? Maybe they were flying a few extra legs for navigational training. With one engine gone, would they have continued training, or headed for base? Or were they orbiting while trying to get a better radio fix to determine their exact position? But why would an experienced TWA crew let themselves get caught in such a situation?

Could it have been a failure in the pitot static system leading to an altimeter error? Perhaps it was structural icing. While it was designed to carry a heavier bomb load than its glamorous cousin, the Flying Fortress, the ungainly Liberator's wings weren't known for their ability to carry ice. The D Model Liberator had de-icing equipment, but it was primitive by today's standards. Equipment failures were common enough, especially early in the war and on early models of airplanes. Maybe they were trying to find their way around the storm and became victims of windshear.

In the final analysis, it was probably a series of errors and mechanical problems that contributed to the disaster. They had "run out of luck and altitude simultaneously," as surviving aircrews would have said in those days.

Lt. Jeffries' Liberator was of interest to me, as were all 24s. While most of my father's flying time had been spent in light bombers and fighters, he had a few hours in 24s. Two of my uncles had also flown the Liberator, and my Aunt Betty's fiance had been killed flying a Liberator in nearly identical circumstances. In appalling weather conditions, he had been ordered, under protest, to fly a VIP to Scotland. The flight ended in tragedy when his B-24 crashed into mountains in Labrador.

I had never seen a Lib up close, and the remains on Trail Peak were scattered widely. The effects of the impact had been magnified by the dynamite that the Air Force had used to obliterate traces of secret equipment on the Liberator. Unless one was an aircraft historian, or knew in advance, it was impossible to tell what kind of plane it was. Then, there was a small cairn with a canister attached to a pole at the edge of the crash site. Inside the canister was a flag, a crew roster, and a request that visitors treat the site with respect, and not remove so much as a sliver of the wreck's remains. Over the years, this ground would be treated with something less than the respect due.

We climbed Trail Peak during Operation Scatter as part of our familiarization with the local area. The climb, while easy in contrast to climbs like Black Mountain, was tough, since we were not yet acclimated to the altitude. Several of us climbed Trail Peak again at the end of the season, and did it in exactly half the time. Trail Peak is so named because it is the dominant peak along the "trail" to Fish Camp via Fowler Pass and Webster Pass. Although two trails would eventually lead to the top, it was strictly a matter of bushwhacking when we climbed Trail Peak from Beaubien.

Pieces of the wreck had been carted off to the Philmont museum at Rayado. Years later the Philmont Staff Association painted a large yellow "X" on the surviving wing to prevent pilots from calling in what they assumed was a recent wreck.

The trail from Beaubien to Red Hills starts at the northwest corner of the meadow above Beaubien. It was the site of another air accident, albeit a much less publicized event. This trail is not especially well traveled. The only reason we were ever on it was to climb Bonita Peak as part of our familiarization process during Operation Scatter. Normally, the trail was used by a few groups coming out of Red Hills Camp, which sent most of its traffic down to Porcupine.

Along the left side of the trail, bent tubing and tattered pieces of aircraft fabric were scattered here and there. Most of it was covered by underbrush. Nobody knew much about the wreck, but it was clear that some light plane, probably a Stinson or a Taylorcraft, had gone down. The fabric was not yellow, so if it was a Piper Cub, it must have been repainted. Why a little ragwing would be flying at such an altitude was a mystery. Most of those little fabric covered ships ran out of steam above ten thousand feet. The nearby peaks, which push towards twelve thousand feet, require hundreds of feet of clearance. Could the pilot have been trying to make an emergency landing in the meadow above Trappers Lodge?

The meadow was long enough for a little taildragger to get in, but it would be a rough landing. Low on fuel, maybe a burst oil line, hemmed in by growing storm clouds—whatever the cause was, the pilot may have overshot the landing, and rolled it up into the edge of the forest.

The entire wreck was not visible, and we never thought to take a shovel out for exploratory excavation. The engine might have been buried, and the site had become overgrown. Maybe the little plane was caught in a storm, and broke up in flight with just a few of the airframe pieces falling by the trail to Red Hills. Perhaps the pilot was sightseeing, banked too tightly, stalled out, and found himself in the classically fatal trap of having too little altitude for recovery. Whatever the case, he, too, ran out of luck and altitude.

Just clearing the ridges was part of the program for the B-52s that we occasionally saw over Philmont. We presumed that they were testing some new terrain avoidance radars since they put a new dimension of meaning into the word "hedgehopping." Seeing the heavy brigades down in the weeds, following the contours of Philmont's terrain with all eight engines thundering, was really inspiring. Since the crews would get little sensation of speed at the high altitudes where they normally flew, those pilots must have been having a ball.

We had to wonder why they were skimming Philmont's ridges. There appeared a routine to their work that suggested some sort of testing or practice. Perhaps there was a former Philmont staffer at the controls, and he couldn't resist the temptation to get on the deck for some real "flat-hatting." In either case, it certainly would have created a stink if a '52 had gone into those mountains, which were hardly unpopulated during the height of the summer.

The B-52s had nothing on Philmont's golden eagles for low level flying. Beaubien was not the best place to watch the eagles, although they frequently soared within sight over the ridges of the Bonita Valley. The best place to watch the great birds of prey was from nearby peaks. While I had not specifically set out to watch the birds when I climbed Black Mountain, that is what I spent much of my time doing.

On July 3, none of the groups in camp was scheduled for the Hunter Safety Course. Since I had the luxury of a little time on my hands, I decided the time was ripe for my jaunt up Black Mountain. "Jaunt" is hardly what it turned out to be, since Black Mountain was rarely climbed, and with good reason. At the time, there were no trails to the top of the mountain, which was one of the steeper, if not steepest, climbs on the Ranch.

Johnny and Skip wished me well, and suggested that I take it easy. The base is not that difficult, and there was plenty of wildlife to distract me. Some of Philmont's rare birds, turkeys and grouse, consumed a few minutes of observation, but I was soon on my way again. A familiar pattern developed about half way up. I got tired and short of breath. Remembering Skip's parting suggestion, I slowed down, and then started setting little goals for myself.

"Go for a hundred paces, and then take a breather," I'd say to myself. I'd give it one hundred ten for good measure, and stop for a minute.

About two-thirds the way up, I was seriously questioning what I was doing on that particular spot of earth. Three-quarters of the way, I resolved that this would be my last trek up any mountain forever. I started thinking that taking a break every fifty paces might be a good idea.

While it looked as though I was running out of steam, it looked like the good earth was too. The trees were starting to look wizened and gnarly. The stunted growth is typical as one approaches the timberline. Black Mountain's crest is just below the timberline, but I did not know it yet. I did know that I certainly wasn't going to go on another lungbusting sidehike again for a long, long time, if ever. Clearly, it was time to haul up for a moment again, and catch my breath.

During one of these breaks, I became aware of a fleeting presence. Whether by sound or shadow, I knew that something had shot past me headed down the mountain. I looked, but saw nothing, so I pushed on figuring I'd better not quit now. Then, just when I thought lungs and legs were about to fold up on me, I got a second wind. Although I was still breathing hard, I could breathe more deeply, and my legs didn't feel as rubbery. I wasn't exactly gliding to the top, but it was definitely not as tough, although the pitch was even steeper than half an hour before. I knew I was near the top because the horizon at the pinnacle was definitely getting lower.

Then again, the shadow flashed by. This time, I turned quickly enough to see what it was. I thought it was a golden eagle plummeting right down the mountain. It was a large raptor, dark all over, but decidedly smaller than a bald eagle. He didn't have much more than twenty or thirty feet clearance, and he was really moving. Then another one screamed past. Then I lost them.

Within twenty minutes, I was at the top. I was rewarded with a view even more breathtaking than the one I had enjoyed on Trail Peak at the beginning of the summer. After taking a few pictures in each direction, and enjoying the view of neighboring peaks, I caught sight of the eagles again. They looked like a family of aerial otters hard at play, romping down some imaginary slide. There was probably some method in their madness—perhaps they were preying on some smaller birds that were also flying above the treetops. Perhaps they were young eagles practicing their newly-won flying talents. Counting those cavorting by the sides of Bear Mountain, there must have been close to half a dozen of these dark raptors. They soared to the tops of the peaks, pushed over, and dove down the length of the mountains. They would pull out just before reaching the base, and then soar skyward with the rising air until they were high enough to push over again.

Black Mountain's crest is stony, and covered with dwarfed trees that resemble shrubbery. I sat on a little stone outcropping surrounded by these Lilliputian trees, and inhaled the scenery. No longer were there any questions about trekking up the next mountain. I was refreshed and, with those magnificent vistas, eagerly awaiting the next climb. The question was, would I be able to get the time off for more sidehikes? I wasn't going to worry about it right then, but I was going to enjoy the moment. All of the major peaks were visible. Bear Mountain was just across the way, and to the west and slightly south loomed the great Mount Phillips massif, which included Comanche and Big Red. To the north were Touch-Me-Not and Baldy, the most distinct of the nearby mountains.

I could see all the way to Colorado and some of its peaks. I thought I could see the curvature of the earth, but that may have been wishful thinking. How easily I started to reflect on the trails that brought me to this magic place. It was so like the mountains, creeks, and glens of my native Bradford County in Pennsylvania. However, there was a major difference in scale and about a mile and half difference in elevation.

My grandfather's farm was located in a Bradford County valley, and was surrounded by ridges of what the tourism bureau would later call the "Endless Mountains." Those Allegheny woods, ridges, and meadows were the playgrounds of my youth. Because I was so closely involved with the rural outdoors from a very early age, I was into "Scouting" long before registering with the B.S.A.

I found the crafts and games of Cub Scouting to be fun, but it was the outdoor aspects and Indian lore of Scouting that made me join a Boy Scout troop. While my knot-tying was workman-like at best, I was well ahead of my peers when it came to nature study. I had always helped my Grandfather Parks chase the cows home for milking, and had made the acquaintance of deer, owls, skunks, snakes, woodchucks, grouse, and most of the creatures of the eastern woodlands long before my contemporaries.

The banks of the Wysox Creek, which flowed along Gramp's farm, provided another link with Scouting. Running beside the creek was the Wysaukin Trail, one of Pennsylvania's major Indian paths. It was along this creek that Great-Grandfather John Allen found many arrowheads for his extensive collection of Indian artifacts.

While I had moved away from the farm before high school, I returned several times a year, and for extended stays in the summer. There was one ritual I always repeated, and was repeating the day I climbed Black Mountain.

I would climb the slopes immediately behind the barn. When I was about two-thirds of the way up, I would lay down on my back, look at the sky with its wandering clouds, and watch the hawks.

Climbing the ridges behind the barn was only a drop in the bucket compared to climbing Black Mountain, although it, too, would put me out of breath if I pushed it. The hawks, usually those magnificent red tails with their piercing "kreeeee" cries commanded my attention for as much as an hour at a time. Unlike the dive-bombing eagles of Black Mountain, my red tails soared with the wind, heads lowered looking for lunch hiding in the grass and brambles below.

Eventually, I'd tire of watching the aerial predators. I'd get up, and climb the rest of the distance to a stately pine that sat on top of the ridge. In the early summer, there were always sweet little wild strawberries for a trail snack, and raspberries later in the year. I'd sit "for a spell" (as Bradford County old-timers would say) under that old pine, which commanded a view of the entire Wysox Valley, and watch the hawks.

How easy it was to slip back in time to my last visit to the grand old tree. I could recall the many trails of Scouting which brought me to Black Mountain, and all of the fun I had along the way.

There was the camaraderie of Scouting that I had discovered in my own Troop 40 in Lancaster County and later at national Jamborees. Dear old Troop 40 was remarkable in many respects of which not the least was its own cabin with a massive fireplace at one end. The community solidly backed the Boy Scout and Girl Scout troops in those, Scouting's halcyon days. Those were the times when Scouts invariably wore uniforms to elementary school on troop meeting days without the fear of jeers from non-Scouts.

The community pitched in especially during our annual newspaper drive fundraiser. We never lacked for merit badge counselors. Interested adults, ranging from the trucking firm owner to the high school librarian, supported our Scoutmaster, Mr. Kenneth Derr, with expertise and enthusiasm. Mr. George Smith, a WWI Marine who had retired as the high school principal to become the editor of our semiweekly newspaper was a naturalist of considerable stature. He had published several books on nature, and was an inspiration to those of us who tromped through his fields in quest of merit badges in nature, weather, and bird study.

My daydreaming was again broken by the eagles and by a now cooler breeze. The shadows were lengthening and it was time to think about getting off the mountain. It was always difficult—leaving the summit. I felt like the little kid who had to turn his toy in. The trip down was typical; easier on the lungs but almost as tough on the legs.

On the way down, I thought about soloing mountains. It was surely against Philmont policy due to the safety aspects. However, it seemed to me that everybody ought to do at least one of Philmont's big climbs alone just to experience the serenity of the experience. To be sure, there is much to be said for climbing in groups, and sharing the joy with others, but the experience just doesn't seem as deep as a solo climb.

It was early evening when I reached Black Mountain's cabin. Johnny had left that afternoon for a day off, and Skip had been kind enough to delay dinner. We had a fine meal of pork chops with mixed vegetables, and then I was off again for the fifty minute hike to Beaubien where I arrived on the edge of darkness. Although bone tired, I attended the evening campfire where Jim's "Silver on the Sage" that night had special meaning for me. I got through the first few minutes of the coffee hour that followed, but excused myself early, and was asleep within a minute or two of hitting the sack.

Until mid-afternoon, the following day was typical. We checked groups out, supervised conservation projects, checked groups in, supplied them with trail food, sold them items from the trading post, and taught them program. By two P.M., it looked like our nearly daily thunderstorm had started making up early. Normally, the afternoon showers started at 3:30 and came from the northwest. We joked with the campers about how they could set their watches by when rain started, but this day was different.

It was hotter than usual without much of the breeze that made the high eighties so very tolerable. There was an unusual hint of the mugginess that we easterners were so used to, and the cumulus buildup had initiated much earlier. The clouds were more impressive than usual with bigger ramparts than I had yet seen that summer. Suddenly they were on top of us with their menacing grayness, and with a surprisingly intense wind.

I had shut down the range as the crack of thunder rolled down the valley. Looking across the pasture, I could see that Jim had already dismissed the western lore program group, and was unsaddling his horse. Jim had prudently decided to remain at the bunkhouse, while I headed for Trappers Lodge. I was bounding up the steps of the lodge when the drops turned into a torrent. There was nothing to be really concerned about. Our groups for the day had all checked in, and had their tents up. Everybody was under shelter, and this wasn't the first or last afternoon storm we would experience.

It was, as my grandfather would say, "coming down in pitchforks and hammer handles." When I had lived on his farm, I actually enjoyed summer thunderstorms. Nestled among the blankets on the front porch glider, I delighted in the cool spray of the rain, the jolts of lightning, and the reverberating thunder. My cousins would usually head for the basement or the centermost closet in the house, but I wanted to be where the action was. And the action was definitely at Beaubien. A few short years later, I acquired the pilot's healthy respect for the power of a thunderstorm, but for my first summer at Philmont, I was going to take it all in.

The visibility went to zero. We couldn't even see the trees outside the lodge. What started out as a strong "pitter-patter" had quickly turned into a roar that became more intense. The wind was not so much shrill as it was a deep howl. As those of us in Trappers Lodge looked outside and then at each other, the mood changed. We sensed in each other the fear that maybe our roof wasn't going to hold up after all. About the time the looks on our faces became much more subdued, the sound changed to a fierce, metallic staccato.

Hailstones! This wasn't your usual hailstorm. We were not on the storm's edge—Beaubien had to be the epicenter of it all. The pounding went on for much longer than the typical hailstorm. Finally, the sound receded, and the darkness started giving way to lighter shades. Shapes became visible outside the lodge as the sound fell off. Within a few minutes it was raining lightly, and then not at all. As we anxiously peered outside the lodge, we were dumbfounded to see what we took to be snow. It was, of course, a thorough coating of hailstones, and not small ones at that. Nearly two inches of granular ice covered the Bonita Valley.

In some places, such as the steps and porch of the lodge, it was even deeper. We burst out of the lodge to behold the results of this atmospherical event first hand. Campers crawled out of their tents, horses started to graze, and Bob Dog sheepishly emerged from beneath the Lodge. The guys who had taken shelter in the bunkhouse started walking over.

When they were within range, the inevitable snowballs were thrown at them. They returned fire. Campers started their own snowball fights. Very quickly, we realized that somebody could get hurt with this stuff, so we got the campers to direct their energies toward trees or other inanimate targets. While we were releasing the pent-up tension brought on by the storm, it occurred to us that we might put all this ice to some logical use while it lasted. Dick Gertler didn't have an ice cream maker, and we didn't have any cones with which to make snow cones or water ices. While we were figuring if we could rig up some Rube Goldberg ice-cream machine, the sun started to reappear. It made short work of the chilly, white patina that covered our surroundings.

Beaubien's porch, which enjoyed a southern exposure and a commanding view of the Bonita Valley to the southeast, was where we usually briefed newly-arrived groups. We always told them to pitch their tents facing downwind or to the south. I never did hear a camper come up to say that he had gotten wet due to poor instructions. It was probably the only case where we were consistently right when it came to the weather.

Keeping a weather eye always paid. On the one occasion I didn't, I was well rewarded for my stupid bliss. It was on my second day off when I had decided to hike down to Abreu, and get a ride into camping headquarters. I didn't have anything firmly lined up for the evening other than maybe going to Raton or Trinidad. I could have ridden down in the same truck that was bringing Dick Gertler back from his day off. I was cook for breakfast and lunch that day, and could not leave until finishing the dishes.

It was a lovely day. Not a cloud in the sky. It was only early afternoon, but I lost track of time as I hiked along the little intermittent creek that flows from the top of the meadow at Beaubien down to the bottom of the Bonita Valley. I was going to stop at Abreu to say hello to a friend who had ridden out on the train with me from Chicago. Then I planned to linger briefly at Olympia for another quick hello. Surely I could catch up with a truck or a jeep somewhere between Abreu and Rayado.

My eyes were riveted on the bottom of the valley and the great blue sky beyond it. My mind was full of thoughts naturally inspired by such a vista. How great it is to be alive, what a view, and how lucky I am to be here were in my thoughts. Suddenly a great shadow covered the valley followed immediately by a gust of wind and the "barroooom" of thunder.

I took my first look behind me in about twenty minutes, and was appalled at the menacing sky, now rent by lightning. I did a quick double take at the beautiful, cloudless sky out in front just as the wind picked up even more. Clearly, I was going to get wet. I decided to make for the woods and reached for my poncho as the first drops hit, but was soaked by the time I got it on. It turned into a general downpour, so I took refuge in the lee of a large fallen pine at the edge of the valley. Down at the end a log was a heap of feathers and some bones. It looked as though some turkey had become a meal for a coyote or possibly a bobcat. We rarely saw bobcats, but occasionally we heard them howling at night. The rain was chilling, but short in duration, and I was soon off again in bright sunshine. I couldn't resist a little sidehike up Rayado Peak even if my feet were wet. I should have resisted.

The descent down into Abreu was as steep as advertised, and I was starting to develop a couple of painful blisters as my reward for not bringing spare socks and shoes. I was behind schedule, so I didn't linger. Abreu would become one of my favorite camps. It is located in a broad glen where the Rayado emerges from its long mountain valley, and becomes a creek of the prairie. Abreu enjoyed the best of both worlds—a sweeping view of mesa and prairie, yet it was dominated by tall pines, rising terrain to the west, and the Rayado's refreshing presence.

I made my apologies and left Abreu, for I still had miles to go. Above the prairie trail along which I was now shuffling, the late afternoon sky was clear and warm. What a difference a few miles make. Beyond Urraca Mesa, the towering storm that had soaked me only a couple hours earlier was now just a few scattered clouds. "Well, that's life in the Rockies. Sun one minute, storm the next. The only constant is unpredictability," I thought, as my prospects for a jeep ride brightened soon after I passed Zastro.

photo courtesy of Fred Blair

Jim Talley (left) and Freddy Blair frolic in the "snow"

5

Night Riders

Beaubien days usually saw cumulus clouds billowing and growing tall by mid-afternoon. More often than not, these mushrooming balls of atmospherical fleece would evolve into the cumulonimbus that would give us a brief drenching by late afternoon. Fortunately, the rains usually came after Jim and I had taught the afternoon program sessions, so camper and staffer alike had time to batten things down. The camp always came to life immediately after the showers with conservation projects, firewood gathering, building the evening campfire, and general maintenance work.

When the rains hit around four P.M. on July 14, we were unaware of the drama that was unfolding on Comanche Pass. On this day, the rain didn't slacken off. It just kept on coming, maybe not as hard as at the peak of one of our typical thunder-storms, but we were certainly getting quantity this time. This rain was just short of a "frog strangler" or "squirrel floater" on the Beaubien rain scale. It was still raining steadily by the time Dick had dinner on the table. It had also turned much colder than usual, and at nearly 9,400 feet above sea level, Beaubien was never warm except in the midday sun. The ridges and mountains to the northwest always threw an early shadow over Trappers Lodge, so we felt the evening chill long before many other camps.

"Well, looks like we'll scrub the campfire tonight," Paul said as we all got up from dinner.

It was still raining hard enough that we wouldn't bother to make the rounds to the campsites to tell advisors to stand down for the campfire. Here was the type of night that campers might laugh about—in a few months, but definitely not then. This was the pre-backpacker stove Philmont. All cooking was done over wood, and when it got wet, the more pragmatic groups would opt for a trail lunch for dinner, especially if they had an easy hike the next day.

On the bright side of things, cancelling the campfire did bring certain advantages such as using the time to write letters and do the inevitable paperwork. In my case this meant filling out requisitions for ammunition, clay pigeons, and other range supplies. I filled out the sales report for ammunition used in extra shooting beyond that which the Hunter Safety course required. If any of us knew what problems were developing over toward Comanche Pass, we would have gotten the searchlights and ponchos, and headed up the ridge trail to Black Mountain. Instead we leaned back in our chairs in front of our warming fireplace.

It was such an unpleasant, chilling night that it didn't look like we were going to get any takers for the advisors' coffee hour until the knock came on the door.

"Guys really must be coffee hounds to come out in this rain."

It wasn't the couple of grizzled old Scouters looking for some caffeine, a warm fire, and conversation. It was a JLT (Junior Leader Training) ranger whose group had just arrived! Two of his charges were in bad shape. This wasn't a surprise, considering what they had been through. We brought the boys into the lodge, and put one on the first aid cot. We hand-carried the other over to the bunkhouse where Bobby Maldonado's cot was available. The boy in Trappers Lodge simply was exhausted. The other clearly had folded up, and looked like he was going into shock, although none of us on the staff had ever seen a real life case of shock. Our first aid stock in trade was the usual laceration, sprained ankle, and the occasional burn from a cooking fire or pot handle. We had all gotten some refresher first aid instruction as part of staff training. That training emphasized the types of problems we could expect, including shock. Of the three staffers in the bunkhouse, I had the most medical training, so I took the boy's temperature and pulse. Clearly, the boy was slipping into shock that was caused by being pushed beyond his endurance. For all we knew, he might have had some underlying problems or source of pain that made matters much worse.

I gave him the classic first aid for shock, which really didn't seem to help much. At least we couldn't harm anybody by treating for shock, or at least we didn't think we could make matters worse. There wasn't much more we could do beside get some dry clothes on him, bundle him up with blankets for warmth, and elevate his legs.

The JLT ranger's job was to shepherd the JLT campers through an abbreviated expedition as part of their training at the Volunteer Training Center (VTC). He looked as frightened as the two boys looked worn out. He had good reason to be worried. Shock can be fatal, and this kid wasn't responding. After some probing, we learned that the ranger had gotten off to an unpardonable midday departure from Cyphers. He then decided to push it to Beaubien instead of stopping at Black Mountain.

The JLT crew was strung out all over the trail, which was infinitely more difficult with rain, cold, and mud. Within the next fifteen minutes the rest of the expedition arrived along with the other JLT ranger. Those rangers had defied conventional wisdom at every turn of the trail. Biting off more than one can chew at Philmont is foolhardy at best. Getting strung out on a trail can always be remedied by putting the slowest camper in the lead and forbidding any other person to pass. They probably should have called it a day at Black Mountain instead of pushing on. If that had happened, perhaps this Scout in our bunkhouse would simply have been bushed, and not in serious trouble. On the other hand, if a camper was in really bad shape, Beaubien certainly was a far better place to be than Red Hills or Black Mountain. Monday morning quarterbacking, however, wasn't going to help the situation. Only one thing was sure at that point. Both rangers would be on their way to the Raton bus or train station within an hour of their arrival back at the VTC, and it wouldn't be a round trip ride.

Thinking about the unpromising future of the rangers did nothing to help their two victims. The boy over at Trappers Lodge was coming around, and since he was clearly not in shock, was eagerly downing soup and hot chocolate.

"Kid's got a real problem, Paul, and what we're doing doesn't look like enough. I don't know what else to do."

With my comment and another look at the Scout, Paul left at once to radio the Control Center, and apprise them of the situation. Control wondered if it was so bad that an ambulance was needed, and if so, could it be delayed until tomorrow when the weather would be better. Paul told them to get an ambulance up to Beaubien right away without fail. A few weeks after this incident, I happened to be in the Control Center waiting for a ride back to Beaubien, and heard Paul's voice on the radio. His deep baritone dropped a couple of octaves in the ether waves, and really sounded like the ultimate authority. "Best not to argue with this man" was probably the reaction of the radio operator that night.

Several of us were watching over the boy when Dimalanty recalled that there was some advisor named "Doc" in a group he had checked in that afternoon. Could this have been a nickname, a veterinarian, college prof, dentist, or might we hit paydirt with a real M.D.? Dimalanty couldn't remember the group number, so we pulled on our ponchos and sloshed our way around to the campsites waking up every advisor. We did indeed hit that paydirt with a mild-mannered general practitioner from a small town in Ohio. He even had a small medical kit with him (bless him for carrying that extra weight).

"Doc" sized up the situation, and was clearly wondering what the New Mexico good Samaritan laws were when he gave the boy an injection. He didn't mention what it was, but it must have been something within the spectrum of a painkiller or cardiovascular stimulant since the Scout seemed to improve.

"If you guys hadn't gotten to him when you did, I'm afraid we could have had some *real* problems on our hands. There's not much else you guys can do, so why don't you call it quits. I'll stay with him until the ambulance gets here."

The physician stayed with the boy until Rans Potter, an ambulance driver, and one of the medics arrived nearly two hours later. When daybreak arrived the rain had stopped, and was replaced with a cold breeze beneath an overcast sky. The mood was somber at breakfast. We were deeply relieved that the night ended with the boy coming around, and that his parents would not suffer a phone call filled with sad news from the Director of Camping. The night served to remind us that life can be snuffed out rather easily. The mountains can be most unforgiving for those foolish enough to forget their training or overstep the bounds of common sense.

Low hanging smoke suggested that most of the groups were up and getting breakfast started. By nine A.M., the expeditions that

were headed on the next leg of their journey had sent a runner up
to ask for a checkout. Some of us were a bit bleary-eyed, but glad
to get the day's activities underway, which helped get thoughts of
what might have happened out of our minds. None of the other
groups in camp knew what was going on, and when the JLT
group checked out, they looked like any other bunch of wet
campers until we saw their faces. Decidedly haggard looking,
they shoved off and headed down the valley toward Abreu. They
could look forward to a pickup in a day or so at the Olympia
turnaround.

We had our usual duties. Clean the lodge, answer questions
for those sidehiking Trail Peak, air out our sleeping bags, help
Dick with the dishes, and assign conservation projects that we
would also supervise. By early afternoon, there were breaks in the
overcast. This eventually gave way to a clearing sky that yielded
some warming rays. We were slipping back into the routine.
Teach program. Check groups in. Help unload the commissary
truck, cut wood for the campfire, split wood for the fireplace. We
were looking forward to a full night's rest after the previous
evening's vigil, but still had to clear that last hurdle—the
advisors' coffee hour—before hitting the sack.

We all enjoyed the coffee hours—up to a point. There were
always a few advisors who wanted to hang on until the early
morning hours. This invariably kept all of us awake since the
bunks were located on one end of the main room of Trappers
Lodge. Paul, the practical engineer, simply requested a few 2x4s
and 1x10s. We quickly built a wall so those of us who wanted to
retire early could do so without fear of being kept awake.

The coffee hours were microcosmic jamborees. We had
advisors from every corner of the country and every walk of life.
While I was not a linguist, I was fascinated by the advisors'
accents. English, or American English, didn't get much better
than that spoken in northern Pennsylvania and upstate New York
as far as I was concerned. Those accents, with their hard long

vowels, and crisply spoken Rs, were the origins of my accent, or lack of it, since I had lived in six other states by the time I got to college.

By summer's end, I could tell where an advisor was from before I saw his council patch or heard him say where his home was. As might be expected, lack of an accent suggested that the speaker was from one of America's melting pots such as California. It always mystified me how going one hundred miles in any direction from my home could turn up a dozen or more accents. There was Philadelphia with its dropped, ending Ds, the almost Elizabethan English of Maryland's lower Eastern Shore, and the most distinct of all, the Pennsylvania "Dutch" (German) of my adopted Lancaster County.

This amateur linguistic streak drove me to get as much give and take as possible in my teaching the hunter Safety Course. I was like a hog in slop if we had some Downeasters from Maine, or a troop of second generation Germans from Wisconsin. To the average Yankee, like myself, the accents of Dixie were all the same—until I had listened to enough of them. By the end of the summer, I was getting to the point where I could distinguish between the many accents of the South. In terms of accents, an advisor from Wichita wasn't nearly as interesting as the one from Asheville or Charleston.

They were all interesting as they talked about their troops, their experiences on the trail to date, and their aspirations. They frequently asked questions about the trails that lay ahead as we lingered over the warmth of the fireplace. More often than not, another advisor would readily answer questions about the nearby trails since Beaubien was really the hub of the South country. Quite early in the summer I resolved that I would do every trail and every mountain in the South country before the summer was over. Little did I know how much time that would take, and that few people, including rangers, ever got to see it all even in a lifetime.

The advisors would show up for coffee within fifteen or twenty minutes after the campfire. We were always ready with freshly brewed coffee and the ubiquitous bug juice.

The other item we had in abundance at coffee hour was oatmeal cookies. We really pushed oatmeal cookies, and with good reason. We were in the midst of the great oatmeal cookie fiasco. It wasn't quite of the proportions that warranted calling it a scandal, but it seemed that we had those cookies running out of our ears. For every sugar cookie or ginger snap, we were pushing ten or fifteen of the oatmeal variety.

Philmont's Commissary Department, while doing a brilliant job year after year, had made one minor typographical error on a purchase order. The effect was to order several hundred cases of oatmeal cookies when only a hundred cases had been required. For some reason, they could not be returned, and they weren't going to be kept for another year. The Commissary Department cancelled or delayed other cookie orders, and instructed us to push the oatmeal cookies.

The advisors, who were at that point used to the amorphously-textured trail food, were delighted with something they could sink their teeth into. They wolfed down the oatmeal cookies with gusto.

"Have another," was the call of the evening at our fireplace.

Pennsylvanians were frequent visitors to the coffee hours. It came as no surprise since that state sent more expeditions to the Ranch than any other. Chester County, York-Adams, Valley Forge, Philadelphia, Lebanon County, Hawk Mountain, and neighboring councils such as Del-Mar-Va all passed through Beaubien. They all got the oatmeal cookie treatment. There were some surprises. The father of one of my fraternity brothers showed up with a younger son in a Baltimore crew. An Assistant Scoutmaster from my old Jamboree troop also came through Beaubien. He had moved to Delaware, and brought a crew out for his third Philmont expedition.

Most of the advisors were in their forties, and had their sons along. Typically, the sons were fourteen or fifteen, had reached Star rank, and were having the time of their lives. It hadn't been that many years before when many of the fathers were in danger of losing their lives. These were the men who had fought the Japanese and mosquitoes on Bougainville, or pushed cargo out of C-47 doors during the invasion of Burma. They were the ones who loaded the 40s on battleships, or hunched over Norden bombsights in the thin air above Germany. When only a few short years older than the average camper, they were fighting frostbite in Belgium during the rough winter of '44-'45 or withstanding many chilling watches on the North Atlantic run.

They rarely talked of that period in their lives. When they did it was usually Army Air Force veterans whose memories of the war years were renewed by visiting the B-24 crash site on Trail Peak. They would fall silent quickly after mentioning that they had flown on '24s, or maybe it was '17s or '25s or whatever. We never pressed them for information, and it was obvious that they were recalling images of smiling, young faces that did not come home. Those were the young men, gunners, pilots, engineers, or navigators who would not marry their sweethearts, build families, careers, or become Scouters who would find their way to Philmont with their sons.

We did, however, serve as host to one reunion that seemed, while not joyous, lighter than most. The advisors had seen each other just once since the war at a reunion of their outfit, the 10th Mountain Division. One vet was originally from Grand Junction, Colorado, and the other's pre-war home was Syracuse, New York. The latter was a salesman in Pennsylvania while the Rocky Mountain native had settled in suburban Chicago where he was a schoolteacher. Both had been avid skiers, which is probably why they wound up as "Phantoms of the Snow." They talked more of their training in Colorado in 1943 and '44 more than the tough days in Italy. Apparently their training, with its emphasis on cross country skiing and rock climbing, was a thoroughly enjoyable continuation of their pre-war sporting life.

These advisors were wearing the hallmarks of early middle age; one wore glasses, and the other was balding, but beyond that they were remarkably fit. Clearly, they weren't having any problems negotiating Philmont's mountains and ridges. They had probably carried many more pounds on their backs before. Like all advisors, though, they enjoyed the creature comforts of our lodge and the warmth of our fire.

Our link with civilization, the VHF transceiver, was mounted on the wall next to the fireplace. While that radio never failed, most of our portable radios were consigned to the bottom of steamer trunks within days of arriving at Beaubien. Reception was terrible, and the only station we could receive well broadcasted in Spanish. On the rarest of occasions, however, one other weak station would come in. To Freddy's delight, and to the dismay of several of us, it was the transcribed sounds of the Grand Ole Opry in Tennessee.

photo courtesy of Fred Blair

Trappers Lodge never lacked for warmth or good music.
Jim Talley with the guitar

On the surface, our "living room" was spartan, but on close examination it really exhibited functional charm. There was a little desk by the front window, a half dozen chairs (not one resembled another except that each had four legs), a large log bin, and a fireplace designed for maximum heat projection. It was wide and had a sloped back that bounced heat well throughout the room. By design, we usually had enough wood on the fire to last for no more than an hour.

We had several items that always drew comments. While we had no organized physical training program at Beaubien, we did have a pair of rings that hung from the rafters. Several of us got to the point where we could do a complete turn in them, although we were clearly not threats to any Olympic gymnastic hopefuls.

There was a stuffed bobcat whose left forepaw was gripped in a small steel trap. The cat crouched with his head turned, fangs bared, and eyes raging at the approach of any tormentor.

The other item was a potentially dangerous trap of gargantuan proportions—the bear trap of all time. This was a wicked looking device with sharp, toothed jaws. To set this contrivance required two of us, and the only thing that made the set easier was to push up against the ceiling beams. The trap would break three inch diameter logs easily, although a trap demo was not part of the evening coffee hour.

Dick Gertler usually attended the coffee hours, and became chief of the fire in addition to being the kitchen's master. He possessed a most extraordinary way of ending the evening, and his technique was worth the wait. He would position himself to the right side of the fire. After about half an hour, he would take a poker and adjust the logs to get more flame. Dick might repeat this once or twice in the next ten minutes, but would draw little attention to himself in the process. As a final preparation, he would rake the coals to an even surface, and then sit back in his chair. There we would be, stifling the occasional yawn, and wondering when the last of the advisors might decide that it was time to head for the land of nod. The last few vestiges of conversation might even mask the soft, rasping sound of Dick's lighting a wooden match, which he then sent flying toward the center of the fireplace.

The result was a roaring "whooomph" and an impressive fireball that would momentarily extend out into the living room. This got everybody's attention instantly. We weren't pyrologists, but we assumed that the match touched off some gaseous byproducts of combustion. That afterburner effect was most spectacular, and was a cap on the evening. It invariably prodded the last of the advisors to his feet for the trudge back to his campsite.

We had a little routine to follow as the advisors departed. Dick would finish a few early preparations for breakfast before heading back to the bunkhouse. Freddy would make a quick round-trip journey up the meadow to turn the water pump off. Paul would check in with the Control Center for any late messages. The night call-in rarely amounted to much more than letting control know that Beaubien was still on the face of the earth. It was usually justified with a time check, although we never had a universal failure of our wristwatches.

On the night of August 15, Control had an unusual request. There had been reports of a fire near Fowler Pass. Would somebody from Beaubien investigate the report? Paul quietly asked me if I would like to accompany him on a little hike down to the bottom of the valley to check out the report. He didn't bother asking anybody else since he obviously knew who the trail hog on his staff was. We left the lodge with Freddy who quickly turned up the meadow path to turn the water pump off.

Night pump duty under Philmont's starry night sky may have, ironically, been one of the more interesting events in Freddy's daily, quartermasterly rounds. QMs rarely got the thanks they deserved for the important work they did. Their position was typically an entry level job that led to better things the following year. I don't recall anybody requesting QM duty two years in a row. Anyhow, Freddy got more opportunity to see the night sky than anyone on the Beaubien staff. When he was gone overnight, I usually looked after the water pump. Unlike some small horsepower engines on the Ranch, Beaubien's ran like a charm. It had no mechanical vices, and didn't even challenge a mechanical klutz like myself.

There always seemed something totally out of place about the job. Here, in one of the most beautiful places in all of the Rockies, beneath a starry sky, and with a gentle breeze, I would walk. My eyes were directed at the heavens. Occasionally I would stumble on a clump of grass, but I was guided in my direction by sound. Not by a distant howl of a coyote, the hoot of an owl, or call of a whip-poor-will, but instead by some sound more akin to your average riding lawn mower engine.

From a couple hundred yards below the corral, Paul and I heard the pump engine die out. It was barely audible in the daytime when overlaid with routine noises, but at night the sound carried further, and the absence of engine noise was noticeable, and welcomed.

Although we had taken flashlights, there was no need for them since the moon was nearly full. While the days were hot, the nights were getting colder as autumn approached. Oddly, this night was not cold at all—just a hint of a chill in the night's gentle breeze. The lighting was eerie. The lunar rays cast everything in muted grays, blues, and greens but with striking definition in the trees and landforms. Now and then the sky, which was brilliantly speckled with stars, would be lanced with a shooting star. We were enjoying the tail end of the Perseid meteor shower.

Eventually, I would study the night sky and astral navigation, but for then, I was gazing upwards with the typical easterner's awe of the western, night sky. Such clarity! I saw more shooting stars that night than I had seen in all my life. I thought of Tom

Whiting who ran the astronomy program down at Crater Lake. A fellow Pennsylvanian, and obviously an amateur astronomer, Tom must have been in hog heaven teaching astronomy at Philmont. Back east, he would have to put up with both air and light pollution, and still rarely get to see the heavens as we routinely could nearly every night.

All we needed were a few owls to make this night hike complete, but they seemed not to be abroad. Maybe they had taken to flying during the day considering the multitudes of ground squirrels that were everywhere. If the owls weren't out, then the steers were. There was a good size herd of cattle in the Bonita Valley, and they were usually found below Trail Peak. We gave them a wide berth since we thought there would be a bull or two in the herd. If there was one thing we didn't want, it was to aggravate three-quarters of a ton of already fractious pot roast. We were past them soon enough.

All too quickly, we reached the end of the valley where the trail drops off in switchbacks down to Crater Lake. We had seen no smoke nor smelled any. No flame or unusual light could be seen save that which came from the moon. Having complied with control's request, we turned around and started back to Beaubien, which we reached well after midnight. We hadn't spoken much on the walk down the valley since we were both entranced with the nocturnal, ethereal beauty of our surroundings, but we did talk on the way back. Paul may have been more pensive than usual when we left Beaubien since he realized that his days at the Ranch were coming to a close. On the other hand, I still had one or two more years left. Paul would be going back to Texas Tech in a few weeks. When next June rolled around, he, with his B.S.M.E., would be entering the engineering profession. Paul would eventually build a highly successful career as an internationally respected consultant and author in project management.

We talked about what a privilege it was to work at Philmont. Paul had enjoyed a copybook Philmont career starting at age eighteen. He had two years in progressively more responsible jobs that led to his becoming Director at Black Mountain the summer before. Black Mountain is one of the most beautiful of all camps at Philmont. To a certain extent, it is a well-kept secret since it appears on only a few itineraries. Paul talked less about the routine affairs such as eager campers and appreciative advisors, but more about the remoteness and tranquility of Black Mountain Camp. While he was now Director of a prestige camp, I could tell that he was reflecting back on his four summers and probably concluding that living within the shadow of that steep, brooding Black Mountain was probably the most intense experience of all.

Paul chuckled as he talked about "Mother," the mule that they used to haul supplies back and forth between Black Mountain and Beaubien. Paul and Dimalanty often told tall tales to the gullible about their stay at Black Mountain. One was how, as mountain men with no modern conveniences, they made orange juice by shoving a handful of oranges into Mother's mouth. They would hold a glass below her grinding jaws to collect the freshly squeezed nectar. Usually, the resulting howls of laughter precluded asking just how such deprived mountain men got real oranges in the first place.

Nearly traumatic events, such as the time Dimalanty almost got hit by lightning on the ridge overlooking Black Mountain, were now becoming treasured memories. The howling of bobcats at night, along with the coldness of Urraca Creek's crystal waters, was going into that special Philmont file in Paul's mind. He would recall these events when he wanted to reflect back on those special, privileged days. All too soon, we were rounding the bunkhouse bend in the road. I wondered if Paul knew it was my birthday. Perhaps he knew it all along when he invited me to go on this little errand. It turned out to be one of the nicest presents I had ever received.

It was near one A.M. when I put "spine to feathers," and then I couldn't get to sleep. I couldn't shake the visions of shadows

across the valley, and the beauty above the ridges. It was like
sitting in a cockpit at the end of a flight, turning off the various
switches before cutting the engines, and eagerly awaiting the
silence that was always minutes away though everything had been
shut down. The flight may have been over, but you would never
know it by the sound of the flight instruments' gyros that would
keep on audibly spinning with their metallic, whirring choruses
before finally winding down. Eventually, my mind's gyros finally
spun to a halt too, thus ending one of the most memorable nights
of the summer.

    We needed all of the sleep we could get. The pace of the last
couple of weeks had been hectic. We had 219 in camp on August
3, and that was about total capacity of my old council camp back
home. Just a few days later, it was 340, and one week before my
birthday, we peaked out with 457 in camp. A couple of days after
my birthday, the pace slowed dramatically, and we had some
spare time on our hands. I had been planning more hiking for my
days off, and had some fairly aggressive diversions lined up. I
was clearly experiencing delusions of grandeur. I planned to head
down to Miners Park, then up Shaefers Pass, sidehiking the
Tooth, going back down the other side of the Pass to Clark's Fork
and finishing at Cito. Then I was going to get up early, hike to
Cyphers, go over Comanche Pass, down to Black Mountain
Camp, sidehike Bear Mountain itself, and then head for Beaubien.
I was going to do all of this within twenty-four hours. It is
possible to do this, but best accomplished by those who are
regulars in iron man competitions. Although I had done Black
Mountain, the Bear was not to be.

    Mount Phillips was to be, however. Groups were drying up
rapidly, and on August 22, there was no prospect of teaching
program. I had been waiting for such a day, and through intercamp mail alerted a friend, Steve Radford, down at Porcupine,
that the first slow day would be a good opportunity to go climb
Phillips. I finished morning chores, and went to Porcupine the

long way, via Webster Pass and Fish Camp, then up to Porky. Steve and I then headed for the mountain by way of Brownsea Camp. Late August can have its brief stretches of cool, rainy weather in the mountains, but this week was a notable exception. It was quite dry and warm, but the trail was well shaded. We happened upon a young porcupine that was making that typical, almost whimpering, mewing sound. These creatures can almost be domesticated. I had seen Jerry Traut, Philmont's Nature Director, hold and pet a porcupine (with the grain of the quills to be sure). The nature center held those animals that, because of injury or abandonment, had come into captivity, and in one sense was almost a petting zoo.

All parties did not hold porcupines in high regard. The foresters who passed through Beaubien said that porcupines killed trees by girdling them. The little critters have been known to chew on axe handles, not for reason of hunger, but for the salt deposits left from sweaty hands. I knew first hand what a porcupine could do when cornered. I had, more than once, helped remove quills from dogs that ran afoul of porcupines back in Bradford County. Maybe Jerry had the right touch, but Steve and I weren't going to push our luck by touching this little guy. I got a long stick, and gently touched the animal with it. I halfway thought he might let fly with that deadly tail, but he seemed more inquisitive than anything else. With a gentle shove from the stick, the little porky rolled himself up into a ball just like a hedgehog. We were wasting too much time, and left the porcupine to his own devices as we pushed off toward Red Hills.

Doing Mount Phillips from this side was almost laughably easy, so gradual was the climb. That mountain, or Clear Creek Mountain as it was originally named, is the central peak in a massif that includes Comanche Peak, Big Red, and Bonita Peak. When climbed from Cyphers Mines, Comanche Peak must first be negotiated, and it is a struggle. Mount Phillips, when done from Clear Creek, is also taxing. From Red Hills or Comanche, it is a piece of cake. We emerged from the spruce trees onto Comanche Peak, and then covered the last three hundred feet of elevation to the top of Phillips almost as an anti-climax. The view was even more spectacular than the scene from the top of Black Mountain, which had been such a grind to climb. To the immediate north was Touch-Me-Not, beyond which stood Old Baldy. We could see well past Colorado's Spanish Peaks.

There was one group up there with us, and they were amusing themselves with the gray jays. Also known as the Canada jay, these birds look like a slender cousin of the Blue Jay, or a very poor relative of the fancy Stellar's jays that are common at lower levels. The gray jay looks more like a mockingbird without the white wing flashes. These trusting jays were quite tame, and would swoop down for any leftovers from a trail lunch. They would even land on a person's head—assuming a few trail lunch crumbs were on his hat. After inhaling the view and amusing ourselves with the jays, Steve and I turned back toward Red Hills. We hadn't seen the pika, a rabbit-like creature that lives only at the highest altitudes, but we weren't complaining. The vistas had been breathtaking, and although I had enjoyed climbing Black Mountain alone, it was also nice to have someone to share the view with. It was especially rewarding to see the enthusiasm of campers and advisors alike at a highpoint of their Philmont Expedition.

The year was winding down rapidly, and each member of the Beaubien staff had some hard decisions to make. The Director of Camping was visiting each camp within a few days after the camp directors had completed the last of the monthly fitness reports on each staff member. Those with favorable reports were encouraged to think about the choices of jobs they wanted the following year. Paul would be ending his Philmont career, and starting the following summer as an engineer somewhere in industry. Our two Jims would not be coming back since earning more money had become a priority. The Ranch didn't pay that badly, but wasn't competitive with many hometown summer jobs. Dimalanty and Freddy had decided to become a team, and put in for Fish Camp. Bobby and Dick would probably return as packer and cook respectively, which left me as the only one who hadn't come to a decision. My situation was a real crossroads. I could have gone on to run the big rifle range at Pueblano or the ranges at Cito. A switch in program specialty was entirely possible since I had credentials for nature, conservation, fly tying, or wilderness survival. I could have tried to get in the fast track, and become an Assistant Director, if not at Beaubien, then at a place like Abreu or Porcupine. Considering my tendency toward wanderlust, there was really only one choice. I would become a ranger.

There were other decisions. There was an announcement that there *might* be a need for temporary staff for the first two weeks of September. Most of this work would be down at Camping Headquarters where Tent City had to be taken down. I didn't have to show up at college until the third week in September, so the prospect of some extra spending money was attractive.

I was also in a quandary as to getting home. I had train tickets, but Dick had asked me if I would like to return home to Lancaster County with him in his Scout. He had also suggested that Freddy join us. We could drop Freddy off somewhere along the way, and he could catch a bus or meet a relative for the rest of the trip to Tennessee. I had already taken a train across country, but hadn't driven it. We got word that there would not be any temporary jobs after all, so that clinched it. On the twenty-seventh, Paul let me have the day off so I could get up to Raton to turn in my train ticket for a refund. This was no leisurely day off. I got a ride down on a Forestry Department jeep, hitched rides to and from Raton, and was back the next morning on the last regular commissary truck. The next time the truck came would be to close Beaubien out for the year.

We were definitely in a closeout mode. The smell of solvent

permeated Trappers Lodge as I cleaned the shotguns. Jimmy was consolidating the unused trail food packs and trading post items into cardboard boxes. We all sat out on the front porch cleaning Dutch ovens, and putting the last film of cooking oil onto the inner surfaces. Along with Fred and Dimalanty, we toured the quiet campsites that no longer contained the curling smoke from cooking fires. Gone were the noises of camping at Beaubien—the "clankety-clank" of pots and pans rattling from the packs of arriving expeditions or the excited yells of pickup football games down in the meadow. The axes had ceased to make their chopping sound, and the woods no longer echoed with the crash of falling trees. Lariats no longer flew in the corral. The curious little running, metallic sounds made by Jim's spurs as he walked across the corral were gone. The ground squirrels must have thought a depression was in the offing since the amount of oats spilled from feedbags diminished by geometric proportions.

Dick, Freddy, and I missed the grand closing since we left early. Dick caught a ride to Camping Headquarters with Hubert Powell, and returned in the late afternoon with his yellow Scout. We weren't there, however, since we decided to go climb Trail Peak for old time's sake. We did it in good time—almost half the time it had taken in June. Clearly, living at altitude and having lots of good food and exercise had done wonders. When we got back, there was still some work to be done, but it was mainly little housekeeping chores. There were some mixed feelings at dinner, but as much as we had enjoyed the summer, we were glad to see it ending. The overwhelming mood was one of excitement and anticipation of getting home, and then back to school. On the other hand, we were realistic enough to know what a privileged bunch we were to serve on the Philmont staff, and that we would probably be homesick for the place by our first midterm exams.

Part II

The Upward Trail

6

Ranger Days

Driving through Kansas was a new experience, and I decided to let Greyhound do the driving the next time. Being a son of the Alleghenies, I didn't take to the flat prairie. Western small town Kansans must love their communities, but I was used to villages with their own unique characters and identities. We rolled on through little towns that differed only in the names on the signs. At the edge of town, there were the service stations and farm implement dealers, then the houses sprinkled throughout the predictable grid of streets, and a central business district bordered by the town park complete with band box.

The two or three churches usually faced the park that seemed to have most of the town's trees. At the other end of town, there were several tall grain elevators. We would speed by them, and look out onto the horizon to see a cluster of little towers. Half an hour later, we would be gathering speed as we whizzed by those "little towers" which were the next town's grain elevators. One town was a carbon copy of the previous community. And so it went on for a hundred miles or so.

These towns must have held something special for their people. It finally dawned on me that there were similarities with the highland towns so dear to me, especially in architecture. Granted, many homes in my native Bradford County were older, but the commercial buildings had been built at the same time. The First National Banks looked alike. The theaters had all started as the town "Opera," a label that was still painted or carved in stone on many edifices. Both had their Scout troops, and Kansas had always sent many staffers and expeditions to the Ranch. Still, I couldn't get used to the flatness, and the crisscross pattern of the streets. What these people needed were some obstacles in which to build their towns—the side of a hill, a creek valley, or maybe a mountain notch.

This repeating small town scenario would continue until we reached Wichita, whose busy skies identified the local Air Force Base and booming aerospace industry. We had settled into a driving routine of three hours on and three off. There was only room for two in the front, so the third slept on the pile of equipment in back. By the time we got to Missouri, I was starting to feel at home. We were in rolling green country again. Freddy's father drove north and met us in Indianapolis where we had lunch. Although Dick, Freddy, and I would serve again at the Ranch, our assignments were very far apart. I was not to know it then, but both of my friends would truly keep the faith in Scouting. They became professional Scouters within just a few years of our cross country journey.

We had been on the road for little more than thirty-six hours; not much more than twelve hours would see us back in Lancaster County. The trip was taking its toll. I nearly hit a logging truck on the Pennsylvania Turnpike simply because my alertness was slipping. We passed through the same mountains that marked my departure nearly three months before. It had been the best summer of my life by far.

Dick drove the last couple of hours, and then we pulled into his driveway in Ephrata. It was two A.M., but my parents were there. I must have sounded like a gusher about the summer. Telling them about my experiences was like a shot of caffeine—I just kept on babbling for the next hour until we got home. I did treat myself to the luxury of sleeping in the next morning. In a couple of days, we were off to Bradford County whose rounded mountains now seemed so pale in comparison even with Trail Peak. Soon enough, I was back at Washington College. There were the usual bull sessions with the other guys about how we spent our summers. My fraternity brothers had spent their vacations as lifeguards, surveyors' assistants, soda truck drivers, and grocery store clerks. Most of them had been in Scouts, but easily confused what I had done with working at the local council camp.

I had looked at our fraternity calendar on the first day back, and noted that we would be having a dance and open house in less than two weeks. I had met a young lady just before final exams the previous May, but had no time to take her out since my life was dominated by economics, philosophy, and the need for some good final exam grades. I called her sorority, and asked for Sarah Mumford. I had not seen her in several months, but she was in my mind's eye. A dark blond, with green eyes, she looked a lot like the singer Doris Day with whom she shared considerable musical talent. Would she like to go to the Lambda Chi Dance on the twenty-seventh? She would. She's been my partner ever since, and is still as lovely as the day I first called her.

Soon, the trees started turning. Autumn is a slow, lazy process on the Eastern Shore where the changing leaves are dominated by brown and yellow hues. People drove long distances to where I came from to see the fiery reds and crimsons of the autumn foliage. As the trees shed their leaves in Bradford County, the first of the Canadian geese flew in great Vee formations, and at tremendous heights. On the Eastern Shore, geese more typically flew low, for this was their winter home—descending to the corn fields, wide rivers, ponds, and marshes. With these signs of winter coming, I wondered how the Ranch looked. The aspens must have been bare because the nights were already getting cold in late August. How many feet of snow would there be in the Bonita Valley? It must have been several—we could still find drifts on Trail Peak in June. If I could have gotten myself up there in the first place, what would it have been like to ski from Beaubien to Lovers Leap? In the dead of winter, my ranger contract arrived. I signed on again, and got a ten dollar per month raise and the guarantee of coping with more ground squirrels.

But Philmont was far away. Sarah was close, there were academic hurdles that had to be surmounted, and it was late spring before I really started getting keyed up for Philmont. While I was excited about heading back to the Ranch, Sarah wasn't. Her lack of enthusiasm was not shared by Steve Gregory, my freshman year "roomie" and fraternity brother. My enthusiasm had been so infectious that Steve applied for a program counselor job at the Ranch. Steve had been a Scout in Chester County Troop 22 that was, and still is, one of the council's strongest troops. While my contract arrived in early January, there was nothing for Steve.

"Where's Lost Cabin?" Steve asked me on March evening in the student union. I could see the excitement in his eyes, and the telltale blue envelope in one hand.

"Beats me. I've been there twice, but never saw the place," I said, recalling fishing trips with Jim Talley. I told Steve that it must have once been a trapper's cabin, but nobody could ever find it, so they called it "Lost Cabin." I explained that it was in a beautiful, remote area of the Ranch, and that he could expect some good fishing. Appropriately enough, he was to be a program counselor in wilderness survival.

The days rolled by, and before we knew it, Steve and I were on the station platform in Lancaster waiting for the night train to Chicago. This year, the scene in Dearborn Station was different. I was a veteran, and made the introductions. Soon, we were boarding the El Cap, and speeding west toward the prairie and another summer of bringing high adventure to thousands of eager Scouts.

"Where's that other guy who's working at Lost Cabin?"

This was the meeting of Steve and his boss for the summer, Ned Gold, Camp Director, Lost Cabin. It was not an auspicious start. Steve and Ned eyed each other warily like cobra and mongoose. Ned was no amateur, although there were stories circulating about how he presided over the melting of a Dutch oven when he was a ranger. In Ned's defense, the rumors were unconfirmed and the oven in question was of the aluminum variety, and therefore had a slightly lower melting temperature than those made of cast iron. Ned was the eldest of three Philmont Gold staffers. A law student, Ned already had several years under his belt as a ranger. Brother Tommy had rangered and would be going to Harlan for the summer, while the youngest, Paul, was headed for his first summer as a ranger. These three Eagles were the sons of an Eagle as well. Ned would go onto a distinguished Scouting volunteer career, and earn the gratitude of all of us when he founded the Philmont Staff Association. Back then, he was the Director of Philmont's smallest camp, although in many ways one of the more beautiful.

I missed the Mississippi again, but apparently some of the hard core hung on for the crossing. We awoke to find ourselves in Kansas listening to the conductors' now familiar station calls over the next few hours. The only break in the monotony was the spectacular sight of a recently derailed freight train on the outskirts of Dodge City.

Garden City, Lamar, La Junta, and Trinidad all came and went. "Raton, Raton," was the conductor's cry, or it may have been the Santa Fe's lament that day. They could not have shown any profit from Raton to Albuquerque considering how many vacant seats were left in Raton.

The drill was a familiar one. Get the steamer trunks and duffel bags, chuck them onto a commissary truck, and get into a waiting school bus for the forty-five minute ride down to the Ranch. Our only responsibilities were to go through the quick meeting with the personnel department, check through the health lodge, pick out a tent in Tent City, and show up in uniform at 6:30 P.M. for the dinner and reception program. Steve and I parted company since he would be spending the next few days with other nature program counselors attending training sessions in the dining hall. As if to emphasize the separateness of rangerdom, I, along with seventy-five others, would move out the next morning for ranger training at Rayado.

Rangering is the best job at Philmont. It takes a "different breed of cat" to be a successful ranger. No other job demands so much in terms of physical stamina, mental fortitude, situational awareness, and in-depth scoutcraft skills. If anything, most rangers have a "rangey" air about them. If they aren't lean mountain men when they show up in June, the combination of carrying a forty-pound pack throughout the summer, and a steady diet of trail food ensures leanness by summer's end.

The average ranger looks the part. While he might appear close-shaven and standing tall in a freshly-pressed uniform at headquarters, the more typical image of a ranger is seen upon his return from an expedition. Because the humidity is so low, perspiration evaporates much more rapidly than most easterners can appreciate. The combination of exertion, low humidity, and enthusiasm for salt shared by all makers of trail food, produces dried deposits of salt on uniforms. This is most noticeable around armpits where the deposits looked just like contour lines on a topo map. Pack backbands produced unique designs that looked like the Rorschach patterns so loved by psychologists. These designs were much more noticeable in bygone days when the deep, polished cotton Explorer green shirt was the standard uniform in contrast to today's light green activity shirts.

There isn't always an opportunity to get a shower in the trail camps where rangers leave their groups, so there might be an occasional whiff of ripeness. If that can't be detected, there is the scent of woodsmoke for which the red Philmont jacket seems to have an especial affinity. Rangers are not big on hats, and this absence allows the wind to tousle already sun-bleached manes.

Boots are well broken in. Doing somewhere between five hundred and eight hundred miles a summer goes a long way to breaking some boots forever. Thus, rangers tend to be pretty well shod. Rangers always have a map of the ranch, if not in a pack pocket, then in one of their own pants pockets. By summer's end with the effects of rain, perspiration, and unfolding, the maps look like something between a papier-maché project gone haywire and some garbage the dog dragged in.

Those maps are a unique link between ranger and Ranch. Probably because I grew up on a farm, I had always felt a oneness with the land. It was very much the same oneness that pilots feel about airplanes—that the craft is an extension of themselves. Sailors feel the same way about sailboats and the sea. At the Ranch that oneness was reversed. We became the logical extension of the land, its peaks, canyons and trails. I felt that way at Beaubien, but even more so as a ranger. Rangers always feel at home whether they are pushing their way up that bearcat, Comanche Peak, or if they are sitting at the edge of Buck Creek watching the antics of a nearby ground squirrel.

Paradoxically, the separateness of rangering was accentuated by Ranger City, then a fenced-in compound of about fifty wall tents at whose center stood a locker building. Rangers always closely guarded access to their place; an elevated gangway made entry difficult. The Ranch had its "cattleguards" while rangers had their own "people guard." The only thing that was missing might have been a moat with hungry boars ensconced therein.

We were at an interesting age—too old to be Scouts and too young to be real Scouters. We enjoyed the best of both worlds. Rangers introduced the expeditions we served to high adventure, and were ideally positioned to partake of some of it ourselves.

About a third of the rangers that year were veterans. The rest of us had to learn rangering. That was Mr. Clarence Dunn's responsibility as Chief Ranger. A retired school principal from the Dallas suburbs, Mr. Dunn was in his seventies when I knew him. He had also served the Ranch for nearly twenty years. He had taken one of the first groups to Philmont during the war years when attendance was severely restricted. Mr. Dunn joined the staff after the war, and created the ranger staff about ten years later when rapidly growing attendance required the use of "guides."

Much has been written about Mr. Dunn. Words alone might not be enough to describe him, his devotion to Philmont, and the esteem his rangers felt for him. He was tall, slender, had snow white hair, and was a sharp judge of character. He and his wife, Ollie, were familiar figures as they strolled, arm in arm, about camping headquarters in the cool of the evening. His voice was mellowing with the passage of his seventy summers, but no one ever questioned his authority.

For the ranger staff, Mr. Dunn overshadowed the Directors of Camping he so faithfully served. While we may have addressed them as "Mister" to their faces, when they were not in our presence, they became "Jack" Rhea, "Skipper" Juncker, or "Joe" Davis.

That was not true with Mr. Dunn. He was, and would remain "Mister" Dunn even when separated by distance and the years. Had we been asked to find a man who embodied the ideals of

Scouting to a greater extent than Mr. Dunn, we would have had a long search.

To learn the rangering business, we got into buses on the morning after our arrival and headed for Rayado, where introductions were made. Mr. Dunn, along with his three Assistant Chief Rangers, then gave us the big picture. During our training, Mr. Dunn was assisted by Bill Wadsworth, a full time professional Scouter from National whose specialty was camping. The other assistants were Al Clemmons, Carl Watson, and Harvey Farmer. Al, who was Buzz Clemmons' son, was a school teacher from Minnesota. The avuncular Harvey Farmer and wispy Carl Watson also were school teachers, and must have had some connections with Mr. Dunn since they all came from the Dallas suburb of Arlington, Texas.

While the more intuitive among us may have realized it, I was unaware that we would embark on a training program that was Philmont's equivalent of the practical session of Wood Badge. In all respects, training was even more intense, particularly in brushing up on advanced scoutcraft skills.

On the surface, a ranger's job description was simple. Meet groups and stay with them a few days until they were ready to function without a guide. The essence of the job was bringing the skill level up to where it was adequate. Occasionally, groups did not need rangers—especially those groups from Rocky Mountain states and places like New Hampshire. A certain amount of re-programming had to be done since Philmont required mastery of some new techniques and an appreciation for the hazards of mountain camping. These skills were not always in evidence, especially among Scouts from eastern cities. There was potential for conflict with advisors who had "taught these boys everything they need to know." Often, some skills needed to be "unlearned" for the next ten days. Getting green groups up to speed required intense training by the ranger.

Like Wood Badge, there was considerable emphasis on leadership and interpersonal skills. There had to be. Rangers are very much on the cusp. We were independent, yet we served many masters: Mr. Dunn, the camping department, directors of the camps we were in, and the advisors and crew chiefs we served. The potential for conflict was enormous, which is why we received several hours of training in behavioral and leadership techniques. Unlike any other summer staff group, ranger training was a patrol experience. We split into eight patrols. Mine was advised by Jim Place, a Training Ranger from Illinois. Along with Joe Martos, who became my tentmate, I became a "Triffid," Jim's name for our patrol. The name had been inspired by some Hollywood science fiction film, ("science friction," as Jim would say). Jim was an easygoing physics major, had several years at Philmont to his credit, and taught us much of what we would learn about rangering in the days ahead.

Ranger training, unlike some of the softer staff jobs back at headquarters, ran dawn to dusk. We were up at six A.M., and had breakfast, installed new patrol leaders, and completed new duty rosters by 8:30. On the fourth day of training, we had a shakedown that was followed by our hike to Abreu, where we were to spend the night. Rayado to Abreu is normally not much more than a walk in the park. We followed a different trail, and hiked by Toothache Springs and Stone Wall Pass. That hike is not normally too taxing, but most of us were fresh from lower elevations. We were also carrying everything on the checklist (three-quarter axe, full mess kit, all ten tent pins, groundcloth and poncho, etc.). In a word, we were heavy. So was the mud that stuck to our boots. It was pouring rain. Often, the brief showers we experienced in the afternoon were welcomed since they were refreshing and cooled the air. This wasn't to be one of those days.

I felt as though I had five pounds of mud on each shoe. Jim was hanging in there, but clearly finding it rough. Nobody complained when he called a periodic break.

There wasn't much that could be done about it so we just kept on plugging away. Bill Bettes, a Training Ranger irreverently known as "Beast" (due to his tenacity) broke his group off, and bushwhacked to Abreu where he arrived early, much to the consternation of Harvey Farmer. Bill was a diminutive sort of chap, but very determined, and probably felt he had done the right thing. The worst was over because we took the trail that tracks just below the edge of Urraca Mesa after leaving Toothache Springs. From Stone Wall Pass it was all downhill. Pulling into Abreu, we all looked like we'd been "rode real hard and hung up wet."

With a canopy of tall pines, big boulders, and a forest floor softened by pine needles, Abreu was a safe haven. We started the fires, relished our trail food supper (something that would not always be the case), and were out within moments of rolling into our sleeping bags. Before dozing off, I wondered what would have happened if Al Clemmons had greeted each of us as we came into Abreu with revised contracts that said "Assistant Camp Director" at some cushy place like Fish Camp or Cito. He might have gotten some raised eyebrows and little more than a moment's dubious thought, but probably no takers. We all knew what we were getting into and had voluntarily asked for the ranger way of life.

I could have pleaded ignorance when it came to trail food, so complete had been Dick Gertler's spoiling of the Beaubien staff. Second and third year rangers might have used temporary insanity, or maybe the institutional food in their college dorms was really dismal. Trail food is the ranger's occupational hazard. Some may claim they like the stuff, which is without doubt great cuisine—for the duration of a single expedition. Fortunately, back in those days, a ranger could look forward to some fresh food on his first night and morning in a starting camp. Cubed steak or ground beef was standard fare, and for breakfast there was bacon and eggs or pancakes. Beyond that, we faced decidedly dehydrated prospects all summer for which the only escape was the headquarters dining hall or some off duty trips to some cafe in Cimarron.

In ranger training, we went through the full gamut of trail foods: menus one through eight. Little did I know that on the first night out of our starting camp on *every* expedition we would face vegetable beef soup, spaghetti, cornbread, and orange drink—the infamous trail supper number one. If we ever got anything else, it was discomforting to know that our good fortune was a mistake.

We would come to look back upon ranger training as a time of plenty, of variety, and what had to be, in retrospect, a grand view of high trail cuisine (had it been trail high cuisine, many would have taken exception). In training, we worked our way through each menu. There was the ham and noodle dinner, chili, beef and potato dinner, or chicken noodle dinner. Those were the core meals. The other dinners were really just a variation on the basic theme with different soups, drinks, or desserts (usually a good counterpoint to the salt-laden main courses). There was a reason for all of the salt. Some felt it was related to the physical exertion of backpacking, which produced buckets of the rapidly evaporated perspiration. I always thought, however, that somebody in power just liked to see the salt designs on our sunlight-absorbing dark green shirts.

Lucky was the ranger who got trail supper #2 after training. Surrounding the main course was beef noodle soup, biscuits, butterscotch creme dessert, and strawberry milkshake. The main course was chicken à la king, which we irreverently called "vejja-vomit." Ours was the last ranger year when the daily menus were issued in regular sequence. Subsequently, meals were rotated largely due to ranger pleas for relief from always having spaghetti dinner on the first night out. In my case, it was too late. I swore off spaghetti, applesauce, cornbread, and orange soda for several years. There was a fringe group within rangerdom who claimed to like trail food; they even thought it possible to gain weight on the stuff. Clearly, these guys were not regularly climbing Comanche, or if they were, the postage on their CARE packages from home must have been impressive.

One ranger, the exuberant son of a Michigan political science professor, was always talking up trail food. The ranger certainly looked like the picture of health. I would like to think, however, that he was like the rest of us. Once a week, we would head for greater downtown Cimarron for some sopapillas, enchiladas, and the biggest steak we could afford.

We also served as guinea pigs for trail food manufacturers. Then, all trail food was "dehydrated." "Freeze-dried" had not really become part of the backpacker's vocabulary, but was just starting to surface. All of the big names in trail food—Seidel, Chuckwagon, and Gumpert—were represented at the Ranch. Here and there were upstarts like Thunderbird that provided some new technology foods. Unfortunately, the new items were always scarce, and never offered more than a tantalizing side course.

The forest floor at New Abreu is so soft, an air mattress is hardly necessary

There was, however, the grudging realization that trail food was the essential evil, and without it the backpacking program, or its logistical costs, would suffer terribly. So, we griped loudly, but kept on eating the stuff.

Any blues over the food were driven away by our ranger campfires. I always enjoyed a good campfire, and especially looked forward to those in ranger training since the training rangers ran them. One night, Giff Kessler was in charge, and he told the story about the Briton who was strolling along the English channel coast near the cliffs of Dover. The man had inherited a strange, amorphous beast called a "rarey." The rarey became demanding and obnoxious—so much so that the gentleman decided that the rarey must go. There was the problem of how to get rid of the animal, but the gent figured that shoving the rarey over the chalk cliffs was the best way to do it. He enticed the blob over to the cliff's edge, and had almost shoved the beast over the brink when another bloke happened by and said, as he looked down to the breakers below, "I say, old chap, that *is* a long way to tip a rarey."

There were groans and guffaws, but whatever one's sense of humor, we couldn't deny the camaraderie that was developing around the campfire. Many years later, I had a troop committee chairman, a dour downeasterner, ask me why Scouting has to have so many campfires loaded with songs, games, and skits. I sympathized with him to a certain extent. Other than enjoying a role in some amateur production during intra-fraternity council weekend, I had never been very big on theatricals. When I read the Hillcourt and Jeal biographies of Lord Baden-Powell I realized that campfires were an extension of Lord Baden-Powell's interest and participation in musicals, especially when he was a subaltern in the British army. In any case, I concluded to my committee chairman, it is the rare campfire that does not build some unity through mirth and song.

Over a quarter of the ranger staff had been to ranger training campfires before. They couldn't get enough of rangering, and it was from this core that the training rangers were picked. For many, rangering was an entry level job. Many of the fellows had been to the Ranch as campers, quite often as crew leaders, and saw rangering as the ultimate expression of Scouting summer employment. The rest of us, guys like Joe Martos, Jack Crider, Don Carlson, and nearly a dozen others, had started as specialists such as program counselors. Buzz Clemmons, the Assistant Director of Camping, tended to direct anybody with a specific talent into a certain niche. One couldn't always control where he wound up during a first year in staff, but the demonstration of any talent would usually ensure getting the job one wanted for the following year.

"Let's get going here, Mr. Cass. It says here that you are still the patrol leader, and your cook and fireman haven't even gotten things started."

Harvey Farmer was trying to wake up each patrol leader that day, and his job was not an easy one. Few heard his words, but I did feel his shoe on my shoulder. It was the sleep of the dead from which we were only begrudgingly emerging. The sky was overcast, and would remain so for the rest of the day, but at least the rain had stopped. Before saddlin' up and heading back to Rayado, we had a power breakfast of eggs and sausage (the latter cooked in their cans at the edge of the fire).

There were still three more days filled with lectures, show and do, role playing, demonstrations, critiques, and cracker barrels before we headed back to Ranger City. Joe Martos and I had become friendly during ranger training, so it was only natural that we became roomies, or tentmates, when we got back to Ranger City.

Ranger City was becoming home, although it would run at only three-quarters capacity that summer. The most prominent feature was the locker building located in the middle of the horseshoe formation of tents. The locker building was a storage facility whose deep walls contained a space for each ranger to throw his pack upon return from an expedition. By the time we got two steamer trunks and two rangers inside a basic wall tent, the addition of two packs would have made living conditions too crowded. While its purpose was storage, the ranger locker building was really a rally point, our clubhouse, our lodge. There was a ramshackle table and several beat-up chairs that were essential for the frequent card games.

We tended to go for the shorter card games, so poker and blackjack were favorites. There was, intermittently, a marginally reliable typewriter for the convenience of chronic letter writers like myself. The recipients of my missives had to be content with the missing Ws, Ts, and oddly, the dollar sign (could this aging Smith Corona have been sent by a shrewd parent?).

June 20 arrived, and with it a streak of boredom that would be alleviated only until the rate of expedition arrivals spooled up to a higher pace. It would take nearly a week before everybody got their first group. It looked as though the selection of rangers was random since some second- and even third-year rangers were sitting around twiddling their thumbs, groupless.

It was during this period that I got better acquainted with my tentmate since, during July and August, we would see each other only fleetingly. Joe was a true ascetic in the strictest sense of the word, and his background was filled with fascinating paradoxes. His diction was without accent, yet he was the son of Hungarian immigrants, and he was from New York City. He was a second year staffer, and had previously taught the western lore program at Clarks Fork. Not bad for a lad whose horizons at home consisted of skyscrapers, "Longg-Guylandt" and "Joisey."

Even rangers had to have some comfort occasionally, and if we had any weakness, it was what went on our backs and feet. Through the generosity of my parents, my feet were clad in Russells and on my back I strapped a Kelty (leading edge back then). Joe's hiking boots were adequate, but he never owned a pack. He simply borrowed an army surplus packboard from trail equipment. We were never told from which war these packboards were surplus, but considering the technology, the War of 1898 would have been a good guess.

Joe was one of the better paid first year rangers since he was in his second year and had been a program specialist the year before. Programs counselors were usually up there on the pay scale, and were eclipsed only by camp directors and their assistants. Joe could easily have bought a new B.S.A. Cruiser pack, which was just becoming available, but he chose not to. He did not have a steamer trunk either, but instead, he built one from materials he purchased in Cimarron. It was a fine piece of carpentry whose construction revealed yet another side of Joe Martos.

About five feet long, the trunk rolled on casters and fit quite conveniently beneath his cot in our tent. He willed this trunk to me at the end of the season. It would travel back east with me after the next season and repose in a garage loft for another eight years. I retrieved the trunk, and converted it into a redwood-finished patio table complete with glass top. After reading Jessica Mitford's, *The American Way of Death*, I decided that this longer than average steamer trunk should also serve as my cremation coffin someday when I head for that great trail camp in the sky. Meanwhile, it serves as a constant reminder of my ranger summer and good friend, Joe Martos.

Joe was twenty years old when I knew him. He was tall, slender, and had eyes that were, on rare occasions, tinged with the Slavic sadness that is sometimes seen in those gray-blue Magyar eyes. Those eyes were usually exuberant and smiling, especially when Joe sang. Each ranger seemed to have a signature of sorts—something that would identify them to their ranger comrades as they moved in time to more decelerating years. For some, like Bobby Rabuck, it was a slow Texas drawl and a perpetual five o'clock shadow. Sometimes, it was wheels (who

could forget Bill Hogg's Karmann-Ghia?). Or our high plains
ranger, Terry Klungseth, and his trademark, a snack of sunflower
seeds sent to him by his hometown sweetheart from Webster,
South Dakota. My trademark was a set of scrawny legs. They
contrasted Phil Yunker's legs, which were so massive one might
imagine there was no piece of Philmont real estate that Phil
would have a hard time negotiating. Ranger accents were
fascinating, of course. Neil Karl spoke perfect English (upstate
New York), but Paul Felty's soft, East Texas accent was more
interesting.

Joe's trademark was the way he looked when heading for the
loading dock—a guitar over his shoulder, a smile on his face, and
a rolled-up paperback copy of *War and Peace* or some other
heavy duty literature in his back pocket.

Joe and I would have some long, deep discussions during the
first couple of weeks that summer. The subjects ranged from girls
to metaphysics. Joe enjoyed our intellectual banter, I hope. I was
skating on thin ice most of the time.

Even then, I was quick to drop labels on people. The "Brain
Trust" was my term for Jim Place, Giff Kessler, and Nick Stroud.

I never told that group that I had secretly appointed Joe as
their academic advisor, though. Giff was a fellow Pennsylvanian,
a student at Williams College, and would eventually pursue a
career in geology with, appropriately enough, Phillips Petroleum.
He was the son of a U.S. Congressman, and hailed from Erie,
which may explain why he found Philmont's usually sunny
climes so appealing.

Nick was from Iowa. He was a student at Grinnell College
where his classmates may have pronounced his name the same
way we did—with an Austrian, uvula rolling "R" that came out
"Shtrrrrrowd." The Brain Trust could easily discuss medieval
literature one minute and the chemical composition of the dining
hall's latest creation the next. All three of them were training
rangers who knew their business very well.

Early in the season with tentmate Joe Martos *(left)*

Another training ranger was Lewis F. "Buster" Simpson from the brewing town of Frankenmuth, Michigan. Buster was a casting director's stereotypical frontier, pony scout. He bore a striking resemblance to Richard Denning, a cinema star of the forties and fifties. Buster's visage was crested with flowing, blond locks, and his tanned appearance was set off by an eagle claw that he wore on a leather thong around his neck.

Buster had caught the attention of the Brain Trust which promptly dubbed him "Bluster" Simpson. The last laugh was Buster's however, and it was a real belly laugh, considering how we were forever talking about the Ranch's "tough" trails. Dave Talliaferro became part of Buster's triumph. Dave, a smiling Arkansan who was as good-natured as he was nearsighted, pronounced his name "Tolliver" although I couldn't quite make the connection. Dave joined Buster the following year in trail development. This wasn't the more familiar trail crew type brush clearing and trail maintenance. This was the real thing—trailblazing. If rangering was Philmont's ultimate, these two guys had the penultimate job. Their prospects boggled the mind. Imagine being turned loose for a whole summer to explore the Ranch, and recommend new trails. It was as close to Lewis and Clark as possible at the Ranch.

Rangers were the largest employee group at the Ranch, and were a good reflection of the diversity within the total ranch staff. We were small town Scouts, big town Scouts, downeasterners, cajuns, coal miners, tarheels, jayhawkers, ivy leaguers, podunkers, phys. ed majors, philosophy majors, pre-enlistees, and one Pennsylvania Dutchman, appropriately named Dick Laudenslager. We were all, quite naturally, believers in the world brotherhood of Scouting.

The average ranger, if there could be such a thing among such a bunch of individualists, was nineteen or twenty years old. He had just completed, or would start, his college sophomore year. The achievement motive ran quite high or he wouldn't have been there in the first place. The red, white, and blue square knots of Eagle rank abounded. The only Life Scout in our midst was Jim Crawford who still had time to work on his Eagle. He wasn't yet eighteen, and was in his second year of staff service. He had been hired right off the trail during the previous summer to fill a vacancy caused by the illness of a staff member at Cito. College majors ran the gamut from chemical engineering to business administration. If any single major was dominant, it may have been political science since more than just a couple rangers were thinking about law school.

Not surprisingly, there were few fellow followers of the "dismal science" (economics). Foremost among my colleagues was Quinton Robert Etzel, who called Corsicana, Texas, his hometown. There were a few other econ majors like Mike Salisbury and Jon Soder, but "Q. Bob," as I called him, went to Oklahoma State and had the author of my micro-economics theory textbook as his professor.

While I knew what *esprit de corps* was from my Beaubien days, I was unprepared for the hubris that marked rangerdom. We knew we were hot stuff. We even had our own "Ranger Song." Seventy red-jacketed, young rangers with their axes and hats were a powerful force. Two things kept that force in check and channeled its energy in positive directions. Primarily it was the deep respect we had for Mr. Dunn. The rangers were really his creation, and we did not want to disappoint him. The other constraint was in the fine print of our contracts. It said that our conduct would have to be of the highest standards all the time, regardless if we were on a day off visiting Colorado, Santa Fe, or anywhere else.

If Judge Roy Bean had been the fastest law west of the Pecos, Buzz Clemmons was the fastest law south and west of the Cimmaroncito Creek. In fact, as Director of Personnel, he was the only law. It was not unknown for rangers and other staffers to enjoy a little night life in nearby towns, but it was done with the strictest comportment. Even giving the appearance of straying from the straight and narrow could spell trouble.

Fortunately, most of our troubles were minor, although I did allow one small matter assume larger importance when I let Mr. Dunn down once. It was easily the worst moment of my ranger service, although I am sure Mr. Dunn forgot it almost immediately.

I had always taken pride in my appearance, and dressed in a clean, recently pressed uniform. We were not required to wear neckerchiefs or neckerchief slides, for which I took a very liberal view of what was "correct." My view of what was proper included belts since I had seen literally hundreds of different belts and buckles in Scouting. So, I extended my view of what was fitting to that which fit around my waist. I had happened to take a fancy to my college roommate's madras belt, which had a clever surcingle buckle.

My college roomie, Bob Warner, gave it to me with his best wishes. He thought I would need all the help I could get considering where I was headed. Little did Bob know then that with the passage of another year, he too would be wearing a Philmont staff patch. The Kingston Trio, one of Bob's favorite groups, was no longer at the top of the charts, but this belt looked like something they might wear. Weren't they a rather clean-cut group? So I couldn't get into trouble wearing a fashionable belt like this blue, white, brown, beige, green, pink, purple, and gray thing, could I?

"Bill, I think you ought to put on a proper Scout belt, don't you?" Mr. Dunn said to me with his soft Texas accent as I walked up to the ranger office one day.

"Yessir, I'll change it right away."

I never wore that belt again until the end of the season when I was getting ready to head back to college. I was furious with myself for having disappointed Mr. Dunn even in the slightest. I hurried back to Ranger City, borrowed an extra belt, and bought a new belt the next day. Mr. Dunn winked at me that evening and said how nice my new belt looked.

Back in Camping Headquarters, we waited for the first expeditions, which were expected on June 20. Everybody was pumped up, but only fifteen rangers got groups on that first day. I couldn't wait to get my first group. The next day came and went without my getting one. Realistically, it might take as much as a week before the last ranger got his first group. Rangers were assigned to larger groups then, and the season didn't always start with a parking lot full of buses.

Next day, no group. Joe didn't get one either. There were second year rangers walking around looking at their shoes. We'd go to briefings, and a few lucky ducks would get called. The rest of us wound up with no more prospects than sitting on the bench for another day. It was like the Crimson Tide not being invited to a big bowl game.

Mr. Dunn didn't want to grant any days off to those of us who were stuck around headquarters. It would not be appropriate for us to be off to Santa Fe or Taos while some of our brothers were struggling in the fields of hard toil. The days off would come after each of us had a trip or two under our belts. What to do until then? The possibilities were not endless. It didn't take long to explore the nooks and crannies of Camping Headquarters. We also made the trip down to the beautiful Villa Philmonte, which had been the residence of Waite Phillips. It spoke volumes about the prosperity and generosity of the man who made Philmont possible. Villa Philmonte is stunning without being decadent. It captures the flavor of the southwest and the man who built it. It is "must" seeing for any visitor or camper. Walking down to the Villa was a pleasant diversion, but we decided to take the grand tour later in the summer.

The walk down the road reminded us of the fact that Philmont was a working ranch as the smell of newly mown hay attested. As we walked along the roadside, with my thoughts going back to cutting hay in Bradford County, we came across a fascinating optical illusion. A little brook flowed on the Villa Philmonte side of the road, and I was not the only one who swore that the little rivulet was flowing *uphill*. The slope in the road and the way the grass had been cut probably caused this illusion. It was a decidedly bizarre experience, especially for the first time.

We used this lull before the storm to get better acquainted with the people in headquarters. People like Duke Towner, who ran the staff services, and Jerry Traut, the nature director, would become familiar faces around headquarters. So was Earl Swope, the school bus magnate in central Colfax County. Earl was "sawed off," and looked like a cross between a beardless Santa Claus and one of the Seven Drawfs. Although he drove the occasional bus full of campers to or from base camps, his official title was, "Greeter."

Earl's joviality was legendary, and stood him in good stead as the unofficial master of the advisors' lounge. Between his own bus trips and supervising the other drivers (most of whom were kin), he regaled advisors with stories of the Ranch and the immediate area. Like any other employee, he wore a uniform although his background as a council or unit Scouter may have been modest. He compensated by having well-pressed pants, Explorer shirt and a lovely plaid neckerchief. His eyes, which were his dominant feature, were cheery, sky blue, and had probably sparkled with mischief in his youth. They still sparkled brightly, even beneath the large cowboy hat that was his other trademark. His complexion, like many native to the area, was a bit weathered. Perhaps he had tired of cowpunching in his youth, and had turned to motorized transport. Earl's legs were bowed, and his walk was a combination of the seaman's swagger and the rolling gait of a cowpoke who had been in the saddle from the age of two.

There was always a crowd around Earl, and he served as one of Philmont's greatest ambassadors of good will. The advisors' lounge, in which the inevitable coffee pot steamed around the clock, was Earl's court. It was also populated by the few advisors who could not complete an expedition, and by those who had already returned and were getting caught up on their coffee quotas after a few days of deprivation.

Earl drove Bluebird buses, the brand to which he was most partial. He certainly should have known about bus construction since those great yellow caravans were subjected to plenty of abuse. I asked him one morning if he ever had to take a wrench and tighten the fasteners due to the endless vibration. He indicated that it was part of their regular maintenance—to go through and torque every fastener as tight as possible.

While Earl's business had started the day campers first arrived, many rangers still languished around headquarters with little to do. The old expression, "Those also serve who only sit and wait," was definitely wearing thin.

But, there was local history to absorb, and much of that was colorful. To experience the best of it one had to go to camps like Rayado, where Kit Carson once lived. While down that way, one could also see the ruts in the prairie that remained from the western spur of the Santa Fe trail. Cimarron had its St. James Hotel that was said to have bullet holes in the ceiling, not to mention the holes in the bodies of some of its late patrons. The guest list at the St. James included famous lawmen and outlaws of the old west. Even Billy the Kid supposedly spent a night in the local slammer. But, when we visited the St. James, then named the Casa de Colores, business looked rather slow. It would pick up as the expedition bus drivers arrived.

During this quiet spell, I wrote a few letters home. There had been little time to do that when we were on ranger training at Rayado. The weather in headquarters was hot enough to require rolling up tent flaps, which is what I did before settling onto my cot, belly down, to start another letter. I became aware of activity just below the back edge of my tent. Here was a little ground squirrel digging a burrow.

Most of our ground squirrels were of the "golden-mantled" variety. These little creatures look like "souped-up" chipmunks with broad, more muted stripes. My little ground squirrel was really busy, which was more than could be said for our own sorry selves. The dirt would fly, and then he would stop, half stand up in that typical crouch, and check things out. The little nostrils would pinch, and the shiny little eyes would look to and fro, after which there would be more furious activity. If only we could have been so occupied. This little ground squirrel was a bona fide thirteen-lined ground squirrel, *Citellus tridecemlineatus*, a high fashion model among the lesser rodents, and definitely not your run-of-the-mill Philmont ground squirrel. He had thirteen lines of light colored spots on his back, and was much more streamlined than the usual ground squirrel. I was delighted with him, and looked forward to the diversion of watching this little guy. Joe and I definitely needed something to occupy our minds before the big day arrived when we would get a group.

The squirrel packed it in. Maybe it was siesta time. At least he had shade, a rare commodity where we were. Rain was also proving elusive. It was a hot June indeed. Rumor was that the local ranchers were in trouble, and were considering selling large portions of their herds since they feared a real drought was in the making. We knew that Philmont had several hundred head, but we also knew that they were up in the highland meadows. Although we were working at a "ranch," we were a bit out of touch. The only other "ranch" we could see was "Nairn Place" which was really a local rancher's residence.

Nairn Place was a large, white structure clearly visible from Camping Headquarters. It was also "off limits." The cattle tycoon living there had an attractive daughter whose aloofness was matched only by her speed as she whizzed by Ranger City in a Chevy El Camino. Where she drove remained a mystery, but one thing was clear; Nairn Place might as well have been on the moon so well was it fenced in.

Things picked up dramatically after the first week. A few of us might have reconsidered our decisions to become rangers had we known how the pace would accelerate in July, and then reach a crescendo in early August. I should have known how the pace would quicken since I had seen Beaubien become so crowded the year before. Yet the twentieth and twenty-first came and went without Joe and me getting a group. Had we said something wrong or possibly offended somebody? No, it was all in the luck of the draw, and our luck changed for the better on the twenty-second.

Trail Talk

The twenty-second of June started like any other day. The more fortunate rangers met their groups for breakfast while the rest of us kicked the stones out of our paths, wondering when our big day would come. We went to our ranger briefing after breakfast, and I learned that the big day had arrived. 622D, or more appropriately, 622D-2 would arrive early that day, and they needed my services. Glory be! I was employed at last. So were Joe Martos and Alan Throop (a fellow Keystone stater from Monessen). The lead ranger for this large group of South Carolinians was Buster Simpson. It was common practice to put first year rangers in the company of their elders on the first trip out.

The group was from the Peedee River Area Council in

northeastern South Carolina, and all forty of them had decided to hike the same itinerary. We started the time-honored drill of taking them through the rounds of headquarters and giving our lectures on the ways of mountain camping at Philmont. I had drawn a crew containing older Scouts. I took an immediate liking to the advisor, Parke Thompson, a nuggety guy with a perpetual five o'clock shadow. We "shook'em down" on the grassy parade ground just south of where the Mabee Services building now stands. Buster, being the senior among us, held center stage, and we turned up a few items that the kids would not need on the trail. Buster should have given the other three rangers their own shakedown since we showed up at the bus with overly full packs. We had not learned our lesson from the shakedown hike. That first expedition, with packs weighing in over sixty pounds, was a real learning experience. When I got back from that trip, I decided right then that the axe would stay in my tent, that one spoon, one cup, and one plate was all of a mess kit I would ever need, and that nobody needed all ten tentpins. We also learned that a poncho made a good groundcloth. On the next expedition, most of us rookie rangers packed out about twenty-five pounds lighter. Eventually, most rangers would buy their issued equipment at half price when the season ended. The one droll touch was that the item we never wore, our campaign "Smokey the Bear" hat, we received without charge. Mine reposes in some dark closet corner, and hasn't been worn since that ranger summer (if it was worn then!).

622D was bound for Cyphers via Clarks Fork. Both would be new experiences for me, although I had been to nearby Cito the previous summer for hunter safety instructor training. Rangers experience more of the Ranch first hand than do other staff groups, and inevitably form preferences for one sector of the Ranch over others. The ranger staff tends to be somewhat opinionated. After all, they don't get there by being shrinking violets. Clarks Fork was never mentioned as a divine locale. I was not that impressed with it, but I had been horribly spoiled by service at Beaubien. The afternoon went smoothly as we wrapped up the last of our lectures on camping skills. The hike to Cyphers was uneventful, and our early arrival placed us in a more conveniently-located Adirondack shelter. And what Adirondacks they were. I was used to your basic eastern Adirondack that might comfortably sleep six to eight people. Here was a shelter that would sleep ten easily, and maybe even fourteen in close proximity.

The previous night, we had enjoyed the luxury of hamburgers, the typical fare of a starting camp, so the Dutch oven held little appeal. On this second night, with a few miles of trail under their belts, these kids were anxious to augment their trail supper #1 with cornbread. Dutch oven cookin' has always been a ranger specialty, and it was my first real test. I started to set them up for the great display of expertise that followed with a stern warning that Dutch oven cooks have to be shrewd judges of the heating value of different kinds of wood.

"As you guys pass through Philmont, you're going to find spruce, aspen, pine, scrub oak, and a couple other varieties of wood. Remember that the harder woods will put out more heat, so you're going to need fewer coals. Stuff like this aspen burns quickly, and doesn't give off as much heat. Don't forget that you'll burn the bottom really fast unless you keep those coals down to a minimum. This iron conducts and holds heat well, so put about three or four times as many coals on the top as you do on the bottom."

Well, I guess I sounded knowledgeable since they were hanging on to every word. "That cornbread better turn out as well as I said it would, or I've got a credibility problem," I was thinking to myself. It did turn out well, but considering our training, there was only a small chance that it wouldn't. I had slept reasonably well the night before, but like a very tired Parke Thompson and his nine campers, I slept like a log that night. In

the morning, these southerners would head west—up to Comanche, a sidehike to Mount Phillips, and then drop down to Red
Hills. After wishing them well, we four rangers hoofed it by way
of the Middle Fork to the Cito turnaround in time to catch a bus
back to headquarters. For Buster, it was just another
well-launched group. For Joe, Alan, and me, it was the beginning
of our ultimate staff adventure.

We couldn't wait to be turned loose again, but we had to put
in some more time on the bench. It would be another week before
we got into the routine of getting in one day, having one day off,
and then getting another group. By mid-July, many of us
wouldn't even get that much of a break.

There was some short-lived talk about working for the Forest
Service as fire fighters on our days off. We were constantly aware
of the fire hazard, and had to conserve water.

Since we had returned from our first groups, a day off was in
order. Several of us went up to Raton where there was a large,
public swimming pool. Most of us had well-tanned arms, legs,
and faces to which we added sunburned backs and bellies
following our afternoon of swimming. When we got back, I saw
that my name was on the list of rangers who were to get groups
the next day. In the briefing after breakfast, I learned that I would
be guiding a group from Washington, D.C. The National Capitol
Area Council probably sent out more Scouts to Philmont than any
other metropolitan area, and I was looking forward to seeing what
these city boys were made of.

The loudspeaker blared several rangers' names, so we knew
the groups had arrived. The rest of the day was spent in the now
familiar headquarters shuffle: health lodge, trail equipment,
laundry, post office, and camp office. If they got in early enough,
we'd shake 'em down the day they arrived. Final stop was the
dispatcher's office to arrange a bus ride to the starting camp.
These Washingtonians were interested in north country programs,
and had scheduled two days of sidehiking out of Ponil.

I was most anxious to see Ponil since this was the ancestral home of the modern day Philmont. Here the first buildings were built after the initial gift of land to Boy Scouting by Waite Phillips. On the day of our arrival, we hiked up to what is now Dean Skyline Camp. We left the sprawling Ponil base camp the next day for a trip over to "Scribblings" to look at the Indian writings on the canyon wall. Having plenty of time, we walked over to Stony Point on the return.

Getting a ride back from Ponil was hardly difficult since it was the hub of the north country. That the pace was picking up was obvious when I got back to headquarters. My name was on the board to pick up a group the next day. I wouldn't get a full day off, but that was no problem since I had the rest of this day. Shepherding groups through H.Q. wasn't very taxing, and I would be off duty the following night. A regular ritual occurs when a ranger returns. First stop is the Ranger Office to fill out a report on the expedition. Less obvious was the report being filled out on the ranger when the group advisor returned to headquarters. Rangers are the most evaluated staff group since there was not only the group critique, but also the fitness report filled out by the Ranger Office itself. The most important headquarters. stop for the returning ranger is the second one: the post office. It never failed to provide me with a letter or two from Sarah. Next was the ranger locker building to store my pack, and then it was off to the showers.

My third group of that summer was from Raleigh, NC. They were also going to Ponil. In those days, one never knew how many crews would form from a council contingent, or what their itinerary was until they sat down in logistics, and figured it out on the spot. It was an occupational hazard in this pre-computerized Philmont era. It could have been worse. Bob Montoya, a tall grinning ranger from West Virginia, went to Ponil six times in a row that summer. That was literally half his total trips. Well, off to Ponil we went. There was a diversion with a sidehike up to the

Ranch boundary to what is now Bent Camp. Now that I had been as far north as possible, I was wondering when I would get to go south. It was all in the luck of the draw. At least the many tame deer offered a distraction at Ponil.

A certain amount of tedium is built-in to the ranger's head-quarters life. When I got back from Ponil, I still had time on my hands after writing several letters and doing laundry. The staff lounge, where we did our laundry, had just received a television set. However, it got very little attention other than for the network news. A few stale newspapers usually held as much or more attraction. In the evening, we frequently went down to Cimarron to have a soda or milkshake at Lambert's drug store. There was a theater in Cimarron, but few of its patrons were staffers since movies were shown at regular intervals in the dining hall. These films included such classics as "My Friend Flicka" and plenty of early Disney fare. On the other hand, the Cimarron Palace did get later run features so there were always a few staff cinema buffs in the audience.

Card games and bull sessions occupied most of our spare time on those days in headquarters when we waited for groups. On a real day off, we might go climbing in Colorado or visit Taos and Santa Fe.

By early July, Ranger City was a base for itinerants. Joe and I wouldn't see each other more than a day or so at a time. Many cots in Ranger City were empty, and there never were more than twenty or thirty of us there at any given time. I joined one group at the last minute since its ranger had reported to the health lodge with abdominal problems just before the group left for Cito. It turned out to be a very routine trip from Cito, where there were rumors of bears, to Cyphers via the North Fork. On the afternoon of my return, I was sitting on an unused tent platform reading an old newspaper when a familiar face passed by. Ned Gold appeared at headquarters for the first of several camp directors' meetings that would be held throughout the summer.

"Bill, we've had seven groups so far, and Steve likes working here."

Ned always came to the point with that breathless, enthusiastic voice of his. I was surprised to learn that they had seen that many groups.

"Joe's out of town, toss your pack in our tent, and stay here," I told him. "We'll paint the town tonight." Our big night on the town was seeing the staff movie, "Drums Along the Mohawk," which we promptly renamed "Drums Along the Rayado." We then got a ride down to Cimarron where we enjoyed a milkshake. At that stage, when we had only been on the trail two or three times, we didn't realize just how important that extra nourishment would become.

My luck turned with 708D, which would take me to the heart of the south country. They were a small group of eight souls advised by Messrs. Hollingsworth and Teter, who worked in Wichita's aerospace industry. Their itinerary was music to my ears: first night at Abreu, second night at the Crags. Those Scouts were older than the average, and were experienced outdoorsmen who frequently camped in Colorado.

Unlike many council contingents that consisted of Scouts from many troops, 708D was from the same troop, and they had their act together. The advisors were ex-infantrymen who knew how to hike. Considering this group's grasp of camping skills, there was little I could do for them except add a modest amount of reinforcement. Basically, I was just along for the ride. What a ride it was to be. The stretch from Abreu to the Crags was among the most beautiful on the Ranch, and made more special because the Crags was a favorite Phillips fishing spot. The fact that it was an unstaffed trail camp, without the hustle and bustle of big camps like Ponil, contributed to its appeal. The Crags was Philmont camping at its best—the steady murmur of a creek, soft ground, and a little drama at night when the bobcats would howl.

There were a few rainshowers as we arrived at Abreu. This

was good news since the Ranch needed the moisture, and bad news because it compressed my map and compass session. A brief shower always seemed to improve the fishing, and these boys were prepared for it. They had all brought their own rods, and everybody had at least one small trout with dinner that evening. This trip was over much too quickly. When I said goodbye to them the next morning, I told them how much I wish I could have gone on with them for their entire expedition. They were most generous in their thanks for my help, but in truth of matter, they were one group that could have gotten by nicely without any ranger. They were one of the most polished groups I worked with all summer.

When I arrived back at headquarters, I ran into Steve Gregory, who was just getting ready to ride back to Fish Camp after a day off. We didn't have much time to talk since he was in a hurry to catch the commissary truck. Big night that evening in headquarters: the "Arizona Cowboy" was playing with Hoot Gibson and Ken Maynard at the staff movies.

We actually got some rain the next day, but not enough to create any standing puddles. I was due for another group the following day, so I caught up on laundry and letters. The next group, 713C was a large bunch of fifty-five to which seven rangers were assigned. The group was from Lansing, MI, and they traveled in style: ten brand new, big white Oldsmobile station wagons. General Motors certainly took care of the local Scout council. Their itinerary looked interesting: first night at the Stockade, and the second night at Miners Park.

Just after the shakedown, I caught sight of Steve Gregory walking down toward the camp office. I made it a point to catch up with him since I had seen him recently, and wondered what he was doing back to headquarters so soon. He was carrying a rolled up, dripping wet tent out of which popped an ice cube.

"Whaddya got in there. Homemade ice cream?"

"Nobody's eating this. Not now anyway."

With that, he unrolled a corner of the folded tent to reveal a monstrous rainbow trout. It was almost two feet long, and clearly had to be a Ranch record. Steve must have found Waite Phillips' private trout pool. As I suspected, the great fish had come from a hole in the upper Agua Fria. It never got the fishing pressure of the waters immediately adjacent to Fish Camp. It had been taken on a black gnat. Steve and Ned had deliberated over what to do with the fish, and figured that it ought to be frozen as soon as possible. It wound up in the Director of Camping's kitchen freezer. Eventually Steve packed it in dry ice, and took it home to Glenwood Springs, Colorado, where it was entrusted to the local taxidermist.

The following afternoon, we were off to the Stockade. I didn't know much about the Stockade other than the fact that it was built to resemble a frontier army post. The continuing orientation of the group went well, and after dinner I found myself having a cup of bug juice with the Stockade staff. A little rainshower came and went. I couldn't believe how dry the summer had been. I had yet to be rained on while hiking, and had never experienced a single raindrop at night (so far).

Stockade's flying flags were easily visible from Ranger City. They might have had one extra red flag that stood for Stockade's reputation as one of several camps with more than just the occasional rattlesnake. In truth, odds were wildly in favor of campers not encountering a rattlesnake anywhere on the ranch. They couldn't be found much over eight thousand feet due to atmospheric conditions. Then, the only people who had been bitten at the ranch had been several staffers who should have known better than to handle rattlers. The approach to the resident rattlers was pretty much "Live and let live." The snakes were supposed to serve a useful function on the Ranch. According to the experts, the snakes kept the rodent population in check. It had to be an uphill battle for the rattlers since there never were any gaps in the ranks of Philmont's legions of ground squirrels.

The prairie rattlesnake, *Crotalis viridius*, as we described it to rapt campers, was hardly on my mind as I turned in for the evening. I rarely had a problem getting to sleep. My thoughts would drift back east to Sarah, I would think about times past, and how much I missed her. Time was flying since the summer was nearly half shot. I would think about the group, and if I was doing any good. Soon enough, I would be sound asleep.

I stirred sometime just before midnight. All was quiet and pitch black. Something had awakened me. Something was in my tent. In fact, something was down at the foot of my sleeping bag. Indeed, it was now *on* my sleeping bag. Whatever it was, it seemed to be moving around in little circles. I shuddered to think that there was a rattlesnake about four feet from my very nervous face. The words, "nocturnal" and "heat-seeking" were assuming a sinister, and much more alarming meaning.

What to do? Try to flick him off by doing a little drop kick from within my sleeping bag. No, I would probably mess that up, and get bitten for my trouble.

"Oh, no, it's moving again, and it's still on my sleeping bag. Well, better on that end of the sleeping bag than this end. Why is this happening to me?" I was thinking as my heart started to pound. I could just see newspaper accounts of a Philmont staffer bitten between the eyes by a rattlesnake. I decided that the best approach was to eject straight out of the back of my tent, which is exactly what I did. Walking quickly away from my tent, I stumbled into another tent in the darkness, scared its occupants half to death, but did manage to borrow a flashlight.

"Well, no point in being a coward about this," I was thinking as I found a large stick. I located the crew shovel with which I planned to decapitate the intruder. I looked around the corner of my tent, and poked at my rumpled sleeping bag. No snake, but then there was some rustling movement on the other side of the tent. There the blighter was. But it wasn't a reptile. It was a skunk! I was thrilled with that little skunk. He was less thrilled with me, but decided I wasn't worth a good spraying as he trundled off into the darkness. It was a while before I managed to drift off to sleep again. When enclosed tents with floors and zippered flaps came into general use years later, I was not slow to appreciate their advantages.

The next day, we hiked up to Miner's Park, which proved to be a delightful camp. I had been past the place several times the year before, but had never camped there. The next morning, I was joined by Steve Smith, a ranger from Utah, and we hiked back to headquarters via the jeep road. When the expedition form was completed, I got cleaned up, caught a ride to Cimarron, and hitchhiked to Raton to have a major problem set right. My wristwatch had packed it in, and I had decided to have it repaired instead of buying some temporary expedient down at Lambert's. Although I did not approve of hitchhiking before signing on at the Ranch, it was often the only way to get to Raton. The sight of a red jacket slung over some lad's shoulder was a good flag. I walked into the first jewelry store I could find on Raton's main drag, and left my watch for repair and cleaning.

Although the tempo of activity was picking up, I was able to get time off before my next group. An intestinal disorder had temporally thinned the ranks of the ranger staff. I hadn't been at the top of my form for the past week or so, but was nowhere as bad off as the nearly half dozen rangers who had spent the past few days flattened at the health lodge. The diarrhea and cramps that had laid them low were traced to some poor water at Ponil. That staff was also under the weather. The whole affair was strong testimony to the perils of drinking water of which one was not absolutely, positively certain of its purification.

There was some good news on the wall before I left for my vacation day. I was next scheduled for duty with 722D-3. Official policy was that no ranger could serve his home council unless he just happened to draw it through good luck. The policy was subsequently changed, but I was favored by the luck of the draw.

722D was from Lancaster County, Pennsylvania. For my day off, I caught the commissary truck as far as Beaubien, and then managed to get a seat on a jeep driven by a chaplain on his way to Porcupine. I hiked from Porky-Ado Junction (present day Phillips Junction) the rest of the way to Fish Camp. There I found John Dimalanta and Freddy Blair installed as the local masters of the realm. I spent the next few minutes trading friendly insults with Freddy, who thought my legs weren't quite as thick as a ranger's should be. I reminded Freddy that my pins had carried me to the tops of more of the Ranch's peaks than he knew the names of. Before Freddy could return the compliment, Ned Gold rounded the corner of the lodge to show me the way up to his digs at Lost Cabin.

The summer that Ned and Steve had Lost Cabin may have been the first and last time there was ever a staffed camp at that location. When they packed in on Scatter, they weren't sure they were at the right place. They couldn't find the "cabin" immediately, but there was a clearing in the woods and a nice spring, so they decided that they had arrived. They had the usual two platform tents (less the platforms), but had seen only a handful of groups at that point. Home being where the heart is, they had settled in and built a table, some rough chairs, and enough camp gadgets to inspire the rewriting of pioneering merit badge. They were enjoying an idyllic summer in one of the Ranch's most pristine settings.

The evening coffee hour was lightly attended since there was only one group in camp, but it was really the best type of advisors' hour—spent around a crackling fire instead of a big camp porch.

Although the summer had been unusually dry, that night we experienced a roaring thunderstorm that just wouldn't quit. I was asleep in the wall tent's dead center when a little trickle of water started running past my nose. For the rest of the night, I tried sleeping beneath Ned's cot where there wasn't much elbow room,

Conversations would drift to biscuits, girls, politics, back to how we cooked pizza in a Dutch oven using the spaghetti sauce mix from trail supper #1. Eventually the conversation would come around to Philmont trails and the inevitable north-south country debate. On a busman's holiday, the average ranger would head for the southwest corner of the Ranch. Most of us considered the Baldy country to be a separate entity since it wasn't really typical north country. Its elevation and vegetation really put it more into the same league with the terrain around Mt. Phillips. Another hot topic was trail signs. Given their way, the fundamentalist rangers would have, in the dark of night, removed every trail sign on the Ranch to put more "wilderness" into expeditions. My view was with the mainstream. We felt that trail signs were a necessary evil. Groups got lost often enough with trail signs, so it was obvious what chaos would result if the signs vanished.

In these conversations, I could just hold my own with most of the second and third year rangers since I had done so much sidehiking the year before. I also had been lucky enough to have well-distributed itineraries so far in ranger service. There was one serious shortcoming in my education. That was Comanche Pass, which was rumored to be a real tough go. I decided that the next time I got to Cyphers, I would hike in via the pass and North Fork Urraca Creek. Although I did not know it at the time, my Lancaster County group would be my ticket to Comanche. What I did know was that I was bone tired from the long, albeit downhill, hike that day and practically no sleep the night before. I got back from the dining hall, hit the sack at seven P.M., and slept soundly until 6:30 A.M.

I decided that I would not tell my Lancaster group where I was from. Most of our uniforms were lacking council insignia anyway other than the OA flaps we wore on the right pockets of our shirts. I thought, however, that it would be easy for them to tell I was a local lad since my Minqua Lodge #519 flap stood out like a sore thumb. Steve Smith, Joe d'Hemecourt, and I greeted 722D at the loading dock after the loudspeakers announced their arrival. Soon I was amid Pennsylvania Dutch accents and sorting out the D-3 crew. By this point, we had the headquarters drill down, and no longer needed the little handbooks that served as the ranger's syllabus. We made it a point to warn about the dangers of messing around with the wildlife as we shepherded the group through headquarters.

"We have bears here at Philmont. There are two types of bears. We've got 'woods' bears that aren't much of a problem since they stay in the woods. Then we've got 'garbage' bears and they are a problem. You can watch'em from a distance, but don't even think about getting close. Above all, don't get between a mama bear and her cubs. Don't be like those tourists up in Yellowstone, and try to feed a bear. Food belongs in your stomachs or run up a tree if you are in a trail camp. The best way to find yourself in big trouble with bears is to keep food in your tent. Bears enjoy a Hershey bar even more than you do, and won't hesitate to run you out of your tent to make sure they can eat your candy at their leisure."

The advice would go on. Similar warnings would follow about getting a modern version of the bubonic plague from the ground squirrels. We also told the campers that their chances of seeing rattlesnakes were remote at best. If they did see one they were to report it to the staff and do nothing else. By the looks on some young faces, I wasn't sure if my admonitions were taken as serious warnings or invitations.

The itinerary was the "Cito-Cyphers milk run," so it looked like I probably could find out if Comanche Pass was really all that tough. While at Cito, two bears, a she bear and yearling, made pests of themselves. However, this encounter was not of the close kind that I would experience in a couple of weeks. Most encounters with bears at that point in Philmont's history were not serious. Bears then were something between a minor nuisance and a curiosity. Serious confrontations were yet to come, and would be aggravated, in my mind, by the replacement of camp commissaries with sector commissaries. With groups carrying food in their packs all of the time, the potential for conflict was substantially increased, and would not diminish until permanent bear cables were installed.

The worst bear incident during my service was when a bear stampeded right through a tent. The campers were more scared than hurt, but it emphasized the point that bears were never to be taken lightly.

The rifle range and poking around Hogback Ridge, Hidden Valley, Window Rock, and Cathedral Rock were the first day activities for my Red Rose County charges. Always game for a new trail, I enjoyed the day with them, especially the views over to Deer Lake Mesa and back toward Camping Headquarters. More of my attention was directed in the other direction toward Bear Mountain and Cyphers, which we reached after lunch the following day. Finally, a Scout from Lititz (a small town north of Lancaster) asked where I was from and why he never saw me at OA weekends. He had seen the roses, blue background, yellow border and turtle totem on my OA flap. The cat was out of the bag, but it had taken them long enough to observe it.

In truth, since going to college I was no longer that active in the Minqua Lodge, and hadn't been to an OA banquet in several years. After the mine tour, I told the advisors how much I enjoyed seeing folks from back home, but that I had to be back to headquarters by noon the next day. I had planned a circuitous return route, and asked if they would mind if I punched out well before breakfast. No, that was OK with them since they were going to have their hands full with Comanche Peak and sidehiking Phillips before spending the night at Red Hills.

I was a bit envious as I turned in for the night since I would love to have gone with them and done Phillips from the Comanche side. So, I started wondering if I could get up early

enough, do Comanche and Phillips, come off via Big Red and
Bonita Peak, and catch a truck or jeep back out of Beaubien. I
could, but wouldn't make it back by noon, which would put me
in hot water with Mr. Dunn. I would be pushing my luck with
Comanche Pass and North Fork Urraca Creek anyway.

I rolled out of the Adirondack before any member of 722D-3
stirred. Then I grubbed a very sketchy breakfast (stale coffee and
some even more stale cookies left over from the previous night's
coffee hour). Shortly after making the turn at Lambert's Mine, it
was obvious why my more experienced ranger peers spoke of
Comanche Pass in hushed tones. All of the usual thoughts were
going through my mind as I trudged up this trail.

"Never do this again. You idiot. I could have slept in. Been
at the Cito turnaround in an hour. Why am I doing this. Cruddy
breakfast. Stale cookies and coffee. Wonderful."

I was not making very good time, and clearly I was going to
have trouble getting back by noon. Finally, I did get to the top of
the saddle after what seemed like hours. It all became worthwhile.
Off to my right was Comanche Peak. It had been almost a year
since I had climbed the peak with Steve Radford. This day was
proving to be as lovely as that day had been. The sky had that
piercing blue so rarely seen back east in the summer, and it
looked like another hot, dry day ahead—for those in the flats
anyway.

Now I had nothing but downhill hiking ahead of me. In
another mile, I would pick up the North Fork Urraca, and a half
hour past that, Black Mountain Camp. I didn't tarry at Black
Mountain, but wanted to since it is a beautiful camp. A ranger
with a full head of steam up can cover a lot of ground in a hurry.
I was making good time now, or assumed so since I was without
my watch. Fortunately, I bummed a jeep ride almost within
minutes of emerging at the Stockade, and just made the noon
deadline.

After signing the paperwork and getting cleaned up, it was off to Raton to get my watch and send Sarah the nicest birthday card and present I could find. I wanted to phone her on her birthday, July 30, but the Ranger Office had other plans for me in 728E. This group was from North Bergen Council in New Jersey, and was arriving in Trinidad, Colorado, on the 5:18 train. This meant they would not reach the Ranch until nine or ten P.M. That was the bad news. The good news was that they would go to their starting camp the next day. I would be with them from there to Webster Lake and Harlan, a couple of new spots on the map for me. Clarks Fork was having bear problems but the bruins left this group alone. It was just as well since this bunch was rather inexperienced. They looked like the types who might forget a ranger's advice when some grubbing black bear stumbled into camp. I was playing catchup with this group since their headquarters orientation had been very abbreviated. One delight of rangering was getting around to the various camps and meeting staffers from all over the country. Each camp had its yarn spinner extraordinaire, and the Clarks Fork cook, Tom Carpenter, was a real story teller. He was from Coffeyville, Kansas, which, according to Tom, was the location of the Dalton Brothers' last confrontation with the law. Those desperadoes were apparently big time gangsters of the early 1890s. They met with some well-publicized frontier justice that really put the town on the map.

Day two saw us on the trail to Webster Lake. This was an easy hike in the flats, but when we arrived, there was a camp complete with a most friendly staff, but no lake. The lake was intermittent, and this being a dry year, the high water mark had long since been past. Tom Guyer, the athletic Alabaman who was the director, extended plenty of southern hospitality. Typically smaller camps in less than glamorous circumstances were among the most friendly. We had arrived late since the group spent the morning taking program at Clarks Fork. As I was so often inclined to do when my rangering duties were discharged, I wandered off on my own, and checked out the local surroundings.

I was poking around the scrub oak when, from a distance, I saw some strange, large birds. They looked like deformed vultures—almost like they had some terrible arthritic condition linked to curvature of the spine. Their bodies were not nearly parallel to the ground like vultures, but were canted upwards at nearly forty-five degrees.

"You dummy, they're turkeys," I muttered to myself. I had seen turkeys at the base of Black Mountain and had seen them occasionally back in Bradford County. It was another one of my wild notions. I thought turkeys were strictly birds of the forests, but here they were right out in the flats.

Webster Lake may not have been a Black Mountain or Abreu, but the company was most pleasant, and the staff had a great view of the mountains. The following day would take us on a short march over gradually rising terrain to Harlan, a camp located between Deer Lake and Antelope Mesas. The advisors on this trip looked upon the expedition as pure vacation, and announced that everybody could sleep in the next morning. Who was I to argue with them? The pace for rangers had picked up, and showed signs that life would become more hectic in the several weeks ahead. We all slept sinfully late the next morning, and might just as well have had lunch at Webster Lake before we finally left.

The hiking patterns of some of the campers never ceased to amaze me. The kneejerk reaction was the chubbiest and skinny, petite boys would be the laggards. This group included one of the scrawniest little kids I had ever seen on the Ranch, but he was the one who set a blistering pace. And his pack was no lighter than any other camper's. We were starting to sweat as we pushed up the approach to Deer Lake Mesa, but I knew we were going to get cooled off soon enough. Developing a weather eye comes easy after spending almost all of the day outside, and I knew that we were going to get spritzed. Just by feeling the wind and looking at the sky, I could tell we probably wouldn't get drenched. When the rain came, it was just a few sprinkles—the kind that refreshes without soaking. We didn't even bother with our ponchos.

Tommy Gold, Ned's brother, greeted us at Harlan, where burros were the program. My infatuation with horses, and their poor relations, had cooled so I held my distance from the burros. I was contemplating dinner. It was comforting to know that I would get a really good dinner tonight, but unfortunately the reason for my good fortune was a mistake. Because I was with this group for three nights on the trail, dinner was the chicken and vegetable with rice menu instead of that occupational hazard: spaghetti, applesauce, and orange drink. I was anxious to get back to headquarters. It was July 31, and I had wanted to call Sarah on her birthday, but it would have to wait until August 1.

When August rolled around, most staffers started thinking about home and going back to college. I wasn't burned out yet by a long shot, but I was thinking about greener pastures. Every camp at Philmont is special in its own way, but because rangers see so many camps, there is a definite preference. Webster Lake and Harlan weren't my favorites, and I was longing for some groups that would take me back to the high, south country.

I said *adios* to my North Jersey group, and hiked down to Route 64 where I caught a ride to Cimarron a few minutes later. From there it was easy catching another ride to headquarters. In later years, I would wish that Philadelphia's subways and commuter trains would run so dependably. When I got to the post office, there were a couple of letters waiting for me. This was the special day when I was going to call Sarah. The phone company made it a lot easier to reach out in subsequent years. Back then, there was only one pay phone available for public use. It was mounted on a pedestal near where the trading post now stands. I had visited the trading post earlier, and had gotten plenty of change for the all important phone call that just wasn't going to last long enough. The call was magic, though. Unfortunately, there wasn't enough magic in my pocket to pay for a half hour of conversation. The sympathetic operator allowed me to charge it to my home phone. Fortunately, my parents were also understanding after reminding me of the benefits of not abusing the privilege. I drifted off on cloud nine that night, but was shaken back into reality the next day with 802E.

In Ranger City with Steve Gregory *(right)*

From Canyon To Crest

I knew 802E was going to be hot stuff. They were fellow highlanders from northern Pennsylvania. Even a ranger could learn a trick or two from a buttoned-down group like this. My Elk Lick Council group was headed for Cito and then Cyphers—another milk run, I thought. They paid respectful attention to my demonstrations, but both parties knew that 802E had its act together. This crowd turned heads on the Cito rifle and shotgun ranges, as well they might have considering they were all deer, turkey, and partridge hunters. Even Cito's bear population wasn't much of a novelty for these boys.

After leaving these fine Pennsylvanians at Cyphers, I opted for a more conventional return to headquarters than Comanche Pass. I could use the energy. It was a sign of the times that rangers were coming in one day, and meeting a group the next day. There had even been a few cases where a ranger came in and was out the same afternoon on the 2:30 bus with a new group.

We had all had lost some weight, and our ranks were definitely thinned. The Ponil plague of early July had reduced our number by two, and four more rangers had bitten the dust the day I headed for Miners Park. In the exuberance of youth, the four had been found behaving in a manner unbecoming Philmont staffers on a day off in Santa Fe. They experienced Buzz Clemmons' wrath upon returning, and learned first hand that justice west of the Cimarroncito was faster than that west of the Pecos.

The group termination of four rangers, all Eagle Scouts, was a watershed event of sorts. We were nearly all college students, and liked a good time. Perhaps we weren't angels, but we had been sufficiently imbued with the Scouting ethic. Our minds were boggled by how anybody could be so stupid as to squander away the privilege of serving on the Philmont staff.

Supposedly, only one percent of all Scouts who register ever become Eagles. I was coming to the conclusion that maybe one percent of all those who made it to Eagle probably should not have gotten past the board of review. On the other hand, perhaps only one rotten apple in a hundred wasn't such a bad statistic. Maybe without constant exposure to Scouting's ideals, the figure might be a lot higher. Still, it was disappointing to find four who couldn't carry the baggage.

Eagles or not, the absence of four rangers was immediately felt. Twenty rangers were leaving headquarters with groups every day. With the occasional sickness or injury, and maybe a few having a rough time getting back by noon, our ranks were stretched. The day off between groups became a distant memory. I had barely seen my tentmate over the past month.

Most rangers were nineteen or twenty years old, which put us in that gray zone between late adolescence and early adulthood. We were not above letting off steam in a few high-spirited, youthful games. I rounded a tent corner late one afternoon to find Giff Kessler and Bob Reeves engaged in a medieval, mock sword fight while Pat LaFrance was alternately playing the role of court jester and magician. Here they were, bobbing around on one of those tentless platforms, slashing and poking at each other with a pair of weathered, yard-long one by fours.

"Aha, it must be the dance of the sugar plum fairies," I announced, borrowing a line from the Nutcracker Suite. To insult Giff, with his rapier swift mind, was to invite a split second comeback even more sharp than the original indignity. Surprisingly, Giff uttered only a deflated gasp. Bob's tastes in music did not include Tchaikovsky. He saw an advantage and promptly skewered Giff, over whose now prostrate form Pat was delivering some final incantation. Giff then rose, not because of Merlin LaFrance's magic, but because it was time to get cleaned up and uniformed for dinner.

The next day, Kalamazoo-zoo-zoo sent me 806C, and all of the bears I ever wanted to see. The advisor was a school teacher and track coach whose enthusiasm bubbled over into his small group of seven campers. Their first day in headquarters was abbreviated through a combination of their early arrival and transportation scheduling problems. Because of this, I spent all of my time with this group on the trail. The Ranch's bears were getting bolder, and now Cito's problems were such that a bear trap was in place. We always went to great lengths to tell our groups to avoid the bears, and these Michigan kids were doing their best, but the bears weren't avoiding us. The trap, essentially a large dog cage on wheels, had been placed among Cito's garbage cans. I decided to stay up, and from the safe distance of about fifty yards, watch the bear get caught.

Cito's staff baited the trap with what would seem irresistible: a Crisco can loaded and smeared with jelly. The bear preferred the garbage, and after watching his antics for about twenty minutes I decided it was time to hit the sack. At 10:30 it was late (for me anyway), so I started walking back to my tent. About fifteen yards away, I was thunderstruck to find a small bear walking a parallel course. He wasn't getting any closer, but I was getting nervous since it was obviously a cub, which meant that mama wasn't far away. I didn't want to break into a run since that might alarm the sow wherever she was. So, I just kept on walking to the waiting wall tent, and tied the flaps tightly once therein. My next close encounter with bears would be of the more unpleasant kind. I wasn't sure where the bear went, but as I was trying to go to sleep, there was a chorus of clanking garbage cans. The little bruin must have gotten his bearings straightened out and headed back to the party after all.

The campers spent day one listening to me and the hunter safety instructors. We spent another full day at Cito sidehiking Hidden Valley and bushwhacking up Cimmaroncito Peak. The second itinerary stop was Clarks Fork, which was having its share of bear troubles as well. For some reason, I didn't expect this camp to have any bear problems. I had developed a theory that camps that had horses were not attractive to the bruins. Had this not been the case at Beaubien? My theory was thoroughly discredited that night. As we were playing cards in the lodge with the Clarks Fork staff, we heard garbage cans being rolled. As we gathered on the porch to see what the commotion was all about, we saw a good-sized bear. By ten P.M., I was in my tent, which was not much more than forty yards from the lodge. Bear bags were not then the rule as they are at Philmont today. The group next to us had apparently put one up on their own, but had not done an especially good job of it. Now there were two bears poking around our campsite. I had pitched my tent in the lazy ranger style, i.e., a diamond shape with three tent pins, one tall pole, and one end of the diamond tied to a tree nearly five feet up from the ground. My pack was stored down at the edge of the tent, not close to me, but within the protection of the tent should it start to rain. This was the pre-"smellables" Philmont where bear protection science was only in its infancy.

I awoke at 2:30 A.M. to more garbage can rolling, and then there came a menacing sniffing and snorting from right next to my tent. It was a well moonlit night, and the moon illuminated something I did not want to see. The big black bear was sniffing at my pack! The bear was between me and the tree—half way into my tent. "It's the cinnamon," I was thinking, "that little can of cinnamon in my pack, the stuff we use to jazz up cobblers. That can is going to be the ruin of my pack and the other tools of my trade." Just as I was about to eject through the back of my tent, the bear started making those half sniff, half snort sounds, turned, and headed across the campsite. I was too pumped up to get to sleep right away. Sometime around 3:30 A.M., after what seemed like a few minutes worth of snoozing, I was awakened by more sniffing.

It was a mama and cub, always a potentially explosive combination. The cub had been attracted to a small pup tent about ten feet away. The tent held the advisor and his son. I could not believe what I was now watching, especially after all I had told these people about messing with the bears. Before my eyes, a raised hand and trench shovel emerged from the darkness of the tent, and squarely bashed the cub on the nose. It must have hurt the cub, because the soft "clonk" was followed by a squeal with which the cub skyrocketed up the nearest tree. The nearest tree, was, of course, the one to which my tent was moored. Mama Bear wheeled around from the other side of the campsite, and charged the advisor's tent. Fortunately, she came to a stop right at the edge of the tent, and turned to look up at the cub. Within a few minutes he came down, and they started sniffing around the campsite again. I was sitting up in my tent watching the incident when suddenly, I sneezed. When I sneeze, it is no small matter. With my nasal thunderclap, the mama turned and faced my tent, but fortunately stayed where she was. I had never been aware that bears could turn so quickly.

I was up early, wished the crew well on their travels, and then said farewell. Earlier, I had taken the advisor aside, and explained how closely he had come to ending his expedition only a few hours before. My words seemed to sink in. I hoped that they had, since he and his crew had been one of the most likable that I had served to date. Tom Guyer at Webster Lake had invited me to "stop in any time." I decided to take him up on his offer, and maybe enjoy a second breakfast as well. It was starting to rain as I caught a commissary truck on the Cito Road. This was the beginning of the monsoon season.

When I got back to headquarters, there were a couple of surprises waiting for me. I found some of Steve Gregory's gear on my cot, and learned that he had spent most of his July paycheck on a new camera. He always had been a good photographer, and Philmont was the place to take pictures (something that I learned too late). I had missed Joe again, as he was off to Olympia shortly after I got back. After showering, I looked at myself in the mirror and was surprised at how my ribs were showing like never before. However, I had never had a summer like this before either.

I met 810C under a dreary sky, and started them on the grand tour of headquarters. Mr. Leroy Tasha and his group were all from the same troop in LaGrange, Illinois. I usually chatted with the advisors as we made the rounds, which started in the health lodge, where I would quickly scan the forms for potential problems. In school I had studied French, and had roomed with guys who had taken Spanish and German. Therefore, I took some pride in being able to reel off names with polished, precision pronunciation. Scandinavian names were not a serious barrier, and

I could pronounce Dutch properly since a close high school friend had been an exchange student from Holland. Slavic names like "Zelenka" or "Blazewicz" were no problem at all. But I absolutely blanched as my eyes glanced over the names on the forms. I was expecting the usual range of names typical of most Scout troops—maybe a Jones, a Plastino, Anderson, Hannifan, Johnson, Mellinger, King, DuVivier, or Schultz. Here were names like Czyzewska, Pietraszkiewicz, Szymkowiak, Wandzilsk, Szelestowski, and Czezowski. I managed to hurdle some easy ones like Gorecki and Kempka, but really had to "wing it" on the rest of them.

"Not bad, Cass. You got about half of them right, and that's about twice the average. Here, let's go through this again. Pronounce Polish 'czy' like..." So I got a good lesson in the pronunciation of Polish names. Modern European history has always interested me. I felt much sympathy for all of the Poles who had been overrun by the Nazis and then the Communists. A Scout in Mr. Tasha's group was a slight, blond fellow who reminded me so much of Stefan Martinski, an elementary school classmate of mine. Martinski was what was then known as a displaced person. His eyes always seemed to have a sad look as well they might have considering what he had gone through. Unlike my childhood friend, Mr. Tasha's boys spoke without accents, and were obviously the sons or grandsons of immigrants. They were anxious to ride, so off to Olympia we went.

Always being a passer-through at Olympia, I had never really gotten acquainted with the staff. The Assistant Director was Jim Delaney. Our paths would cross many years later when he was a *Boy's Life* editor. The Camp Director was Bill Benner, a gent whose greeting was unique. Bill walked very quickly, as if he couldn't wait to meet you. His head tilted to starboard, and his hand extended well before the handshake. He also had his right thumb pointed toward the ground. I wondered how we were going to shake hands with thumbs aimed downward, but at the last minute, Bill would roll his hand right side up, and pump his guest's hand furiously. He was the type who was kind to children, small animals, and rangers. I concluded that he must have been a ranger early in his Philmont career.

Olympia had none of the charm of its neighbors, Abreu and Crater Lake, and was not soaked in history like Rayado, which was then known as Carson-Maxwell. Olympia had a shotgun range, and made up for the natural beauty with considerable down-home hospitality. We were now in the rainy season. However, the occasional sprinkle did not interfere with the trip down to Rayado for horseback riding and the tour through the Kit Carson museum. We had a go at the shotgun range the next morning. Clearly, breaking the clay pigeons required more practice on my part. I had brought a couple of boxes of twelve-gauge shells of my own, but didn't make much of a showing on the range.

We left Olympia as it started to rain. It was a typical mid-August shower: bright and sunny one minute, raining the next, with a rainbow forming down toward Rayado. I took an opportunity of having my picture taken with me at the end of the rainbow arc. It would make a nice gift for Sarah. Fishing and conservation took up most of the afternoon at Abreu, our next stop. This was my first real visit to Abreu since Ranger Training and my trip with the Kansas group. I was really beginning to enjoy Abreu, which seemed to have it all: the fast flowing Rayado, a great view of Urraca Mesa, good fishing, lovely campsites with tall pines, and a sweeping view of the prairie.

My orientation with this group was basically finished, and with the group off on their conservation project, I walked up the meadow to visit New Abreu. It proved to be a wooden version of the stone lodge at Crater Lake. A breezeway separated the trading post and the staff/kitchen/dining room. The view from the front of the lodge seemed to go on forever.

I sat on a porch chair to write a letter to Sarah. Greg

Schondel, the camp director, had musical tastes that paralleled my own. There was a Liszt piano concerto on his record player (electricity was another of Abreu's amenities). There were still rainshowers about, and a low cloud hovered over a small mesa to the southeast of Rayado Camp. The sun was low enough on this late afternoon to light the mesa top which now looked like a silver platter beneath a gray sky. "Ah, could life be any better?" I was thinking to myself. The visual effect of rain and light on the prairie was striking. It was typical of some skyscapes where mountains give way to foothills and then the flatlands.

"To be a ranger, to be in such a special place, to listen to good music, and to be writing to my gal. Oh, surely life couldn't get any better than this." Actually, life could be better. Much better in some respects. It would be nice to have my beloved right there with me instead of half a country away. And Mr. Tasha, I thought, was something less than universally pleased with my services.

It was the old story of some stranger trying to teach the advisor's boys a few new tricks. After all, what could some college kid, who probably had less than five or six active years in Scouting, possibly add to what *he* had already taught his Scouts. I already knew the eventual outcome of that attitude, and hoped I would be in headquarters when they came off the trail to see the transformation.

I decided, therefore, that my Dutch oven performance that evening had to be top drawer. So, we were going to have a Dutch oven treat beyond the cornbread that would accompany the unappetizing spaghetti and applesauce. With a couple of Scouts acting as assistant pastry chefs, we were on our way to jelly roll. We made the jelly, trail food variety, by adding water to a grape bug juice (beverage) base. It was rolled in a sweetened dough, and popped into the Dutch oven. The result may not have been up to LaGrange's better bakeries' standards, but there were no complaints.

The birthday boy with his group of Texans prior to the descent into
Red Hills Camp

There were a few signs that the camping season was coming
to a close. There weren't food shortages as such, but there were
substitutions here and there. The number of groups would soon
slacken, and be composed largely of short, seven day expeditions.
But for now, things were still red hot. I left my group at Abreu,
and caught a ride below Olympia. When I arrived at headquarters,
I found I was scheduled to go back on the trail that afternoon.
814A had arrived early, and another ranger had already completed
the headquarters tour and shakedown.

As we were about to head for the loading dock, the sky
opened up, and wouldn't slacken. Then the loudspeakers announced that all transportation for the afternoon was cancelled
due to the heavy rain. In the hurry, I had only managed a brief
glimpse of the itinerary, which started at Cito. Due to the
cancellation, the starting camp was omitted, and we departed from
the Cito turnaround for Lambert's Mine. The next day, this group
would give me a nice birthday present, a climb of Comanche
Peak from Cyphers followed by a night at Red Hills.

Although ranger contracts ended on the twenty-fifth of August, several rangers had already finished with their last groups. They were now hanging around, as some of us had at the beginning of the season. It was rumored that only the talented rangers would carry on until the end. I still had another trip after this group so my ego was in high gear. If only my stomach could have been in the same speed. If I had been faced with another trip to Ponil, I am sure that burnout would have started setting in, but I was really excited about this itinerary. On the other hand, I was less enthused about the advisors. One was frail while the other had a heart condition. Still, I had seen some scrawny kids eat up trails like professionals, and the health lodge had not held this guy back. So, off to Cito turnaround we went the next morning.

I had been through Lamberts only once before. The camp proved to be a stony clearing at the edge of which reposed a small shack very much in its decline. Interestingly, there was fresh evidence of beaver activity in the area. Another distraction was the menu for the evening. One consolation of the end-of-the-season food problems was that we got some different meals on those last trips. Dessert that evening was chocolate pudding, which was not too popular. The boys said they were saving it for a snack to have later. I gently reminded the advisor of the consequences of leaving food out overnight. The boy leader assured the advisors that the pans would be clean before dark. I wound up sleeping on a bed of rain-softened porcupine quills in the line shack after our little campfire wound down.

The stars had come out, which encouraged us. We were going to need good weather for our big climb the next day. I was looking forward to the ascent since it was the only standard approach to Phillips that I had not done to date. My mood shifted in the morning when I saw what was in the pudding pans of the previous night. They were loaded with drowned mice! Although the advisor was more than twenty years my senior, we had a little peer review of some camping basics. He apparently got the message since the pots were thoroughly cleaned with remarkable dispatch after dinner that night.

We got off to an early start. However, since we traveled at such a slow pace, it would have been better if we had spent the night at Cyphers. The boys were more than up to the task, though. They were among the oldest boys I had guided that summer, and many would be going back to high school as seniors in just a couple of weeks. It was the advisors who had a rough go. Clearly, we were going to get strung out on the side of Comanche Peak. I called an impromptu conference, and suggested that the advisors move up front and set the pace. I took a position just a few steps behind the chubby advisor. We took a lot of rest stops, but that was better than having a medical problem on our hands. I had hoped that we would make it to the top of Comanche by lunch, but that was not to be. When we finally got there it was mid-afternoon. We took a long break, and were amused by the antics of three Canada jays. After the novelty wore off, we left our packs in a line and sidehiked the remaining easy mile to the top of Mount Phillips.

We were blessed by grand weather. August at Philmont is a time of unsettled, and usually wet, weather, but on this day the sun shone and the visibility was unlimited. We backtracked, heaved our packs on, and were off to Red Hills, which we reached at the rather late hour of 4:30 P.M. It was my birthday. The Red Hills staff invited me to dine with them, and I gladly accepted since I knew that the Beaubien packer had been through that very afternoon. First, I would break a modest amount of bread with my Houstonians. The advisors had met the challenge head-on, survived it, and were delighted to know that all trails from that point were easier, if not all downhill. After a taste of ham and noodle dinner, I made my apologies, and was treated to fried shrimp. Red Hills was a more primitive camp, almost a high altitude Lost Cabin without refrigerator or running water. But they ate well on the nights that the packer had come through.

After a sound night's sleep, I headed down the Comanche Creek trail, and soon found myself at Porky, which was having its bear problems.

They had not yet caught their most troublesome bear, "Big Otis," but had caught one of his relatives, "Little Al." This young bear sat at the edge of the cage and cried. Yessir, he had tears at the corners of his moistened ursine eyes. I made the mistake of casually resting my hand on the wire cage. Fortunately, my reflexes were quick enough to avoid Little Al's teeth as he lunged at me from his sitting position. After failing to lunch on my fingers, the little bear just huddled back in his corner, put his head on his paws and cried some more. On top of all of his other problems, he could have used a little deodorant too. Little Al was my ticket to headquarters since I rode in the pickup that towed the trailer cage out of the high country. Little Al was released on top of Urraca Mesa later that day, and within a few more days he was back home at Porky living the good life again.

When I got back to headquarters, I learned that Steve Gregory was in the health lodge, and taking some pretty strong pain killers. He had been driven in from Abreu after having taken a bad spill while crossing a log over the Rayado during his hike down for a day off. The culprit was a wet log, and the poor balancing characteristics typical of external frame packs.

At least I now had a full day to get cleaned and rested before the next group. Rangers and wranglers were the ones who needed the washing machines. We could occasionally be a dirty lot in the literal sense of the word. It was an occupational hazard. My once proud, red wool shirt jacket was sorry looking. It had absorbed the smoke of scores of campfires, and when wrapped in a T-shirt it served as my pillow on the trail. As the washing machines and dryers did their thing, I was losing my focus on the old newspaper I was holding. I wasn't seeing the headlines, subheads, captions, and copy about what was happening back east or around the world.

I was looking at Jim Place as he led us up to Toothache Springs on that raw, rainy day in early June. I was comparing Neil Karl's upstate New York accent with Carl Manning's Tennessee drawl. Now, the "rattlesnake" at the Stockade was good for a laugh instead of a knot in my stomach.

Somebody reminded me that the dryer buzzer had gone off, and maybe I should make room for the next guy. For nearly all of us, this was a period of reflection. The summer was almost over, and I knew that it had been the best summer of my life by far, as I am sure it had been for every other first year ranger. Part of each of us was still the young Scout enjoying the summer and the Ranch for all the adventure it could provide. The peaks and fast cold streams, the sudden showers and the heavily timbered mountains were intoxicating. And they actually paid us to guide people through all of this! There was, though, another aspect of rangering that made it obvious that we were crossing the boundary between Scout and Scouter. It came from being around headquarters when one of our groups came off the trail. It was in their eyes and voices as they told us of their adventures, and how much they appreciated what we had imparted. Often, we started young dreams that would be realized in just a few years when some of these Scouts would apply to work at Philmont. The advisors, most of them almost old enough to be our fathers, returned from their trails a little more ragged looking. They now looked at us more as their equals since we were, on a daily basis, going through what they thought was a real grind.

Hot dog! Last group, 819S. Appropriately enough, they were from Warren, Ohio, which would eventually be home to Ned Gold. Messrs. Heltzel and Clifford were taking the now familiar south country itinerary that started at Olympia after the bus ride to Rayado. At this point, I was beginning to burn out, although I tried to retain my enthusiasm when I was with the group. In another couple of weeks I would have Sarah with me, and would be getting back to good food (even college food appealed). There would be new courses, the Greek social scene, and friends to share stories with.

Bill Benner was as cordial as ever, and had some Canadians in camp. I made it a point to visit with them, and talked at length with their advisor about the differences and similarities in our respective Scouting organizations. I had planned to take my leave, and return to headquarters via Stone Wall Pass since I had never traversed it before. The more pragmatic side took over, and said that Stone Wall could wait. I caught a jeep at Zastro, and came home to Ranger City on the twenty-second of August to find that place in a state of flux. Some guys were packing, several had already left, and there was a banquet planned for that evening. We were ready. In our best uniforms and red jackets, nearly all of the ranger staff boarded two of Earl Swope's buses. We then took a short journey to the Stockade for our annual banquet. Although there were nearly a dozen of our brothers out on the trail, this was the one day when most of us were in headquarters. The baked potatoes had already been started, and when the fire was burning down to coals, the steaks were put over cots that served as grills.

There were no scraps that night. Mr. Dunn said a few words to his hushed audience, and then we broke into song. There were the usual Scouting melodies, but the obvious favorites were "Silver on the Sage" and the "Ranger Song."

Cleaning up and packing was the first order of business in the morning. Joe was among those who would be leaving early. I hated to see him go. We hadn't seen that much of each other over the summer. Oddly enough, since June we had never run into each other on the trail.

"Want to buy my boots, Bill? I'm not going to need them where I'm headed."

I did buy his boots. I had borrowed them several times over the summer, and was anxious to buy them. They would remind me of a close friend.

Joe was headed for a monastic way of life. He would travel to Rome, and receive his Bachelor of Sacred Theology degree in the Gregorian University. Then he would return to the United States and earn a Ph.D. in Philosophy. In my mind's eye, I saw Joe becoming a Philosophy and Religion Professor, department head, and respected author. I also saw him as the father of a couple of young lads who would find their way to a Cub Scout Pack. When we reestablished contact many years later, I was absolutely correct in my vision of Joe's future.

I wasn't headed anywhere soon. My parents were going to drive out and pick me up at the beginning of the Labor Day weekend. We planned some vacation time before returning to the East. For me, this meant remaining at the Ranch for another week.

Several of us who had come in on the twenty-second or twenty-third were talking about how to spend our free time. We knew we would be put to work at odd jobs around headquarters or sent to close down camps during the last few days of August. We decided that it was time to climb Baldy and throw in Wheeler Peak for good measure. At something over thirteen thousand feet, Wheeler is just across the valley from Baldy, and is the highest point in New Mexico. The plan was simple. We would get some trail food (not supper number one, for which the supplies had been exhausted anyway), and go on our own two-day expedition. Since we had wheels, we would drive to Eagle Nest, take jeep trails as far as we could, and then bushwhack it. We might even take in the night life in Red River the night before. The night life in Red River turned out to be not all that bright, and it was raining when we got to our hastily set up camp near Pine Gulch.

The climb was not difficult when compared to other trails with a full pack on. What made it difficult was the weather. What awaited us on top was not the ideal, bright, sunny view of Philmont's peaks to the south, Wheeler Peak, or the broad sheet of Eagle Nest Lake. The surrounding clouds only occasionally parted to reveal a misty view of the town of Eagle Nest. Baldy has always had a reputation as a mountain that rewards one forward step with two backward steps. The constant cycle of freezing and thawing has reduced the sandstones and shales to an obstacle course that tries the mind and boot soles of all hikers, especially in wet weather. The weather didn't look like it was going to improve. What would improve our spirits was a steak at Miss Dee's, and maybe an evening at the cozy staff lounge. Even the breezy ranger locker building was better than our prospects on Wheeler, which we duly decided to save for another day.

Ranger contracts expired on the twenty-fifth, and after that I was still doing some packing. Autumn had come to Philmont. The nights were much colder, and we were getting more rain. For the first time this summer, there were a few mosquitoes about. Most of us had taken to wearing long levis in the evenings. Joe's boots came in handy. The fine gravel around headquarters had worn out the soles of the penny loafers I wore when not in hiking boots. August 26 came, and only six rangers were left. I was assigned to work in the post office. It was managed by Rick Garcia, a widely respected young man, and former ranger, who had developed arthritis to the extent that continued ranger service was not possible.

I had hoped for a posting to some camp as part of the closeout staff. However, the post office had its advantages—I got Sarah's letters faster. I had already received more letters than any other ranger. The real question was whether I had received more from Sarah than Freddy Blair had received from his Gwendolyn. Freddy would show up soon since the far northern and southern camps would close first. When Freddy appeared, the letter contest remained in dispute. Dimalanty wouldn't be coming back the following year, and Freddy was undecided. He thought he would ask for Beaubien, but had also been considering the top youth job at Boxwell Reservation, his home council camp in Tennessee.

Headquarters services were picking up. The food had improved, and even the movies were more recent. We watched Disney's "Living Desert," and it was a film to which we could easily relate. Music was played over the loudspeakers each night just before the closing campfire: the Grand Canyon Suite was a favorite, and on the night Steve and Ned came down it was very appropriate. These early autumn sunsets seemed more striking than those of high summer. Sunsets now were darker, limned with silver and the warmer colors of the fading sun, and set off by the jagged outlines of Tooth Ridge and Trail Peak.

Senior staffers who planned to return the next year usually had an employment interview with the Director of Camping. I had been thinking about my future and was torn between more rangering, and maybe getting a camp of my own. The thought of some managerial experience was appealing, but so was the nomadic life of the ranger. I had one of the better experiences among rangers that year—good groups and a phenomenal spread in itineraries. In the end, I decided that, although being a training ranger was assured, I would ask for some camp in the south. Accordingly, my choices as a prospective Camp Director were for Black Mountain, Crater Lake, and Miners Park in that order. Ned and Steve would set their sights higher and request Fish Camp and Abreu, respectively. Steve had passed through Abreu enough to appreciate its beauty and the rush of the Rayado. The fact that there was good fishing nearby was not lost on him either.

Meanwhile, there was still work to be done. I had graduated from postal service to the repair of packframes. Then Buzz Clemmons interrupted my work to request my services as a chauffeur. I was to drive a couple of staffers up to Raton in Buzz's station wagon. Three quarters of the way up the fifty-two mile ride there awaited a sight that drove us into gales of laughter. Here, in the broad valley, barren of any trees, a black bear had climbed a telephone pole! The *Raton Range* reporter and photographer were both there covering the oddity, which was still perched on the cross tie when I drove back.

Ranger City was a ghost town. Most of my buddies had left. The nights were getting much colder. Ned and Steve had come down to find me as the last ranger in Ranger City. At that point I had found further employment as a tent packer at the polo barns. We decided that it was high time to get ourselves ready for re-entry into the college way of life. What better way to do it than get a real, professional haircut. The trip to Raton was also an opportunity to ship my steamer trunk home. We got shorn, but were disappointed to find that the municipal swimming pool had closed two days before. That evening, we used our one-time only pass at the Training Center to have dinner at their dining hall. Under a bright sky in the morning, Ned and his brothers pulled out for St. Louis. Steve headed for Glenwood Springs and relatives. Unfortunately, he forgot his fishing gear and treasured elk antler, a souvenir found exactly on the spot where he and Ned had set up camp at Lost Cabin.

At two P.M. on September 1, my parents drove through the Philmont gateway. They found a son somewhat more slender than the lad they had seen off at the train nearly three months before. After loading my pack and Steve's items, we were off to Albuquerque and the biggest steakhouse in the city. I polished off the most massive sirloin I had ever seen, and then devoured the remains of my parents' steaks. Getting to sleep was an unusual experience. For the first time in months I was in novel surroundings: four walls and a ceiling. I had come close at Cyphers in an Adirondack with three walls and a ceiling, but still couldn't quite get adjusted to a ceiling that was perfectly flat. It would take a while to readjust. My first instinct at any faucet was to cup my hands before taking a drink. I had forgotten what carefully wrapped drinking glasses were for.

We enjoyed a marvelous vacation; we saw the Grand Canyon, took the narrow gauge railroad at Durango, Colorado, and swam in the Great Salt Lake. After the Tetons and Yellowstone, we did some serious fishing in the legendary trout streams of Wyoming,

Idaho, and Montana. I could not imagine then how that experience would pay big dividends the following summer.

Within a week, I had Sarah in my arms again, and Economics bouncing around in my head a week after that. But the Ranch would not let go. The experience of that summer was always just beneath the surface, and after many years, Philmont still has not let go (not that any Ranch alumni would have it any other way).

Arriving at Comanche Peak

9

Old, New, and Improved Abreu

Steve and I quickly settled back into the routine of college life. As autumn was turning into winter, we reminisced about the summer past. My roommate, Bob Warner, better known as "Wally," would listen in, with seemingly growing interest. Wally had acquired his nickname from an absent-minded Spanish professor who consistently referred to Bob as "Senor Wallace." So "Wallace" Bob became; the contraction to "Wally" was a natural.

I had never talked much about Scouting with Wally, although he had attained Eagle rank before starting college. Steve's and my enthusiasm over the Ranch proved to be infectious, and with Wally's credentials, he would have no problem getting a Philmont staff job if he wanted to.

I was studying Economics harder than ever since Washington College required comprehensive exams in one's major before granting a diploma. We took these "comps" seriously since ten percent of the preceding senior class had not been invited to graduation due to shortcomings on the two-day test. I became a more serious student because of the comps, but still found time to promote Ranch employment to Wally. I knew that his application would be favorably reviewed, and that he would get the job based on his own background and not just the glowing recommendations of Messrs. Cass and Gregory. I also knew that he probably wouldn't receive his contract until sometime in early spring. Steve and I were getting itchy about what camps we would get or if the competition was such that we both might wind up as Assistant Camp Directors someplace. It was to be a Jamboree year, and that meant a smaller staff with more competition than usual for the best jobs.

The big day came when I opened the mailbox to find the blue envelope. Inside were those two magic words—"Camp Director."

However, I was to be Camp Director at Clarks Fork. This was actually a compliment since Clarks Fork was much larger than anything I had asked for. The camp had a staff big enough to have its own cook and many horses. Clarks Fork was a key starting/ending camp where there would be plenty of activity. Camping Headquarters usually tried to place ex-rangers in such camps since they were familiar with the needs of groups just getting started on the trail. Figuring that there might be room for a little wheeling and dealing though, I decided to call Buzz Clemmons for the purpose of a little trading. First, however, I called the omniscient Ned Gold who always seemed to have the latest information on anything to do with the Ranch.

Meanwhile, Steve's little blue envelope said "Director—Porcupine." It wasn't his first choice, but Porky was a lovely camp, and Steve was not unhappy with the appointment.

Ned had gotten Fish Camp, and had heard that Freddy Blair was offered Abreu. I knew that Freddy was entertaining other possibilities, and decided to invest in a weekend phone call to Middle Tennessee State College. Freddy mistook me for some big shot, and called me "Sir" when the operator said long distance was calling for "a Mister Frederick Blair, please." After a few pleasantries, Freddy said that he had decided to take the big job at Boxwell. We wished each other well, and I waited until Monday evening to call Buzz Clemmons to see if I could line up more suitable employment. I had to sit and think out how I was going to handle the call. I figured that my first three choices went to others, and that Buzz wouldn't think much of my calling up and pleading for Black Mountain or Crater. After all, I had been offered a big camp, and to parade an inclination for downward mobility probably wasn't a good indicator of managerial talent.

When I reached him, Buzz Clemmons was surprised to hear of Freddy's plans, but seemed to appreciate the thrust of my suggestion that I take Abreu. Abreu was to have a fine, new rifle range put in, and how convenient it was that I was already an NRA-certified instructor. As for the fly tying/fishing program—I laid it on somewhat thickly by mentioning my vast experience on the Loyalsock and Pine Creeks in Pennsylvania, and the Madison, Gallatin, and Jefferson in the west, not to mention the Green and Salmon Rivers. Did Buzz know that I was already an accomplished fisherman on the Rayado and Agua Fria, etc., etc.?

I was really getting wound up when I said that one of the greatest moments in my life as an outdoorsman was pulling a few cutthroats out of the Snake up in Wyoming using a fly that I had tied by candlelight at Beaubien the previous year. Buzz Clemmons had probably heard several sales pitches like this before. He most likely thought that the voice on the other end of the line might well eventually find employment somewhere in the fishing tackle industry. But there was logic in my proposal. Mr. Clemmons saw an ex-ranger at an important base camp, and a double rated guy who could run both the fly tying program and the rifle range when the regular program counselors were off. So the deal was struck.

"By the way, Mr. Clemmons, I've got an Eagle Scout roommate here, and both Steve Gregory and I think he would make a wonderful addition to the Philmont staff. I believe his application was mailed several weeks ago. His name is Bob Warner, and we can assure you that he more than lives up to..."

"Well, Bill, I'll see that he gets all of the consideration he deserves. Look for a revised contract in the mail, and say hello to Steve won't you?"

I had probably been holding Mr. Clemmons up from leaving his office at five P.M., but I couldn't resist getting a good word in for Bob, whose contract as Top Gun on the Cito ranges arrived a few weeks later. I was on cloud nine, and had the world by the scruff of the neck.

The damp Eastern Shore winter gave way to the lacrosse season and soon enough to exams. Then we took the dreaded comps, which proved to be not so frightful after all. Graduation followed which meant that my last season at the Ranch was only ten days away. Wally and I had decided to drive out together in his station wagon.

Sarah was rather distressed by my decision to put in one last season at the Ranch, but had found a temporary solution to the distance that separated us. Her family would vacation in the southwest, and they would swing by the Ranch on the way out and back. So we would get to see each other twice that summer. It wasn't much, but it was a whole lot better than not at all.

Wally and I planned our trip out. It would take us along Virginia's Blue Ridge, and on through Tennessee, Arkansas, Oklahoma, Texas, and to Albuquerque where we would spend an evening with Jim Talley. We arrived in Albuquerque earlier than planned, so we drove up to Sandia Crest before showing up at Jim's house. Jim suggested that we all go down to Vicente's Dining Rooms in Old Town Albuquerque for dinner. It turned out to be quite an evening. Vicente was a classical guitarist who would sing to his guests. On the walls, there were faded pictures of Vicente in his youth. He had been a troubadour, and there were pictures of his associates, all dressed up with those great Mexican hats. Vicente would sing for about fifteen minutes at a time, and then, after some yells from the kitchen, he would retire. He likely left to wash dishes or cook more enchiladas. He would reappear, and sing for another fifteen minutes, and then the cycle would start again.

Jim Talley was no slouch with a guitar, and was invited to come forward and accompany Vicente, whose fame had apparently spread throughout the southwest. Vicente's little establishment was filled with visitors, many of whom had come from Colorado or Texas just to hear this man sing and play his many-stringed guitar. Wally was rapt since he had occasionally played guitar in a band at Washington College. We eventually returned to Jim's home to spend half the night reminiscing about Beaubien days. The ride from Albuquerque seemed to take forever. We passed through Santa Fe, Espanola, and Taos, but when we got to Eagle Nest, we were as good as home. There was Baldy in all of its glory, much sunnier and warmer than my last visit.

It was mid-afternoon when we arrived, and we immediately went through all of the check-in procedures.

"What am I supposed to do with this thing?"

"That's your staff patch, Wally. Hang it off your right pocket button, but don't lose it. They're valuable."

"Willee, you think I'm a patch collector, or what?"

"Put it in your steamer trunk, that's what I do."

There was a lot of catching up to do. It seemed like all of the veteran rangers had regained most of the previous season's lost weight. Yet there were many faces missing. It was a low attendance year due to the Jamboree. There were less than sixty rangers, but almost half already had one or more years of rangering under their belts. Maybe there wouldn't be as many campers, but at least those that came were going to get off to a good start. I was anxious to show Cito to Wally, so we drove up there late in the afternoon. On the way back, we encountered another driver, a young man with blond hair and blue eyes. He did not recognize me at first, but I remembered Frank Estes from two summers before when he was camp director at Crater. I made the introductions, and both Wally and Frank seemed impressed with each other from the moment they met. They looked so much alike that they could have passed for brothers.

There were only sixteen camps in operation that year. Old time rangers hadn't done too badly, and wound up in charge at many of the camps. Ned Gold had Fish Camp, Jerry Thatcher had Olympia, and I rounded out the far South Country directors. Way up North, Doug Trevett was directing French Henry. Dick Pate, Phil Yunker's former tentmate in Ranger City, was running Clark's Fork. Phil had the plum—Black Mountain.

The roster, which had been mailed in May, hadn't said much about my staff other than Ron Price would be directing the new rifle range. Ron and I had done Hunter Safety Instructor training together, so I knew the range would be in good hands. I was disappointed to learn that he had been reassigned to another range, but was equally pleased to find that his place had been taken by none other than Wayne Woods, who had also been in our training class. There was another name in the roster: Bob Wert from Chattanooga would be our quartermaster/commissary manager, but I was in the dark about the other range officer and the fly tying instructor. As I would learn later in the day, I had also struck paydirt when the other two Abreu staffers introduced themselves. The biggest surprise happened when the camp directors had their first meeting.

The New Abreu cabin, which overlooked the Rayado and the

rolling prairie to the southeast, was being put out to pasture for a while. A new trading post had been built next to the creek and the jeep trail that led up to the Old Abreu Lodge. Two of the five members of the Abreu staff would live in a separate room within the trading post/commissary. I was wondering where the rest of us would live, and just assumed that it would be in a pair of wall tents.

We were to live in the Old Abreu Lodge itself! Somebody was making good decisions where the fate of William Cass was concerned. Posted from Rayado to Beaubien at the last minute two years before, handed itineraries that I couldn't have picked better as a ranger, and now to live in an original Phillips hunting lodge. It was almost too good to be true. Indoor hot running water and a shower stall inside the lodge, too. Eat your hearts out Fish Camp and Cito!

My remaining staffers emerged from the crowd after the staff opening banquet. Tom Leightenheimer hailed from Portsmouth, Ohio, and would be Wayne's assistant on the big, new .22 range. They made an ideal team. Tall, slender Wayne was introspective where the shorter "Light" was irrepressibly enthusiastic. Clint Wethered, the fly tying instructor, was younger than most counselors, but vastly more experienced in his craft than other fishing program people. He was quite resourceful, and his talents would literally save the day on Operation Scatter.

Always quick to form opinions, I sized up my staff as being top drawer, and knew that we were going to have a solid summer of bringing high adventure to Scouting youth. First, we had to get prepared for this adventure. For Camp Directors, it meant training that emphasized leadership, camp operations and how to handle any emergencies that might come our way. We were also encouraged (in our copious free time) to attend the training sessions of our program staffers. I concentrated on fly tying with Clint. Teaching Hunter Safety was still fresh in my mind from Beaubien days.

One remarkable aspect of Philmont staff training is the quality of instructors. Top experts with Scouting ties descend on Philmont in early June to get the staff up to speed in all of the program disciplines. Our fly tying instructor sold his flies to the then exclusive sporting goods emporium, Abercrombie & Fitch. It was immediately clear that Clint had enough talent to qualify as a subcontractor. Clint was from Ephrata, Washington State. He pronounced it Eee-Fray-tuh. Dick Gertler also came from an Ephrata (in Pennsylvania) where it was pronounced Effer-tuh. Somehow, something got lost in the transition from east to west, but one thing for sure was the fact that Clint's flies were light years ahead of anybody else's. No wonder he sold flies back home. Sport fishing was big business back in eastern Washington, and Clint had the dexterity to make money at it.

Much of my time was spent in the company of other camp directors that first day back at the Ranch. Still, I had to make a quick visit over to Ranger City to see who had come back.

Mr. Dunn was rolling on like Ol' Man River of course. Paul Felty, Giff Kessler, and Greg Hobbs were among the ranger Crew Leaders. Times hadn't changed; Terry Klungseth offered me a sunflower seed, and by the look in Terry Denton's eyes, I suspected that a card game might be in the offing. Those very self-assured youngsters, Steve Haynes and Jim Crawford, had returned, but they weren't such youngsters in staff service anymore—collectively they were starting their fifth year. Joel Lewitz had breezed in from the Windy City again, and Tom Tucker's smile was bigger than ever. A few of the familiar faces that were missing in Ranger City had surfaced elsewhere. Some rangers, such as Neil Karl, had returned as Assistant Camp Directors. Others had opted for program jobs. I wondered how many guitars Hillbilly Ashby would batter into splinters while running the campfire at Beaubien.

Operation Scatter started, and for the Abreu staff, it was just one foul-up after another. I had decided that we would rotate sleeping quarters so that by the end of the summer we would all have a chance to live in the Old Lodge. For openers, Bob Wert, our Commissary/QM man, and I would stay at the lower cabin. This was a recently constructed building complete with electricity. After offloading Bob's gear and mine, we drove up to the old lodge to find that it had not been left in very good condition. It was normally used by JLT expeditions, and its last use had obviously been during heavy rain. The mud from many boots had dried on the floor, which closely resembled a carpet of small, brown stalagmites. We had to chip them away with shovels before having at it with soap and water.

Once we cleaned that up, we could appreciate the lodge for what it was. There was the "Great Room" with a mounted deer above the fireplace, which had the usual Phillips fine touches on the screen. There was a bunkroom and a large kitchen. There also was a double-padlocked pantry built from heavy timbers that seemed to shout "bearproof." At the end of the kitchen was the shower that gave forth hot water. This was real style. Somebody had obviously been through quite recently to make sure that the stove and refrigerator would work, but it would take a couple of weeks before we mastered the refrigerator's balky pilot light.

It was Bob's responsibility to make sure that the water pump was working. Located at the edge of the Rayado, it was a simple affair and consisted of a pump and small gasoline engine that fed our water tower. This engine, unlike the highly reliable pump engine at Beaubien, was an evil contrivance that regularly tried our patience. On our first day we were spared of water problems, only to find that the commissary truck driver had brought his share of woes for us.

There was a heavy wire rope gate that blocked the way into Abreu. Our first awareness of this problem was seeing the truck driver walking forlornly toward our lower cabin. He had forgotten or lost the key. He had already supplied Rayado and Olympia. By the time he got back to headquarters to get the key, all of those cartons of milk, meat, and eggs would probably go bad. Time for a command decision. We dug a post out, and replaced it as best we could. For the next week I lived in fear that the fresh dirt mound at its base would betray our rather hasty improvisation. Luckily, nothing ever came of it. Then we got all of the perishables into our refrigerator before offloading trail food and trading post items at the lower cabin.

I could see that the truck driver was nervous since he was looking throughout the truck's cab, his pockets, and then in the cabin itself. Sure enough, now he had lost the keys to his truck.

"Big deal, I'll just call the Control Center, and they'll have a jeep down here in forty-five minutes with another key."

That was the obvious solution, but the driver clearly saw that as the last resort. Then Clint did something quite remarkable. He asked permission to jump start the truck using nothing more than pliers and a screwdriver. Was this the same young, wholesome Clint from rural Washington State? Maybe we had all been mistaken, and Clint had misspent some of his youth as a hoodlum on the mean streets of New York or Newark. Within two minutes of entering the cab and laying down on its floor, Clint had tinkered his way to success. It became something of a joke, but we always asked the driver if he had his keys in his pocket whenever he came our way again.

We still had all of the Scatter jobs ahead of us. Get the lay of the land, cross-train ourselves, open the rifle range, number the campsites, paint a little here and there, put together our duty rosters, and do all of the other tasks that would make Abreu a successful camp. We would host two hundred and nineteen groups that summer, and would serve nearly one camper in three who came through the Ranch that year. When Scatter was over, we went back to headquarters for the last of our training, reviews of any glitches, and our final pep talks. Then we shipped out again to bring high adventure to thousands of eager Scouts.

Three days after the ranch officially opened, four groups came to Abreu; two groups from Texas, some Kansans, and a small bunch from New Orleans. We were ready for them. Shortly after their arrival, Clint had his first customers at the fly tying table. It wasn't much longer before we heard the sharp rattle of .22 fire from the rifle range. We were off to a good start, and it would be more than a week before we would run into our first problem. Some groups coming down from Fish Camp asked to be checked in at the old lodge where they wanted to establish their campsite for the night. The two cabins were separated by more than a quarter mile, and there wasn't room at the old lodge. So, we cleared it with Control, and thereafter all groups were checked in for camping at the newest Abreu.

There was a pleasant surprise on June 27 when Jim Talley showed up at Abreu. Clearly Jim missed the Ranch, but the economics of pursuing his Master of Fine Arts required the higher earning potential of a summer job in Albuquerque. We enjoyed a nice lunch together, and although we would correspond for several years, our paths never crossed after that day.

Jim's musical abilities would carry him to Nashville where he balanced careers in music and real estate. The same talent that so impressed us at Beaubien led to albums and the White House where he was occasionally a guest entertainer. Jim's critically acclaimed CD/book set, *The Road to Torreón*, traces its origins to northern New Mexico, and, indirectly, to the Ranch, which he credits as the springboard to his professional music.

As I had sensed from my first day at headquarters, I had been given a top notch staff. We were running like a well-oiled machine, which was more than could be said for our pump engine and refrigerator. We eventually learned to readjust the pilot light on the refrigerator to bring back the chill. This seemed to be an epidemic problem.

"Fish Camp to Abreu. Come in Abreu."

"Abreu. Go ahead Fish Camp."

"Bill could you relay a message down to Control, and have

them send Pappy Scholl up to fix our refrigerator?"

"Ned, you got a large, flickering orange flame behind the lower front access panel?"

"Huh?"

"Take the panel off, and tell me if there's a big flickering flame."

I had taken notes on the servicing procedure when Pappy had fixed our refrigerator, and then talked Ned through the repair. Operating the radio was normally the right of the camp director, and the Ranch had gotten us the VHF transceiver permits from the FCC to operate the radios. Those radios were a godsend in emergencies, but they had their humorous moments as well. Since VHF transmissions are pretty much line of sight, camps like Porcupine and Fish Camp couldn't communicate directly with the Control Center, so messages had to be relayed. Ned's childhood nickname had been "Corky," so calls between Porcupine and Fish Camp were initiated as "Porky-Corky." We used the Radio Ten code with its familiar 10-4 for "Yes" and 10-20 for "what's your location?"

To this we added a whole litany of other codes that ranged from 10-26 (Help, we're out of food) to 10-15 (Clean your desk, C-1 approaches). A "C-1" was the sector director, and his role was much like that of a district commissioner or regional manager. He was charged with the successful operation of camps in his sector. There were three sector directors that year, and Duke Towner was ours. Duke was a school teacher from Lexington, Illinois. He had previously served in headquarters management jobs, and by his looks must have also been a basketball coach. Duke was tall, sinewy, and took a real interest in the success of each camp in his sector. He had a way with each camp staff that made them feel that they alone were Duke's favorite. It was a nice touch.

When everything was running pretty smoothly, I granted myself a day off. I hiked down to Rayado, caught a ride to headquarters, put up at Ranger City that night, and was on the way to Fish Camp the next morning in a chaplain's jeep. Ned seemed well settled in, but what I had in mind was a fishing trip down the Rayado. Those crazy little dippers were still there, as were some nice trout that we cooked for dinner at Abreu that night. It was that night that my staff bestowed on me my nickname for the rest of the summer. It was "Daddy." I was only the oldest by a year, but the tag said all of those wonderful things about seniority and respect. I ate it up. They even reacted well when I occasionally called them "my sons, my sons." Then I would spread my arms like some biblical prophet calling his flock together.

"Hey Daddy, let's make up some hush puppies to have with these fish."

Dumb yankee that I was, I couldn't quite make the connection between fresh trout and casual shoes. Thus, Wayne and Bob started the rest of us on the way to appreciating southern cuisine.

The next morning, we had a celebrity in camp. When I was through Ranger City the night before, Skip Stephen said that Greg Hobbs had been assigned to some advisor who was a Hollywood star. I found it a bit incongruous that anybody from Tinseltown would be attracted to the tough life of ten days on the trail. However, it seemed that the veteran character actor Jack Kruschen was cut from different cloth. Jack was not a big matinee idol, but had regularly appeared in wide screen, western epics in such typical roles as the town dentist or hardware store owner. He looked like any other advisor, and probably had more gumption than most. He came hobbling into Abreu with a broken foot. A wet Rayado log crossing had claimed yet another in a long list of victims. He didn't want to leave in the ambulance, but I told him that it was firm policy.

I was starting to question the wisdom of having taken a camp director's job. We tried to maintain a quick pace at camp with conservation projects and all of the program that the campers could absorb. Somebody had to man the fort at our lower cabin, and that frequently was me when Bob was out quartermastering.

However, headquarters life for a ranger could be quiet as well. At least we were getting three squares a day. We were also getting more rain than usual, but after the previous summer, any rain would have been a quantum increase. In the quiet moments, I would tie a few flies with young Clint, the old master. I was a hopeless pragmatist about the flies that I wanted to use for fishing. Clint was actually not that enthusiastic about fishing, and seemed to regard the tying as an end in itself. Not surprising considering what little works of art he produced. He had it all down cold; even wings were easy for him.

There were a few personal surprises in store for me. In early July, I noticed a family of three walking up the jeep trail. The lady was wearing a billowing light-colored dress, and the man and boy were in Scout uniforms. Doggoned if it wasn't Mr. Dunlap, principal of my old elementary school. He had moved to Lancaster even before I reached high school, but here he was with his son Robin. They were at the Training Center. We had a nice reunion that was followed the very next day by another. One small camper from the Del-Mar-Va Council found me and said, "My big brother said I had to come say hello to you because he's going to marry your girl's college roommate." It was Dave Smith's little brother. It was strange how this great Scouting community could be such a small world sometimes.

Within a couple of nights at our Old Lodge coffee hour, I noticed one advisor looking as though he knew me. It turned out to be Gil Turner, a tall, ruddy-faced advisor from Lake Charles, Louisiana with whom I had another coffee hour conversation two years before at Beaubien. But the reunion I was waiting for was the one with Sarah. She was due out at the Ranch soon with her parents, and I could hardly wait for the day.

Meanwhile, Abreu was running smoothly. There was usually something to do between checking groups in and out and supervising conservation projects. I knew that there would be some monotonous moments as well. So, I had subscribed to the Sunday edition of the *New York Times*. I figured that all the news that was fit to print Sunday would keep us going for the rest of the week. It turned out to be a real hit with advisors even if the news was a bit stale. Since I was now in the ·autumn of my Philmont staff years, I had decided that it would be especially appropriate to have some proper music at Abreu. Greg Schondel's classical music tradition was kept alive by my record player and a modest collection of albums. My tastes were eclectic. They included dixieland, instrumental bluegrass, and the big bands, but my true love was the romantic era with Brahms and Beethoven leading the pack—the sterner the better. We had no electricity at Old Abreu Lodge, so all of the culture was delivered down at the lower cabin. Clint's program was served up on the porch, or in the commissary area on rainy or windy days, to a background of symphonic music.

Old Abreu—an original Phillips lodge

Because the other guys were wrapped up in program, Bob Wert and I usually checked most of the groups in. I was on the front porch watching our nesting Say's phoebes one morning when I saw a group coming up the trail from Olympia. They struck me as kind of an odd lot, but I couldn't figure out why at first. Then it dawned on me that a ranger was first in the file. Not only that, he was wearing gloves, something normally expected only of wranglers. Philmont does its best to screen applicants, but as I had learned so well the previous summer, there is the occasional odd bird who slips between the cracks. It looked like one was headed our way. The first year ranger seemed visibly insulted when I asked for the group advisor and boy leader. I checked them in, and got them across the creek to their campsite. As Bob was leading another group across the bridge, I saw yet *another* group coming up the trail. After getting our third group signed in and over to their campsite, I crossed the bridge, and thought I heard music. This struck me as odd since our record player was in the bunk room, and had not been running when I left the cabin.

Sure enough, there was the gloved ranger listening to the Brahms violin concerto.

"I don't want to see you on this side of the creek until your group goes to program. You belong with them until tomorrow morning. Next time you want to use somebody's property, you ask for it. Please rejoin your group now."

"I don't have to take orders from you."

"You obviously didn't read the fine print in your contract. It says that you will consider yourself a member of any camp director's staff while you are in his camp. I'll see to it that your contract is read to you when you check in back at the ranger office. Now get out of here."

I was almost hoping that some future group would bring him back to Abreu, but I never got the satisfaction. What really pleased me was the number of old ranger friends who did come through Abreu that summer. Bob Bingham, Alan Throop, Jack Crider, and Paul Felty were among the first to pass through Abreu. The old guard, guys like Rick Vuylsteke, Steve Smith, and Bob Stepp would say hello, and then I wouldn't see them until much later. They were still plying the old ranger trade—always imparting something to their groups as long as they could.

In addition to my immediate boss, Duke Towner, we had only one other visitor besides the commissary truck driver. This was James R. "Booger" Brown of the cattle department. Booger was second of the two real cowboys I got to know while at Philmont. He was as different from Bobby Maldonado as night and day. Bobby's sense of humor ran to the droll and occasionally very dry while Booger was purely a slapstick comedian. Bobby was lanky, Booger short, wiry, and bowlegged. Booger had a mild speech impediment related to his cleft palate, but it was barely noticeable considering his ultra-salty speech. Booger's jokes and guffaws would never quit—except for his brief nap for which he had appropriated Wayne's cot.

We would see Booger about once a week as he came to check the cattle that summered in the Abreu area. He would park his pickup and horse trailer in the little meadow in front of Old Abreu, and ride off toward La Grulla Ridge. He would show up a couple of hours later, and have some of our coffee. He declared our brew to be drinkable, but little more. At least Abreu coffee was reasonably fresh. There was a Philmont tradition of using the same pot, and just adding a little fresh coffee to the grounds already in the pot. When the grounds reached the top of the pot, it was time to start from scratch again. Most of Booger's coffee was just reheated remains from the previous night's advisors' hour, so it hadn't really aged to true Philmont standards.

Booger took great pride in his horsemanship, and was appalled that we were so unmoved by it. He challenged Tom Leightenheimer to get on the horse properly. Light finally got aboard, but it was not by the conventional means. Wayne demurred, and then it was Bob's turn. He swung into the saddle, but still we were not up to Booger's idea of promising cow-punchers. My eyes met Boogers', and the challenge was on. I still remembered what Bobby and Jim Talley had taught me, so with a reversed stirrup, and a handful of reins, I swung up, around, and into the saddle. This brought great whoops of amusement from Booger who said that maybe I ought to apply for a job with the horse department next summer.

Booger offered to bring up another horse and take me on one of his inspection trips. For some reason, I never took him up on it, and now look back upon that as a great mistake. Booger tread where there were few trails, and saw much of the Ranch rarely seen by camper or staffer.

He said that there were very active signs of mountain lions just up the Rayado Canyon, but we never did see the elusive cats. Nor did we see their little cousins, the bobcats, although hearing them at night was not unusual. Abreu was probably a rich camp in terms of wildlife because we were right on the border between two of Philmont's life zones. While the prairie was within view, we were on the boundary between the pinon-juniper and Ponderosa pine forest zones. The fact that the Rayado flows through Abreu contributes to the variety of wildlife. The usual mule deer, rabbits, squirrels, and ground squirrels prevailed, but we also had visitors that crawled and slithered.

Our first introduction to the prairie rattlesnake was late one afternoon when Light rounded the corner of the porch with a wild glint in his eye.

"Daddy, guess what I got?"

I could see what Light had gotten, and it was a well-ventilated sight. Of all places to cross in broad daylight, this poor snake had chosen the rifle range. He had been perforated to the extent that he wasn't worth eating, let alone being made into a hatband. Our policy with rattlesnakes on the trail was pretty much "live and let live." If we saw one in the confines of a camp or thought there was some enduring menace, we would simply pin the snake's head down and decapitate it, making sure to bury the head quickly and deeply. I wasn't anxious to have campers getting excited on the rifle range, nor had I forgotten my experience with the skunk from the previous summer. The next rattlesnake was found a bit closer to home—too close in fact: on our back porch. The lower cabin had a little concrete step in the back. One morning Bob opened the door and almost stepped on the snake. After dispatching the rattler, we decided to have it for dinner since it was an unusually large specimen—well over three feet. Unfortunately, I was the cook that day, so it fell to me to clean the snake. I had cleaned plenty of small game and fish, but that was little preparation for the production that followed. Rattlesnakes are well assembled, and are held together by a variety of membranes and plenty of bones. After getting it skinned and cleaned, we probably should have boiled it, and then fried it, but we just settled for frying. The meat was strikingly white, but not especially flavorful.

Abreu was generally free of pests other than the ubiquitous ground squirrels, which were really more amusing than anything else. We did, however, have the occasional rhinoceros beetle. We first encountered these overgrown specimens on the rifle range where they were definitely distracting and, therefore, a safety hazard. I gave Wayne a box of .22 bird shot, and told him to discretely shoot any beetle he saw when campers were not on the range. That may sound like overkill, but a full-grown rhinoceros beetle is not something easily taken care of with a fly swatter. Wayne said he and Light had gotten rid of quite a few of the beetles, which had the annoying habit of landing on the rails separating the various firing positions on the range. After a few days, they seemed less bothersome, so I assumed that we had gotten rid of the local population. Perhaps they had migrated to another, lower risk environment.

Then one afternoon, I was doing some paperwork in the lower

cabin. An advisor and a couple of kids from a Memphis crew stopped into the commissary to pick up some trail food. The advisor lingered, and was reading the remains of a recent newspaper while halfheartedly keeping up a conversation with me. It was just idle chatter since I was trying to be polite while filling out requisition forms. I thought I had seen some movement in one of his shirt pockets, but didn't pay much attention to it. I finished the last line of the commissary requisition, and looked up to see the man's face suddenly contort into the most terrible grimace. Then the sounds started. It was a sort of grunt that quickly evolved into a full fledged, painful scream. Then the sound turned into a fast, throaty little series of deeper grunts. His face was turning red, his teeth were bared, and he was starting to clutch at his left shirt pocket. "Oh, Lord, the guy's having a heart attack," I thought. What should I do? Get to him, treat him for a heart attack, and then get on the radio fast.

I ran down to the end of the counter, but by then the episode was over. He had reached into his uniform pocket, and pulled out this black, three-inch long rhinoceros beetle that had just pinched him.

"Darned thing just bit me! Caught'm up on the rifle range this afternoon. My brother's a biology teacher, and I thought this might make a nice looking specimen for his display case. Say, can you give me one of those envelopes? I don't want to get bit like that again."

The rest of the wildlife was much less intimidating, or at least had proven so up to that point in the summer. We were free of most insect pests, including mosquitos. Campers occasionally asked us about the dreaded tarantulas and scorpions. Although they were supposed to exist within the Ranch's life zones, we never saw any nor did we ever talk to anybody who had. Still, the wild kingdom had some surprises in store for us, but they would not become obvious until later in the summer.

The day I was waiting for finally arrived. I rode back to

headquarters with the commissary truck driver one Tuesday in early July knowing that Sarah and her family would be arriving sometime that afternoon. I tossed my pack into a vacant tent in Ranger City and took up my vigil down at the loading dock. Two o'clock came and went, and there was no family Mumford motoring through the gateway. After what seemed to take millennia, they arrived. The scene that followed was reminiscent of one of the television commercials of the day where the young couple run along the beach and leap into each others arms in a loving embrace. We were lucky not to chip a couple of teeth. I swung my girl around almost as though she was a little rag doll. It seemed like ages since I had last held her close, but it hadn't been much more than a month. Those moments were easily the best of the entire summer.

Sarah's father shook my hand, and said how much they were enjoying the trip, and how beautiful northern New Mexico was, but I barely heard a word. Then he said they were going to go down to Cimarron, and check into the motel, but would be back at five o'clock to take us out to dinner. Two hours alone with my lady and probably a hundred staffers looking on! Holding hands, we walked around headquarters, and sat in the shade of the trees near the camping office. Every second was ticking by much too fast. We walked past Jerry Traut's nature exhibit, and then strolled down to Villa Philmonte where we were much more alone.

The rest of the day flew by much too quickly. We wound up the evening at Lambert's where staffers couldn't keep their eyes away from us. Most girlfriends were just black and white, framed pictures, but I was one of the lucky few who got to share the Ranch with his girl.

The next morning we drove down to Rayado, out to the Stockade, and then down to Villa Philmonte. I knew it wasn't going to last long enough, but Sarah and her family had to leave right after lunch for Albuquerque, and then the Grand Canyon.

But they would be back in a week.

I held Sarah close, and kissed her knowing that what seemed like every pair of eyes in headquarters must be watching us. The departure was bittersweet. At least I would see her again before the summer was over. Then, as they drove out beneath the gateway in a cloud of dust, the ego trip began. Old ranger buddies were suddenly surrounding me wanting to know who that attractive girl was with whom I had been walking around headquarters.

Duke Towner gave me a ride back to Abreu where I tried to throw myself into my work again. There wasn't a whole lot of time to daydream since we had a busy daily schedule which started with a routine that was becoming almost a fetish with me. Abreu was the location of one of Philmont's weather stations. Weather had always fascinated me as it would in years to follow when I had to fly through all sorts of it. Our station was not that sophisticated, but did require observing sky conditions, measuring rainfall, reading the humidity with a sling psychrometer, and recording the maximum and minimum temperatures of the previous twenty-four hours. Every morning, I was out there at 7:30 A.M. sharp getting Abreu's Accu-weather sorted out.

Our daytime highs were typically in the upper eighties, and nights in midsummer were usually in the forties. Once this ritual was completed, I checked on our little Say's phoebe family, which had its nest on one of our porch beams, then declared Abreu open for business.

Unfortunately, it seemed that the Mumford family departure created a vacuum that was filled by rotten weather. We had several days of intermittent rain and low stratus cloud. The only break in all of this overcast was a letter Sarah had sent before arriving at the Ranch. Sarah's visit seemed to bring home an inescapable fact—my days at Philmont were numbered. I knew that Sarah and I would have each other for the rest of our lives, but the Philmont era in my life was going to end soon. There would be no more "going back to the Ranch" after exams. For that reason, I decided that I would experience as much of the Ranch as I could in the waning weeks of the summer and try to leave some mark on Abreu if possible. While I obviously couldn't take time off and go hiking, I decided that I would excuse Bob from evening pump starting duty, and do it myself. It gave me a few minutes alone by the Rayado, and afforded me the opportunity to try to put some fish in the refrigerator.

I enjoyed those evening forays immensely—although it meant doing battle with our cantankerous pump engine. With priming, readjusting the valves, and checking the fuel supply, I could usually get it going. The pump would run until after the coffee hour was done, by which time our water tower would be full, and could serve campers through breakfast cleanup. Occasionally, I would see a water ouzel, but more often just the deer and rabbits played as I trudged up to the pump after dinner. I would continue up on the south side of the creek until I was out of earshot of the pump engine, and then would start fishing. On the opposite side of one of my favorite pools was a badger den. Its occupant wasn't always out when I happened by, but when he was, I would stop and sit on a rock to watch.

The badger had that grumpy look of all badgers, and he seemed quite put out with me for interrupting his household cleaning chores. He was frequently digging around his den entrance when I saw him. Like the badger of Beaubien, this low-slung guy would turn around and glower at me before resuming his digging. I could just read his thoughts.

"You're just summer help here. I wish you riff-raff college kids would get out of here, and leave the place to us year round residents. You think you own this place or something?"

No, I didn't own any of the Ranch, but in the larger sense, it probably owned a bit of me. My mind was elsewhere, thinking about Sarah's return to the Ranch. I couldn't take two full days off when the Mumfords returned. I got down to headquarters early since they were driving up from Taos, met them, and then brought them back to Abreu for the grand tour and a late lunch. Sarah couldn't have been more beautiful. She wasn't dressed for traveling—she was all dolled for me and was wearing a lovely black and white outfit. Unfortunately, their vacation was ending. Sarah was lucky to get that much time off from her summer job, and it would just be another five or six weeks before we would be together again. We drove back to headquarters where, after an embrace that wouldn't last long enough, Sarah was on her way back east.

10

Rayado Vistas

There were problems waiting for me when I got back to Abreu. One problem was not, however, created by my lady's appearance. She had clearly made her mark. Wayne quietly said, "Daddy, she's real purty." That almost made my day, but unfortunately, a bear rolled us on the night of my return. I had heard that Ned was having a few problems with bears, and wondered if he had sent his troubles down the valley. Our bear was medium-sized, and had shown up around 9:15 P.M. when we heard trash cans rolling around. I was in a dark mood. Sarah was gone, and I had a bear to deal with. The bear was my problem, not the campers', and not an itinerant ranger's. Clearly we had to double our attempts at garbage control, and make sure that the groups in camp did the same. I became convinced that they were Ned's bears. I momentarily considered sending Clint and Light up the valley in the dark of night to plaster the side and roof of every building in Fish Camp with jelly, syrup, and molasses.

Unlike some of Cito's more brazen critters, this bear was easily frightened. We dashed out onto our little porch and let fly with some blood curdling Indian war whoops. The bear bolted off into the bushes for the rest of the night. I decided that if he came back and got close enough to the lodge, we would empty our fire extinguishers on him from the porch or a window. Our lodge was quite secure. Even if a bear had gotten inside, it would have been impossible for it to break into our sturdy, padlocked pantry, which was going to be our bunker if things really got bad.

We got hit again the next night—at both Old and New Abreu. Fortunately, the bruins stayed on the north side of the Rayado, and left the campers alone.

A medical emergency marked my second day after Sarah's departure. A group from Wichita came down from Crater, and their advisor appeared in rocky shape. I recognized the name, J.D. Spitzengel, since he had been through Beaubien two years before. He barely made it into the lower cabin before collapsing. He had all of the signs of shock, so I had him put into Bob's cot, got his feet elevated, and put some blankets over him before getting on the radio. The ambulance arrived within forty-five minutes. Mr. Spitzengel had obviously been pushing it too hard, but now was in professional hands.

"Say, wasn't it you with that chick at headquarters last week? Man, she really turned some heads. Who is she?"

Sarah had obviously made a bigger impression on this medical student than poor Mr. Spitzengel was making. The advisor's son decided to accompany his dad back to headquarters since there was another adult with the group, and they had only one more day on the trail anyway. They forgot his walking stick, which we sent down by commissary truck the next day. It was a lovely stick, but I was secretly hoping that it would never get much further than Mr. Spitzengel's den in the future.

Abreu was getting busier, and we were averaging ten groups in camp per night. Our little bridge, which led to the campsites on the south side of the Rayado, was barely up to the traffic. I decided that we really needed a proper bridge that would be wide enough to accommodate two-way traffic. We had one large pine that had fallen across the creek only about fifty yards west of the little bridge. I decided we would use it as the foundation for our new bridge over the Rayado. My requisition for nails, 2x4s, and 1x4s was met with something less than enthusiasm. It seemed that I would have to provide plans for approval before the supplies could be released. So the Abreu staff became structural engineers.

We decided to take down another pine whose girth was similar to the one already crossing the creek. We would roll it into a position next to the log that was already across the Rayado. Then we would place a smaller diameter log in the gap between the two big logs, and nail the 1x4s across the logs. To make a rail, we would build side supports in the shape of the number 4, using some 1x4s cut long for that purpose. The rails would be nailed onto the top of the "4"-shaped posts to complete the project. Our plan was finally approved, and we had plenty of free labor for the project.

Christmas intervened, however. The practice of having a "Christmas" party would eventually be replaced with "Fiesta," which was more in keeping with local traditions. Ned Gold decided to play Santa Claus, and invited all of the south country camp directors up to Fish Camp for the festivities. It was not all party, though, since Duke Towner would be having a sector meeting that day. It was just as easy to meet at Fish Camp as headquarters. I was all in favor of it since it meant fishing my way back to Abreu after the meeting.

Deciding to maintain my ranger skills, I hiked from Abreu to Beaubien via Lower Bonita in little more than two and half hours. An ambulance was passing through Beaubien on its way to Fish

Camp to pick up a burn case, so I rode in comfort the rest of the way. Ned had invited the Director of Camping and other dignitaries, who showed up with Steve Gregory. Ned always knew how to pull strings and his table was well prepared. I buzzed out quite early the next morning, and caught enough trout for dinner on the way back to Abreu. We were eating pretty high off the hog at Abreu due in no small measure to Wayne's talents as a cook and the fact that some of the best fishing on the Ranch was just a stone's throw from our lodge.

Occasionally, we would get a real treat like frozen shrimp, but we also got a lot of cubed steak, hamburger, Dinty Moore stews, and cold cuts. Because of our fishing forays, we built up a canned goods inventory. We had so much food that it was almost embarrassing. I had heard that the Clarks Fork staff was suffering from the opposite problem. We boxed up much of the surplus, and prominently marked "CARE" on the packages. We then shipped them to Dick Pate at Clarks Fork. Unfortunately, the commissary intercepted the packages. They informed me by intercamp memo that they would take care of Dick's feeding problems by themselves, and no further intervention was necessary.

We consumed a lot of "bug juice" as might be expected since we spent very active days working in low humidity. We were all walking three to four miles per day, and burning up shoe leather at an alarming rate since the distance between the two Abreus was nearly a half mile. Because we had a good refrigerator, we also had ice. Thus, our bug juice was much more inviting than the average. The "beverage base" as they now call it, came in three varieties: cherry, lemon, and grape, or at least that's what we thought they were. Eventually, we just started calling it by color.

"Hey Light, pour me some red, will ya?"

It was our long-suffering commissary truck driver who really savored our bug juice, though. His was an unrewarding job, and he was on the road six days a week with fresh food for camp staffs and trail food for their commissaries. He hauled and shoved more crates and cartons than anyone, and his reward was only the occasional lunch of cold cut sandwiches and bug juice.

"J.B., stay for lunch, we got purple today."

So we would have a guest for lunch, and get caught up on the latest headquarters gossip. It took a while for us to learn that the best bug juice was a blend of the red and purple. Unfortunately, we always seemed to get more yellow than anything else.

The bridge over the River Rayado was now a top priority. We had taken down the big pine, and used small logs to roll it into place. This proved to be the most difficult part of the entire job, and for me the most painful. I was at the end of the log, guiding it as my small army pushed it across the creek. Unfortunately, the log got jammed just about a foot short of the little stone foundation we had built to function as the log's northern base. Using a 2x4 as a crowbar, Bob levered it up as I held onto the bottom of the far end. With a mighty heave, we moved it again, but also jammed my left hand into the stone base as the log dropped into place. I howled in pain, but quick thinking Bob levered the log up just long enough for me to get my bloody hand out. It didn't look good. My knuckles were a mess, and the nail on my left index finger was ripped and bleeding.

There wasn't much left to do, but get down to the cabin, clean it up, and see how bad it really was. I knew that the iodine was going to make me sing this time. Once the cuts were cleaned up and the bleeding stopped, I took stock of the situation. I had had stitches for injuries before, and decided that a few good butterfly bandages would do. My hand was throbbing for hours from the accident that never should have happened in the first place.

My days as a bridge laborer were over. The bridge was finished in the next couple of days much to everybody's satisfaction. The next milestone was our staff banquet. This was a more formal affair to which Duke Towner would be invited. I also decided that Mr. Dunn should be our special guest. After checking calendars, Thursday, August 6 was selected as the big day. Duke Towner would bring seven prime steaks as the main course, and we would be on our own to provide the rest.

"My sons, my sons, gather 'round so we can plan our feast."

So, we planned a full ten course dinner. We would lead off with chilled tomato juice followed by vegetable soup and blushing pear salad. Naturally, we would have a fish course which would consist of shrimp, trout, and oysters. To add to the class, we would have a cheese course. The main event would be buffalo steak, creamed potatoes and spinach. We would close with homemade ice cream, cake, and coffee, tea, or milk. I filled out the commissary request, and next to the oysters I wrote mushrooms. Fat chance we would get either, but a little humor never hurt. After all, what would steak be if we couldn't have mushrooms. When the commissary truck delivered our special request items, I was absolutely flabbergasted. Our banquet box did indeed contain one can of B&B mushrooms and a small can of smoked oysters.

Then our banquet day arrived, and with it Messrs. Towner and Dunn who had brought along some fresh sweet corn. We were ready in our best uniforms, and had the place ship shape. As it turned out, nobody was big on mushrooms, so I enjoyed our special treat by myself. Wayne and I were the only parties interested in the oysters of which we made short work. Dinner was topped off by the trays of homemade ice cream, and the French apple pie that we substituted for the cake. It was one of the more memorable evenings of my three years at Philmont. Although we only had about three more weeks left to the season, I was riding high. Here we were in an original Phillips lodge located in one of Philmont's most beautiful settings. The Chief Ranger was our guest, and my staff had really shone all summer. Even our local bears were respecting the occasion by leaving us alone.

Staff banquet in Old Abreu Lodge
Clockwise from left: Tom Leightenheimer, Wayne Woods, Mr. Dunn,
Duke Towner, Bob Wert, and Clint Wethered

Periodically, there would be a camp directors' meeting at headquarters. They would start early in the morning, but be over in time for us to catch some transportation back to our camp by early afternoon. For one of these, I got on the radio to see when and how Jerry Thatcher was going to leave for the meeting. We decided that a little sidehike was in order. Accordingly Jerry showed up at Abreu around three P.M., and we lit out for Stonewall Pass together. We were going to have dinner with Del Crowther, the camp director at the Stockade, and then hike into Ranger City. I had never done Stonewall Pass, and was finding it difficult to keep up with Jerry. Stonewall is not difficult, but I was running out of steam. As we approached Lovers Leap, my head started aching and was still throbbing when we pulled into the Stockade. Del was older than most of us, and had done a hitch in the Air Force. He was now thinking about joining another branch of the service. The Stockade, built to recapture the flavor of frontier army forts, has one of the more commanding views of any camp at the Ranch. My headache was receding after dinner, but we still had the better part of an hour's walk in front of us. I decided to make the health lodge my first stop where a surprise awaited me.

The "take two aspirins and stop back tomorrow morning" came as no surprise, but finding Steve Gregory getting a physical exam before joining the professional scouting service was an eye-opener. He was getting his forms filled out, and after forty-five days of training at Schiff Scout Reservation in Mendham, New Jersey, would become a district executive in Green Bay, Wisconsin. Still, I probably shouldn't have been so surprised. More than just a couple of Philmont staff alumni go onto the professional service every year, and what more inspiring jump off point than Philmont?

I also ran into Wally after the directors' meeting. That was the first of only two times I saw him during the summer until I went up to Cito to help close the place out. He had made a big impression. Wally had been asked to consider coming back next year as Director of Pueblano, which then was home of the 30:06 rifle range. He was more immediately interested in going to the Santa Fe Opera. Unfortunately, seats were sold out on the day he wanted to go. So Wally chose the next best thing—a drive up Pike's Peak.

Whatever bug I had picked up, it proved to be short-lived. Returning to Abreu, I found that the bears seemed to have deserted us in permanent favor of Fish Camp. Our camping load had gotten quite erratic. One day we would have only one or two crews in camp, and the next day we would have ten or twelve groups. We were coming down to the end of the season since nights were getting colder, and the rains were more frequent. All of us seemed to be enjoying the wildlife more than usual. Each night after dinner, we would sit on our modest front porch and watch the hummingbirds. There were a few down at the lower lodge too, but they seemed to work in groups around Old Abreu Lodge. They would fly almost as a swarm, and hover among the flowers at the edge of the meadow until it grew dark. Frequently deer would cross the jeep trail that led away from our lodge. We knew there were also several other creatures that we would have a hard time seeing. Chief among these was the ringtail cat, a cousin of the raccoon. We never saw the ringtails although Wayne and I saw their tracks. They were supposed to be found in Philmont's inter-life zone camps such as the Stockade and Abreu. Not seeing the nocturnal, ultra-secretive ringtail was a real disappointment, but like missing the elusive bobcats, it was just not to be. I was smugly content merely to have seen ringtail tracks until looking at our nature guide on animal tracks. It suggested that a weasel had fooled us.

Our chief visitors to the lower cabin were the plentiful deer. Three of the deer seemed much tamer than most, so we named them: "Bud," "Delilah," and "Lurline." We could almost set our watches by another local, a weasel. Every afternoon around 4:30, the weasel would appear at the upper end of the meadow. He would scamper ten or twelve yards through the tall grass before stopping to survey the scene. He would scan the meadow intensely for a couple of seconds, and then disappear only to show up in a few more seconds further down the meadow. Then he would repeat the process until he crossed the road in front of the lodge. I usually took his arrival as my signal to cross the creek and chat with the advisors, and to make sure they had been invited to coffee hour.

Not everybody wanted to hike uphill for nearly a half mile, but we usually had a few hardy souls for whom caffeine was a strong attraction. One night, we hit double paydirt when two groups each brought up a Dutch oven full of cobbler. We only ate one cobbler, but I thanked both advisors profusely, and said we'd attack the remaining cobbler for breakfast. Just for safekeeping, I put it in the cupboard beneath the sink. I wasn't worried about bears, but we occasionally had ground squirrels in the lodge, and I thought the smells of cleaners and steel wool might mask that of the cobbler.

These were enjoyable evenings. There were expeditions from all over the country, and Wayne, Light, and Bob each got to chat with groups from their home states. Clint, however, from rural Washington State, was not so lucky. Del-Mar-Va, Daniel Boone, York-Adams, Chester County, and Hiawatha (Syracuse, New York) Councils all sent groups through Abreu. Lancaster County did not, but from Bradford County came Bill Baker with ten General Sullivan Council explorers. When Waite Phillips built the Old Abreu Lodge, he probably did not know then how much satisfaction it would bring to us and our guests.

The lodge was a bit unusual—it had a very high ceiling in the great room. There were two windows mounted above a deer's head that was far above the fireplace. The windows were so high that they functioned as sky lights for all practical purposes. With nights being crystal clear most of the time, the stars, moon, and light from our fireplace provided most of the illumination we needed during the advisors' hour.

We were living in the lap of luxury, and had some conveniences of which Cito and Fish Camp could not even boast. Hot running water was probably the chief of these amenities. It certainly made taking a shower less time-consuming. It also simplified shaving. At that point I had taken to shaving with a straight razor, and brought stone and strop with me. One morning in mid-August, I was irritated to find that my youngest "son," Clint, had improperly taken a fish knife to the strop, and had all but ruined it. After a brief discussion, we decided that Clint would buy the strop for the generous sum of four dollars, which

I used to buy more conventional shaving gear.

We were living the good life. At least our dining hall had not suffered a fire, which had been the case at headquarters. Apparently there had been a grease fire which was quickly controlled, but it was a few days before service returned to normal. At the same time, we found that we had vandals in camp.

One morning, I arrived at the lower lodge, wetted the psychrometer's bulb, and went up the meadow for the ritual swinging before reading the humidity. That done, I looked on the porch post to check our thermometer for the maximum and minimum temperatures, and did a double take. Our Taylor thermometer had been ripped away. I could hardly believe my eyes. Putting two and two together, I had a pretty good idea of where the problem came from.

Jerry Thatcher had been on the radio the previous morning. He warned me of a troublesome bunch from north Jersey, and said I should keep my eye on them. Nothing got me more irritable in a hurry than seeing boys who were not living up to the ideals of the Scouting program. It appeared that Scouting could take the boy out of the city, but apparently not always the city's less desirable sides out of all of the boys. I knew what I had in mind would create a real stink, so I called the Control Center to ask permission to shake down the group right then. Control Center denied permission, but indicated that the group would be dealt with when they came off the trail. The group would wind up their expedition at Cito about a week later, and proved to be a nuisance in every camp they visited. They proved so obnoxious at Cyphers that Big Bob Mahn got on the radio to warn other camps about the approaching swarm of vandals.

There were other frustrations. One day practically no campers, the next day we'd have over a hundred. Needless to say, our infernal pump engine decided to quit on the day we were loaded with campers. Bob had thrown up his arms in despair, and I had exhausted my patience over that mechanical terror. There was nothing left to do but get on the radio, announce our incompetence to the listening world, and request professional help. Pappy Scholl, the Ranch's wizard mechanic, arrived and finally got it going after about half an hour of tinkering. He had been up to see us three or four times that summer, but fortunately, this was the last fix it would need.

Duke Towner had been most generous in his evaluation of me and the Abreu staff. We all got good reports, and I decided that the vacation policy should be liberalized starting from the top down. After all, my "sons" were planning on returning the following year, but I was going into retirement. If that had to be, I was going to go in style. I had sent Wally an intercamp memo, and suggested that we meet at headquarters, and go on the grand tour with Duke Towner during one of his weekly south country inspections. It was a real treat for Wally who got to see the Stockade, Miners Park, Crater Lake, Beaubien, Porky, and Fish Camp all in one day. We even had time for some fishing, the results of which were left for Ned's table. For me, it was a last hurrah in the south country. I knew I would not see Beaubien again for many years. In my mind's eye, I had already pictured my future in Scouting and how I would next see Beaubien. I envisioned myself as involved with Scouting on the unit level, and returning to the Ranch as an ordinary expedition advisor. Fortune, always cruel to some, smiled on me however, for that is exactly how I would return. It would just take a lot longer than I ever thought it would.

At that age, thinking so far into the future was rare. Wally and I still had the evening off, so we drove over to Springer to go to the movies.

"You ever see any cops around here?"

"It's my third summer here, and I've never even seen a state trooper."

Wally always was a mite heavy on the pedal. Unfortunately, it was noticed by one of New Mexico's finest—and the only state policeman I ever saw out there. Wally's need for speed cost us $22.50, more than ten percent of a month's pay in those days. After the movies, the sky opened up on us, and poured so hard we had to stop on the side of the road. The speeding bug was catching. Ned and Steve had recently been to Santa Fe, and also contributed to New Mexico Highway Department coffers.

The end of the season was really closing in on us. We did our best to maintain enthusiasm, but when the going got tough, the tough went fishing. I had turned pump duty back to Bob, and had taken to heading up the Rayado immediately after dinner, and returning just in time for the advisor's hour. I rarely returned empty handed, but just spending two hours along the Rayado was enriching. Since we only had about a week to go before closing out Abreu, I tried to enjoy as much of the Ranch as possible. Normally, I fished from the south side of the creek. In the few remaining days I pushed well past the Bonita Valley trail, and tried the north side. There were some nice pools that were not accessible from the main trail on the other side.

It looked like there had once been a path on the north side, but it was obviously no longer in use. Unfortunately, the old trail did not always follow the edge of the creek, and I found myself up on a steep cliffside. I could see two nice deep pools just ahead, but the trail wasn't very appealing. It looked as though it had been washed out, and all that was left was a very fine gravel crust that offered poor footing.

The bad stretch was only about ten feet long. I didn't have a pack on, and if I crouched low with my uphill hand close to the stones I probably wouldn't have a problem, or so I thought. Still, it was all of twenty-five feet or more down to the creek. Hesitatingly, I started across, and before I knew it, the gravel gave way and I started to fall. I felt like I had somersaulted on the way down, and had the wind knocked squarely out of me upon arrival. This was not the stuff of which agile rangers are made, I was thinking as I took stock of myself. I was lucky that I didn't break anything since I had landed among rocks. I was bleeding from brush burns on both elbows and my left knee was also cut. My pants were embarrassingly split right up the seat, but my fly rod had survived intact. The fishing was the best I had all summer. Within twenty minutes I had seven trout, including two that were almost a foot long. Clearly, getting off the beaten track was worth it, even if I got banged up in the process. "No Dinty Moore for dinner tomorrow," I was thinking on the way back. Unfortunately, there wouldn't be much flycasting for the rest of the summer either.

I had been using an eight-foot fly rod that was really overkill for anything at the Ranch. Most of the Ranch's waters are so tight that even a six-foot rod is too long. So tall were our ceilings at Abreu that we stacked fly rods straight up without even taking them down. I had taken to opening the door, thrusting the handle end of the rod inside, then quickly pushing the screen door wide open, and dashing inside with the rest of the rod before the door could swing back and close. Well, I wasn't up to the task that night, and the door swung back, and snapped off the last foot of the rod. The whole evening was enough to make me wonder if I had become accident-prone.

On the next day we were visited by Philmont's Director of Maintenance, the wizened, little Charlie Rosenfield. He usually made one or two tours of each camp over the summer to make sure everything was functional, and to inspect the water system. After he finished his inspections, he would have a seat on the bench of the lower cabin, and light up one of his trademark L&Ms. Within a few minutes, he would be coughing and gurgling with what seemed to be the most terrible, tubercular death rattles. His little red face would pinch up, and he would curse "these danged cigarettes," but soon he'd light up again, and repeat the cycle once more. Fortunately, there were very few staff smokers. On the trail, smoking was a very dangerous habit indeed.

Most of the people who had the weed habit were at Zastro, a

camp located between Abreu and Olympia. It was used for Wood Badge about which, then anyway, none of us had the slightest clue. All we knew was that "Disastro," as we called it, was periodically full of oldsters (they all must have been over forty). Those old coots had a low powered radio that could reach Olympia and Abreu, but not the Control Center at headquarters. Whatever Wood Badge was, it obviously was fueled by Campbell's tomato soup, Folger's coffee, and Marlboros. Now and then, our radio would crackle to life with a request for so many cans of soup, so many packets of coffee, and so many cartons of cigarettes. The Zastro residents would then ask us to please relay this request to Camping Headquarters. Dave Bates was then in charge at control, and did not tolerate the use of the airwaves for such requests. With great pleasure, I relayed control's message to Zastro that supplies should be requisitioned through normal channels. The nicotine addicted were just plain out of luck since the Ranch didn't stock smokes. Unfortunately, the players down at Zastro were a revolving cast of characters whose rosters changed every other week. They never seemed to get the message about reserving radio use for real problems.

We were now down to the last couple of days. In the last two years, I hadn't been responsible for much at the end of the season, but now was charged with closing out a camp. I was determined that we would leave it in better shape than we found it. Our riflemen were cleaning and lubricating the tools of their trade, and Bob was inventorying and packing trail food. Then we started giving the Dutch ovens the once over just as Dimalanty, Jim Talley, and I had done at Beaubien two years before.

"Daddy, we're short one Dutch oven. I've looked everywhere, latrines, camp sites, and still can't find it."

As Bob spoke, the unsettling reality of the missing Dutch oven's location came to me. I knew exactly where it was, and worse, I knew what was still in it. Or at least I knew what its contents might have become by now. We removed the oven from beneath the sink, and it proved to be every bit as bad as I had imagined. I lifted the lid to see what looked like multi-colored cotton candy dominated by greens and oranges. At least it wasn't moving, although the bottom had become a decidedly putrescent sludge. Clearly, what we had created was something that would excite only a bacteriologist or mad dermatologist. The contents were consigned to our garbage barrel, and then properly cremated.

Abreu and Olympia would be among the first to close out, and the last afternoon would be spent packing personal gear. We would ride out on the regular commissary truck. The day before we closed out, I hopped a ride to headquarters from Olympia with a chaplain, drove Wally's car back to Abreu, and loaded most of my personal gear. My sons and I had spent a quiet evening in front of the fireplace looking back over the summer. The fire felt good as well it might have; autumn was approaching, and our nights were much colder. Wayne wasn't sure about the following summer, but knew that he would be going up to Cito with me for the next few days. Light, with his boundless enthusiasm, would be back—to stay in the hunter safety game probably at Cito or Pueblano. The program business appealed to Bob, but he hadn't decided, although I had done my best to sell the rangering life to him. My youngest son, Clint, was also undecided. I hoped he would come back, perhaps at Fish Camp where he could continue to pass along his fly tying wisdom.

August 26 came. After breakfast, we moved our personal gear to the porches of both of the Abreus, and gave the place its last scrub down. We spent the first part of the morning taking pictures, and hiking through the campsites. Around eleven, our truck arrived, and we loaded up. Although I was anxious to leave, I knew that an important era was coming to a close. It would be a long, long time before I would see Abreu again. How lucky I had been to have spent my last summer at Abreu. Here I hiked on my first day off two years before, here Jim Place had led us on ranger training, and here the Phillips presence still lingered.

photo courtesy of Steve Gregory

Living the good life at Fish Camp—
Steve Gregory, John Dimalanta, Freddy Blair, and Ned Gold

Then we were off. Wayne and I did little more than check into headquarters and toss some gear into the lockers before we caught a truck up to Cito. There we would join Wally as Hunter Safety instructors. Cito was the last camp to close, and we served as replacements for several of its program personnel who had to leave by the twenty-fifth. Frank Estes, of Yale Whiffenpoof fame, was laird o' the glen. He presided over a happy family, right down to the camp mascots, the Huey, Dewey, and Louie of the ground squirrel world. Rather in conflict with Ranch guidelines, the Cito staff had adopted an orphan ground squirrel family. The squirrels were named Skinny, Medium-size, and Chubs. They got plenty of attention, had their own wired-in quarters, and were exercised on a circular treadmill built into their not-so-little cage.

We had only a couple of days as program instructors before becoming a skeleton crew charged with shutting Cito down. Cito had its creature comforts, but I didn't hesitate to remind Frank Estes that as Abreu staffers, we were really slumming it. After all, we now had to walk to the showers, and wait for the hot water. On the other hand, we had the services of a semi-professional cook at Cito, so life wasn't all that bad. We went through the closing of Cito, which was just a large scale version of closing out Abreu. The only remaining excitement was taking out a large pine that was starting to threaten the structural integrity of Cito's commissary. I was the only one with any significant experience in handling a crosscut saw. Most onlookers thought I had gone 'round the bend when I started to take the tree out by driving a stake into the ground about seventy-five feet from the southeast corner of the commissary.

There wasn't a whole lot of room between the tree and the corner of the building. However, there was enough for Wally and me to cut through to the notch we had made on the other side. There was the usual creaking and groaning, followed by the "whoomph," and clouds of dust as the pine went over. I missed the mark by several feet, but at least didn't dent the commissary. The irony of the afternoon wasn't lost on me. I was ending my staff days the same way I had started them two years before—cutting down trees.

Part III

The Return

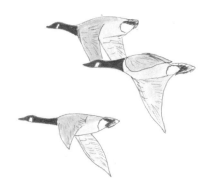

11

Interlude

My last night at the Ranch could not have been spent more appropriately. My college roomie of three years and I found a tent in Ranger City after having a pleasant dinner in Cimarron. The weather had turned foul. It was almost like my last day of the previous year. The sky was leaden. The gloaming had obscured Trail Peak and was settling down over the top of Urraca Mesa. Even the Solar Molar was partially obscured. Camping Headquarters was almost a ghost town, and what few staffers were left had opted for more comfortable quarters in the staff cottages. For me, the choice of lodging had been automatic. To stay anyplace but Ranger City would almost break those ties that had been so firmly established the previous summer. I didn't think my old ranger buddies would have minded a non-ranger bunking in for one night within those barbed wire confines. Besides, Wally would have made a terrific ranger had he come to the Ranch a year or so earlier.

When we got back from dinner, darkness was scuttling in. The tent we had selected was not exactly standard for Ranger City. Apparently, some new Assistant Chief Ranger had decided to reside in Ranger City proper, and had a substantially larger tent moved in for that purpose. The tent contained a metal frame bed with a mattress far more luxurious than the regular ranger issue. I won the flip for the choice bedding, and then helped Wally drag a regular cot into the tent. Wally was asleep quickly, but it took a while for me to power down. It was a repeat of the night two years before when Paul Dinsmore and I walked down the valley to look for fire near Fowler Pass. My body was tired, but my mind's gyros kept on spinning. Their song was full of indelible memories about high adventure in Philmont's mountains.

The chorus was filled with the sad knowledge that I would not be coming back. Instead of counting sheep or the Bonita Valley's Herefords, I purposely reflected on the great moments of the three years that were ending that night. Sarah's visit to the Ranch was paramount. The excitement at Dearborn Station, teaching campers in sight of Trappers Lodge, watching the raptors from Black Mountain's crest, and shakedowns on the parade ground drifted through my mind. Mr. Dunn's gentle voice, the sweat and exhaustion of climbing Comanche from Cyphers, those crazy water ouzels along the Rayado, fishing the Agua Fria—before long I was drifting away. Daybreak brought weather no more promising than the night before. For breakfast, Wally and I had some doughnuts and milk that the night had chilled. Then we drove out beneath that Philmont Gateway for the last time, and out of Scouting for many years.

We weren't alone. Our contracts had expired so we felt free to bring Chubs along for the ride. Cito's Grand Ground Squirrel Trio was headed for the big time. Medium Sized went to Texas with Frank Estes, and Skinny, the laid back ground squirrel, traveled, appropriately enough, to San Bernadino, CA. Chubs was about to become the most widely traveled ground squirrel in America. Wally and I had decided to duplicate the route of my previous year's return home, which meant we were headed for Albuquerque's biggest steak house. Our track was a familiar journey for me. Out route 64 by Touch-Me-Not and Baldy into Eagle Nest. Over Palo Flechado Pass and into the artsy community of Taos. That night we found a modest motel, and a really immodest steak in Albuquerque.

We were bound for the Grand Canyon the next day, and put up that night in Flagstaff. We got another early start, and were at the great chasm in the sunrise chill. Assuming that Chubs would be disappointed at not seeing this landmark, I kept him in my red jacket's left breast pocket as we pulled up at the South Rim.

"Aaach! Loook at zee little anny-maul."

Bob Warner, packing up the station wagon

It was the "anny-maul" part that really slayed me. I wondered what Chubs would have thought about being called an "anny-maul." The German (or were they Austrian?) tourists couldn't get enough of our pint-sized passenger. They wanted pictures, so we obliged. The "anny-maul" looked great perched on Wally's head. We were on a tight timetable, so we stuffed Chubs back into my pocket, and headed off for Durango, Colorado. The ride from Durango to Silverton was as stunning as ever, and made especially so by the early turning of the aspen leaves. Next stop was Salt Lake, and the visit to the Tabernacle. Dusk found us among fraternity brothers in Logan at the University. The next day, when we got to Jackson, Wyoming, we slowed down, and decided to do some serious fishing. We got provisions in town, and headed back south along the Snake River. There we found a nice spot where we could pitch my old ranger tent, and tie into some legendary cutthroat trout.

We decided to separate, and I found myself on a jetty-like rock formation that stuck out into the Snake at an odd angle. The Snake was impressive. There were rapids, boiling deep holes, falls, and rich pine woods on the other side. There were a few sandbars, but most banks were stony, and there was no shortage of steep drop-offs. We loved the place. We were also going to be pragmatic about the fishing. That meant using "hardware." While I had never used anything but a fly rod at the Ranch, I had brought spinning gear for the Snake. I figured that we would catch dinner and breakfast by the most practical means possible, and then we might switch to the more gentlemanly, sporting methods. Wally and I split up to enhance our chances of bringing home the bacon. Wally said he'd hike upstream for half an hour, and then fish his way back. I decided to try that big jetty.

Ever the egomaniac, I suggested that Wally take the only net we had, and I would keep the creel. It was yet another in my long string of fishing blunders. Even a history of fishing gaffes hadn't sharpened my outlook with the slightest hint of sensibility. Here was a guy who would go seining for minnows to use as bait, and dredge up a snapping turtle. I once tied into a tremendous shad while wading below the Conowingo Dam on the Susquehanna only to lose my footing on the slippery rocks. In the full view of scores of other shad fishermen, I sank ignominiously beneath the waters, and emerged only to find the shad had gotten off the hook. Another time I latched onto what I thought had to be a monster trout in Lancaster County's Stewart's Run, only to find a rather modest eel on the end of the line.

Here on the Snake, I tied on a red and white DareDevil, my old standby. I started casting into a deep pool formed by the jetty I was on and another, shorter rock formation about thirty yards upstream. I was standing about seven or eight feet above the water, but there was a little ledge below me that was right at the water line. The rod tip bent sharply after my third cast. I knew there was a big fish at the other end from the force of the pull. I kept the tip up high, and tried to tire the trout, but it wasn't working. I would get a few feet on him, and then lose it. I didn't have the highest test line on, so I was reluctant to readjust the drag. Several minutes went by (a lifetime considering the size of the fish). I was starting to win because I could see him rolling, and coming closer to the surface.

My problem was my location. I couldn't land this fish eight feet in the air. I couldn't jump down onto the rocks. I couldn't move back, since there were more rocks to be negotiated behind me. Wally and the net were my only option. After yelling myself hoarse, it became obvious that Wally wasn't going to solve the problem. The big cutthroat had by then gotten his second wind, and went deep. Maybe he got behind another rock or something, but I lost him. It was sickening. Clearly, it was the biggest trout that had ever come my way. Well, I had to catch some meat for dinner, and I wasn't going to make the same mistake twice. Leaving the accursed rock, I moved upstream to the next pool, and lost another good sized fish on my first cast. The third cast was lucky again, and I had a gradual stony shore to bring this fish onto. It was a fat cutthroat, and while it may not have been much by Wyoming standards, it was clearly the biggest trout I had ever landed. There would be plenty for both of us that night at dinner.

Wally showed up troutless, took the obligatory picture of me with the fish, and then I cleaned it. With fresh sweet corn, sauteed trout, and canned peaches for dessert I was thinking that life didn't get much better than this. The river was audible over the crackling of our campfire and the rustle of wind through the pines. Sleep came quickly, but I woke up stiff and sore, and no wonder. My air mattress, veteran of many nights on Philmont's ground, had sprung a leak. We planned to catch breakfast, and within fifteen minutes, I caught two average-sized trout. I didn't have the creel to tie the fish up with this time, so I just found a forked stick. I ran one end of the stick through the fish gills, and anchored the stake back in the sand at the water's edge.

I went back to fishing and hooked another trout that was almost fourteen inches long. Unhooking the lure, I turned to tie up this trout with the others. The sight that greeted me from the sand was discouraging. My two trout and the stake were gone. There were raccoon tracks all around where the fish had been. The fourteen-incher made a fine breakfast though.

After breakfast, we were off to see the Grand Tetons and Yellowstone. Late afternoon found us fishing from the bridge at Yellowstone Lake. My little white flies tied on #16 hooks didn't do the job on the big trout that were visible in the clear waters. But if the fishing was disappointing, the wonders of Yellowstone weren't. We made the grand, if somewhat hurried, tour before camping in the park that night. The next morning found us starting the homeward trek back East. The Badlands, Black Hills, Mt. Rushmore, and Devil's Tower were the highpoints of the return. We had a few anxious moments when we nearly lost Chubs in an Albert Lea, Minnesota motel. We had a flat tire in Indiana that drew the attention of one of Indiana's state policemen. He was a courteous officer who helped us unload Wally's station wagon so we could get at the spare (Wally's Ford was loaded to the point of endangering its springs). We were still wearing Scout shorts, and that instantly translated into a reverse good turn for the officer who gladly recalled his days in a small town troop.

Sunset found us in the Alleghenies, which was ironic. Here, over two years before, the train was speeding west through the same mountains to take me to the Ranch. Now, that period of my life was ending amid the same darkening ridges. Wally and I pulled into the driveway around three in the morning. My parents were thrilled to see us, but maybe not so gladdened to see Chubs. He took their lack of enthusiasm calmly by curling up in a living room corner for a little snooze. After a hearty breakfast, and some fresh garden greens for Chubs, Wally was on his way back to New Jersey.

◆ ◆ ◆

There is life after Philmont. It follows the predictable path of military service, perhaps graduate education, entering a career field, and probably a few job changes along the way. Twelve years after leaving the ranch, I was firmly ensconced in center city Philadelphia's corporate community. Sarah and I had been married, had two kids, a house in the suburbs, and very little to do with Scouting. Our daughter Holly was in kindergarten, and son Will was a diapered, custard-covered little toddler not yet a year old. At 7:30 A.M., I was not out in the Abreu meadow swinging the sling psychrometer or checking out departing groups. I was standing in a group of clean-shaven, business-suited, briefcased men waiting for the commuter train to whisk us into the concrete canyons of Philly's business world. Sarah and I had made our home in West Chester, Pennsylvania. At the time we moved there, I was not aware what a good decision it was from a Scouting perspective. West Chester is in the heart of Chester County Council, which is not large as councils go. However, it is well blessed with professional talent, and enjoys the efforts of many enthusiastic and dedicated volunteers. The OA Lodge, Octoraro #22, is exceptionally active, and is one of a handful of honor lodges in the Northeast Region. I later remembered that this relatively small council consistently ranks among the top ten in the country in numbers of crews sent to Philmont. However, during our first years in West Chester, there were very few contacts with Scouting, and only one from the Ranch.

When Mr. Dunn retired from Ranch service, the call went far and wide to "his" rangers to write a reminiscence. These were bound in a special volume for presentation at a banquet in his honor. The response rate to that request must have been extraordinary. If published, surely its recollections would make it the definitive book on the Ranch. A couple of years after Mr. Dunn's retirement, the Philmont Staff Association (PSA) was formed. I had several conversations with Ned Gold about his plans for starting the Association, but played only a modest, sounding board type role in the group's formation.

I had lost touch with Steve Gregory, but not Wally. We got together occasionally for sailing and duck hunting on the Chesapeake. The years hadn't been so kind to Chubs, the fearless ground squirrel. He had faced down several neighborhood dogs, but met a feline who didn't bluff so easily. One thing about Chubs, while he was alive down here on earth, he really lived. I am sure he is in that great granary in the sky, content with his oats and memories of a very rich life.

My life was certainly busy enough. At one point I had to be in Chicago one day a week, was driving a minimum of four hundred miles a week to handle client business in the mid-Atlantic area, and still found time for a busy office schedule. Occasionally, I got a phone call from Ned Gold, especially while he was serving as the PSA's first president. Ned is a night person,

I am a morning person. Ned usually calls somewhere between 11:30 P.M. and midnight when I barely have my act together. Luckily, one of his most memorable calls came one summer evening just as I arrived home from the office.

"Guess who I've got standing next to me, Bill."

"Steve Gregory."

Steve had settled down in the Los Angeles area after corporate transfers to Seattle and Orlando. As it turned out, Steve had not become a professional Scouter, but instead became a credit analyst with the west coast branch of a large computer company. A business trip had taken him through Cleveland so he drove over to Warren to see Ned. Steve had always been a rotten correspondent so it was a pleasant surprise getting caught up on the years that were starting to roll by much too quickly. Ned's client responsibilities periodically brought him to Philadelphia while my occasional trade show trips took me to Cleveland, so we could get together now and then.

With Ned Gold at Fish Camp

Between our visits were the late night phone calls that would start with a somewhat breathless Ned saying, "Bill, let's get a conference call going with Steve." Lucky Steve, it would only be nine P.M. on the coast. By the time we would get through, I was usually sufficiently wakened to carry on a lucid conversation.

Ned called me at the office one day, and asked if our company might be interested in doing a *pro bono* project for Joe Davis, who had retired from Philmont. He was then Director of High Adventure Promotion at BSA headquarters in North Brunswick, New Jersey. We were interested, and it seemed only like a few minutes after Ned called, I was on the phone again talking to Joe. I made a mental note to prepare myself for Joe's extraordinarily vigorous handshake at the meeting that was sure to follow in the near future.

We met in Philadelphia, and had lunch at the Hoffman House, a German restaurant that was one of my favorites. Joe was no stranger to Philadelphia where he had been a professional Scouter, and from whose council he had taken the first American Wood Badge course. I enjoyed the project immensely, going to BSA's headquarters, seeing all of the Norman Rockwell originals on the walls, and meeting Joe's staff. Jim Delaney, who had been the Assistant Director at Olympia during my ranger summer, was working on *Boy's Life*, and it was great to see him again. The project ended all too quickly, and once more I drifted away from Scouting.

My only other contacts with Scouting were putting news-papers out for a local troop's paper drive and reading news articles of local lads making Eagle. Occasionally I remembered Lancaster County Council days with a client, John Reid of the Woodstream Corporation in Lititz. An avid Scouter and Wood Badger, John was a great client whose product line, outdoor sporting goods, required me to spend time in the woods again. It was a deeply appreciated opportunity to dust off some of those old ranger tricks, especially when we went to Canada on fishing trips. Several more years would pass before I became deeply involved in Scouting. My daughter, Holly, had tried Girl Scouts, but the program seemed more directed toward entertainment than outings, so she dropped out quickly.

John gave me two books that I enjoyed immensely. Larry Murphy had been a staff contemporary of mine, which made reading his *Philmont* even more enjoyable. It filled many gaps in my knowledge of ranch history. If I had been asked who Charles Beaubien was when I served on the Beaubien staff, the answer would have been limited to one short sentence. The other book was Dave Caffey's *Head for the High Country*, which stirred up recollections of happy days spent as a ranger.

There were a few other reminders of Philmont in the intervening years, and they were usually from magazine articles. The Sunday Magazine section of the *Denver Post* had a section on the Ranch at the time my parents happened to be passing through Denver. Ever thoughtful, Mom had picked up some extra copies and sent them to me. I wrote to the photographer in an attempt to buy some dupe shots, but my letters went unanswered. I will always kick myself for not having had a good 35mm camera with me when I worked at the Ranch. For that reason I'm still terribly jealous of my training ranger, Jim Place, who had the wisdom to always carry a good camera. I decided that when I got back to the Ranch, I was going to carry enough film to make up for my past sins, even if it weighed my pack down.

When my son Will joined Cub Scouts I was starting up a new company, and putting in the weekends and long, long hours that are the curse of entrepreneurialism. By the time Will graduated into Scouts, I was still putting in long hours, but things had settled down. I could spare time for meetings and the occasional weekend to go camping with his troop. I rarely talked about my Philmont background. Nobody ever asked, and I thought that talking about it might be misinterpreted as bragging. I was also determined not to take a particularly active role in my son's troop since I felt it was important that he make his mark on his own. So, I became an ordinary member of the committee.

Several new Dads took Scout Leader Basic Training. The course obviously was a major learning experience for the men who had never been Scouts, but in my case it proved not to be very enlightening. My Wood Badge practical experience was not an eye opener either although I enjoyed working with the other patrol members. The reason for my ambivalent reaction was clearly rooted in Philmont ranger training. Since working at the Ranch, I had undergone several other intense learning experiences, ranging from flight training to AMA courses in management, marketing, and communications. I found ranger training to be an extraordinarily lasting experience though its duration had been limited to little more than a week. It was also about as close to the Wood Badge practical session as one could get without actually taking it. In many ways ranger training was much more demanding.

In retrospect, I have come to the conclusion that the ranger experience was built upon the Wood Badge program. We had the same patrol learning experience, and the rest of the summer to apply what we learned just like working a ticket. Working my real Wood Badge ticket was a delight, and I enjoyed it immensely. One reason for this enjoyment was my ticket counselor, Jim Smith, an Eagle and '37 Jamboree Scouter. I have called Jim "Counselor" ever since, and although I am young enough to be his son, he calls me "Mr. Bill."

One of my ticket items was making feature presentations at a year's worth of regular district roundtable meetings. For one of these presentations, I developed a slide show on the ideals and traditions of Scouting as seen through the history of Scouting art. This was a tremendous learning experience. When I started it, I was unaware that it would lead to another, subtle calling card from the Ranch. In preparing the presentation, I learned that each of the great names in the development of Scouting (Lord Baden-

Powell, Ernest Thompson Seton, and Dan Beard) were all talented artists. Indeed, both Seton and Beard were professionally trained. But the slide presentation was closer to a one-man show of Norman Rockwell's calendar art. I had always admired Rockwell's work, and considered him a real artist even if his detractors might have dismissed him as a sentimental illustrator. Before researching for the show, I, like most Scouters of my generation, was familiar with some of the most popular calendars. There were two Rockwell paintings that were a bit before my time, and both stopped me dead in my tracks.

Each of these paintings had been preceded by his beloved "The Scoutmaster." This painting featured Marshall Ammerman, a Jamboree official, looking over a moonlit campsite at the 1953 Jamboree. On the way back east from the Jamboree, Rockwell stopped at Philmont where he painted "High Adventure." There was a little artistic license taken in the view of the explorers from Albany Post Nine approaching the Tooth of Time. Rockwell portrayed that great rock formation more dramatically than it can be seen in reality. The painting was pure Rockwell—there was drama, and the beholder was suddenly thrust into the climb by the inviting gestures of the campers. I had not recalled seeing the picture before: it made the Ranch beckon even more.

The other post-Jamboree painting was also done on the return from the '53 Jamboree, although the art never appeared on a Scout calendar. Rather, "Breaking Home Ties" became a *Saturday Evening Post* cover. The scene is of a rancher, sitting wearily on the running board of an old pickup truck. He is waiting for the bus that will take his perky young son off to the state university. The painting had been inspired by a setting in Cimarron. It took me back to days when I was leaving for college and high adventure. It also reminded me that it wouldn't be too many years before I would be packing Will, that "Young Scout" of mine, off to some far destination.

Watching my son and other boys grow in Scouting was a

richly rewarding experience, although there were a few rough edges. I took the autocratic road during Will's first year in Scouts, and told him, "You're going to the meeting tonight." The second year, things had relaxed, but only slightly when I would say, "You better have a good reason if you're not going to Scouts tonight."

By his third year, I was asking, "Going to Scouts tonight?" In his fourth year, it had become, "You are not going unless your studying is done and your chores are wrapped up." In that year, I had, however, assumed a major role in the troop. The adult leadership of the troop was turning over as many of their boys were leaving the troop after reaching Eagle and turning eighteen. Fortunately, we recruited a new Scoutmaster, but he was only two meetings into the job when he was transferred to Atlanta. So, with the encouragement of our district executive, Tom Dintaman, I became a Scoutmaster.

With the help of our Scouting Coordinator, "Counselor" Jim Smith, and Assistants Bob McElroy, Larry Hillhouse, Bob Groff, the boy leaders and I were able to reinvigorate the troop, and build membership to an all-time high. By this time, Will had already made his mark in the troop, so I re-registered as an Assistant Scoutmaster, after our search committee found my replacement as Scoutmaster. The year spent guiding the troop taught me that serving as a Scoutmaster is truly where the rubber meets the runway in Scouting.

As part of my Wood Badge ticket, I also became a unit commissioner. I had seen this as a one year tour, but now, several years later, I am still at it. I look forward to it as my tie with Scouting someday when I bow out of Chester County Council Troop 21.

I had started with 21 as the Advancement Chairman. Part of the job involved running Eagle Courts of Honor to which we added an interesting twist. Sarah had suggested that we have some background music or a prelude since our Eagle Courts are held in a church. Sarah, a superb pipe organist, volunteered to play on those Eagle occasions. I got her a Boy Scout songbook, and told her to just pick out seven or eight of the old warhorses. She would play for fifteen or twenty minutes before the actual start of the ceremony. We went over to the church so she could practice. She started with some familiar tunes: "Green Grow the Rushes," "The Happy Wanderer," "Scout Hearted Men," "Trail the Eagle," "God Bless America," "America the Beautiful," "I've Got that Scouting Spirit." Then she played one that raised goosebumps. I hadn't heard it in many, many years. It was, of course, "The Philmont Hymn."

I knew I would go back to the Ranch someday, but there were more immediate activities. Pitching in on weekend camping trips, spending a night or two to help at summer camp, and going to OA service weekends were a lot of fun. I enjoyed pulling out the old trappings of my Philmont days—my ranger axe, canteen, and compass. Scouting equipment had certainly changed. My ranger tarp tent was an antique, and we quickly replaced it with a modern tent complete with a floor. My trusty Kelty pack wasn't that outdated. There was no reason to replace it, although I did weaken and buy a padded hipbelt replacement for the pack's original web strap.

Seeing my son inducted into the OA was a wonderful experience. Shortly after that, he was off to the Jamboree, and so was I. I decided that he ought to do his own thing at the Jamboree, and not be fettered with his old man always in the background as a troop leader. Therefore, I applied to serve on the Public Relations staff as a photographer. I had always enjoyed photography, but at that point my cameras were just gathering dust. The Jamboree seemed like a logical outlet for my interest in using them again. The Director of Public Relations from BSA headquarters called me at my office from Dallas, and offered me the job as director of the souvenir video project. Although it wasn't what I asked for, it seemed like a good posting, so I took it. It turned out to be a wise move, and I became convinced that I had the best job of any volunteer Scouter at the Jamboree.

I worked with Roger Olson of STS Productions in Salt Lake City. Not only were Roger and his staff top flight cinematographers, they were all dedicated Scouters. We split into two crews and covered the Jamboree from dawn to dusk, from opening day to the closing moments. We shot both the big and small events. Coverage of talks by the Chief Scout Executive, visiting VIPs, and that irrepressible, veteran Scouter Willard Scott, was great fun. The best part of the job was doing interviews in the campsites where we taped Scout reactions to this great event. We covered it on foot, by helicopter, but mostly by vans, whose air conditioning was deeply appreciated.

There were a few Philmont staff veterans here and there, but there was no organized rendezvous. The Philmont Staff Association had missed a great opportunity, but Jamboree logistics were difficult. Still, the '37 Jamboree Scouts had their reunion, so I thought that someday the PSA might get its act together. At the Public Relations headquarters tent, there was a Jamboree registration printout that did contain the names of several Philmont staffer acquaintances. But with our shooting schedules, free time was just about nonexistent. I only got to see Will three times, and in each case the meeting occurred only because our shooting schedule happened to coincide with his whereabouts.

On a Monday evening, we were taping the Brownsea Island exhibit, when I became aware of two men walking up to the encampment. The elder man was instantly recognizable as Green Bar Bill. The other was Joe Davis. It had been thirteen years since I had shaken his hand, and I had not forgotten to "Be Prepared" when it came to his handshake. It was a great reunion, but, like the rest of the Jamboree, it was a fleeting event in a blur of activity.

Ned Gold came to the Jamboree on the day of the big arena show, so we got caught up on old times and Philmont friends.

Ned, by then a Silver Antelope Scouter, took his seat in the VIP section, and I hastened back to my crew to cover the great night. Every day and night seemed to shoot by so quickly. Before we knew it, we were packing up, and heading back to our home councils. It had been my third Jamboree, and the first for son Will. It was a great event for both of us—and our meetings were classic. On our first encounter, I was covering the arrival of the Northeast Region into the Arena Show. Out of the columns that were entering, a dusty, sweaty young camper marched up and gave me an exuberant high five. Several days later, I ran into him while taping gateways and patch trading sessions.

"Hey, Dad, can I have five bucks? You don't have any extra Octoraro flaps do you? There's this guy in Hunnikick who wants to trade with me. You gotta see this Kahila I just picked up!"

"You hungry? Let's go over to the trading post?" Will had been up and down on Scouting during his first year. This was largely due to the isolation that young, first year Scouts often felt before the new program emphasizing more attention to younger Scouts was put in place. However, with his induction into the OA and the spirit of the Jamboree, he became firmly committed to Scouting.

Will asked about Mr. Gold, if I had seen him, and if I had seen any other Philmont buddies. Ned Gold had been back to the Ranch several times, and had, of course, been to most of the PSA meetings. I had planned to make several of these, but something always seemed to come up. My travel schedule was ridiculous, and I seemed to always be in the wrong place at the wrong time (Tampa in August or Buffalo in January). Being back in Scouting, and especially seeing acquaintances with their newly-won tan arrowheads come to the September roundtables, was starting to take its toll.

It was following the Jamboree that I started thinking very seriously about returning to the Ranch. At first, I wasn't sure I was up to the task. I was old enough to be entering heart attack country. Some acquaintances younger than I had already developed cardiac problems. I decided to take a hard look at the pros and cons of returning. Our Wood Badge Course Director, "Hab" Butler, had said that of the many "summits of Scouting" in his experience, going through Philmont with his son was the highest. I certainly knew the Ranch well enough to get through without a map even these many years later. The question was, could I cut it on the tough trails? I had long since traded in my lacrosse stick for golf clubs, but unlike some friends, I hadn't run to fat in these, my "mellowing" years. In fact, I weighed less than I did on the day I left Philmont. My old uniform still fit comfortably!

A health freak I was not. But I had always eaten very sensibly, and lead an active life. Once, I thought tennis was a game fit only for mad dogs and Englishmen, but while helping my daughter practice for her high school team, I came to enjoy the sport. I had always done most of the yard work around our home, and constantly had some major project going, like building a stone wall or fireplace. So, I decided I could cut it after all. Still, I was occasionally inclined to believe in the words of one of Philmont's visiting astronauts. He believed he came into this world with a finite number of heartbeats, and he certainly wasn't going to use them up too quickly running around in some jogging suit. I had always been healthy, and rarely had a cold in the winter, but I was starting to have my share of bursitis and tendinitis.

I decided that I would get the Philmont physical and have some extra tests done. Doctor Harold Orvis, a local aviation merit badge counselor and still-flying, ex-Army Air Force pilot, concluded I was fit for the trip. Granted, my blood pressure and cholesterol level were on the high side, but still within the normal range and without need for medication. Pulmonary capacity was average for my age and build. Of course, I had already decided to go. I also decided that some form of conditioning was needed, so I bought a stepper/treadmill.

So started a love-hate relationship with that maddening contrivance. When I first got on it, I was gasping after a hundred steps. It occurred to me that maybe I should just visit the Training Center instead of going on the trail with these teenagers. Each day, I covered a little more ground. I added sit-ups and a few more exercises, but decided that pull-ups just might be asking too much of my bony elbows. In the morning, I would do a quarter mile or more before driving to the office. In the evening, I would do an eighth of a mile with my old Kelty filled with forty pounds of bricks. It proved to be a good regimen. My traditionally scrawny legs didn't get much thicker, but there was new, firm definition. I noticed that about the time I thought I should get off the miserable device, I would get a second wind and could carry on for another stretch. It was like doing Black Mountain again. I got the old last minute push, a second breath. Instead of the inspiring view out in front, I watched the network news. Still, it was progress. There wasn't much reason to worry about son Will who had just completed his high school freshman year. A season playing attack on the JV lacrosse team had put him in good physical shape, which was maintained by his own workouts on the stepper.

After deciding for sure that I would go, I tried to peel away a few years by reading some nearly forgotten letters. For letters sent to Sarah, I hauled out my old steamer trunk. Then I called my parents to find that Mom had carefully stored all of my letters home. While the freezing rain of February fell, and March winds howled, Sarah and I read of hot days, dusty trails, and sunswept heights when our love was so new. It was a wonderful trip with Sarah, to still be with the lady to whom all of those letters were lovingly sent.

Since a Philmont trip really belonged to the boys in the crews, we let them choose the program activities through an informal ballot. I breathed a sigh of relief as the scales tipped in favor of a southern itinerary. Our council Philmont "veterans" were

constantly pushing northern itineraries. They were blinded by the
pull of Old Baldy. In one of our High Adventure meetings, I
asked if anybody could name all of Philmont's peaks over ten
thousand feet north of Route 64. The answer came in only one
word. While Baldy's view of Eagle Nest Lake and Wheeler Peak
is spectacular, there are many more opportunities to climb in the
South. It always struck me that a southern route was the best
choice for a first expedition. I never really could see Baldy as
"north" country anyway. Its topography and life zones are all
much more closely allied with the southwest corner of the Ranch.
I also took some exception to the "typical" and "rugged" descrip-
tions given to itineraries. Most of the southern trips are described
as typical only because they are shorter in total miles. They are
not shorter in vertical distance covered, excluding sidehikes. Even
then the south offers more sidehikes with such worthwhile
diversions as Trail Peak and Black Mountain.

To my way of thinking, Philmont's central and southern
sectors are the real Phillips country. Here was where Waite
Phillips spent most of his time, and built his hunting and fishing
lodges. It is the heart of the ranching operation too. Granted, the
Ranch as a Boy Scout property started in the north at Ponil, but,
for me, the golden quadrangle was formed by Abreu, Fish Camp,
Mount Phillips, and Cito Hunting Lodge. The only way to see
Philmont is to go there every summer for a lifetime, or at least
for as long as your legs and lungs hold out. Even long-legged,
long term rangers will readily admit that their knowledge of the
Ranch is superficial at best.

In going through the backpacking equipment checklist, I
became a real bean-counter, or more appropriately, an "ounce-
counter." I would never forget my first Philmont expedition with
the Peedee River Council when I was carrying a pack that was far
too heavy. I dredged up an old postal scale and weighed the
alternatives. The Scout canteens weighed too much, and were
replaced with plastic bottles. A light microwave dish replaced the

mess kit pan. I had an ulterior motive since I knew I was going to be carrying some extra weight. I had the crew first aid kit, on which I would not skimp. This time, I wasn't going to make the mistake of going without a camera. My photographer lent me a versatile 28-105 Macro Zoom for use with my Nikon. Unfortunately, it was not a light lens, but its versatility was worth the weight penalty.

Most of the boys in our crew had obtained sophisticated-looking Camp Trails packs that made my veteran Kelty look like an antique. It may have been an antique, but I noticed that the newer packs had only cosmetic improvements such as extra pockets and map flaps. The hip belt, contoured frame, and nylon bag construction were essentially the same. I decided to copy some improvements though, and added a frame extender. Having mastered Sarah's sewing machine, I added a quick access compartment to the upper section of the pack, sewed on a few loops, and added a strap that covered a new, velcro-detachable day-pack. I was looking forward to taking the updated antique back to the ranch. Many years before, my pack had already been back to the Ranch with my own Scoutmaster, Mr. Kenny Derr, from Troop 40, Lancaster County Council. He had gone to Philmont the year after I left Abreu.

The year was slipping by, and I started wondering how our Troop 21 boys would fare. Would they pass muster or be found wanting by Philmont's special demands? I decided that we would add a program feature to each of our Monday night meetings. "Trail Talk" was launched in early March, and took up the first few minutes of each meeting. There was something in it for every boy in the troop, but the message was directed at the older boys who would head to the Ranch. As the weeks passed, Trail Talk would cover just about everything the boys would need. It was both a reinforcement of what they had already been taught, plus a taste of what would come from their Philmont ranger.

Trail Talk was running smoothly, but our expedition crew

selection was definitely not. Because we had only five boys and myself from our troop, it appeared that we would have to be separated. That was the last thing I wanted to happen. The same problem was being faced by another advisor, Vic Dinnocenti, an Assistant Scoutmaster in Troop Four. Vic had been in my Leader Basic Training patrol, and we had always had a brief reunion at council camporees and OA weekends over the last few years. Our council high adventure committee chairman, the urbane Aussie, Greg Acland, was trying his best with our council office to get that extra crew, which would have solved my problems. If we got an extra crew, we could join forces with another group. We would then form two crews which would hike an "A" and "B" itinerary. I discussed this with Fletcher Swanson, whose Troop Six was sending nine boys and three adults. They also were interested in a southern itinerary. Fletcher agreed to my plan calling for him to lend me a father and son from his troop to form the eleventh crew. It would make a natural fit since I was also Troop Six's unit commissioner. Six is one of Chester County's oldest and best troops, and I knew most of the older boys since I had served them as a merit badge counselor.

Unfortunately, the Chester County contingent didn't have an "E-11" to add to its 730E expedition. Council had locked in on its ten crews, so it looked like we were going to be split up until a little networking produced the eleventh crew. This solved my problems but not Vic Dinnocenti's. Vic had wanted a northern itinerary, but was now considering withdrawing from the expedition since he couldn't keep his Scouts in the same crew. That seemed a shame, so I called Vic and said that if he wanted to follow a southern itinerary as part of our eleventh crew, he would be more than welcome. After discussing it with his boys, Vic accepted our offer. Now, we were enjoying the best of all worlds.

I was looking forward to hiking with Vic who had been in my leader basic training "Swoose" patrol. "Swoose" (half swan, half goose) was the personal aircraft of a prominent WWII general, and a send-up of the local OA lodge totem, the Canada goose. The Chester County Council high adventure committee had put together a good shakedown weekend at Camp Ware, one of the two adjoining camps at Horseshoe Scout Reservation. This involved some vigorous scrambling up the steep slopes above the Octoraro Creek, a deeply carved tributary of the Susquehanna River. We climbed three ridges during the shakedown weekend, but none was more than three hundred and fifty feet high. It was not much of a simulation of doing Mount Phillips out of Clear Creek, but it at least reminded us that there were tougher climbs ahead. If only we could have simulated an additional ten thousand feet of elevation. I hadn't expected to get much out of the shakedown, but I did learn a few lessons about cooking equipment in my getting reacquainted with trail food. The council would provide us with propane stoves, but we decided to invest in some white gas backpacking stoves that were lighter. Besides, we didn't want to haul prope bottles all over creation. It was a wise decision.

One aspect of the shakedown weekend had special meaning. To occupy part of the evening, slides of past Philmont expeditions were shown. These were slides taken with a light weight, Instamatic type camera. Although the quality wasn't up to single lens reflex standards, there were slides of Black Mountain and of Beaubien. I was riveted, and asked to have the slides held on the screen a little longer. Then the slides continued. Dean Cow, camping headquarters, Ponil, Cito, and several other central and north country scenes came and went. I wasn't watching very closely since I was drifting, slipping back in time. The slide on the screen may have been Indian Writings or Harlan's burros, but I was somewhere between the Beaubien range and Trappers Lodge. Dick Gertler was ringing the triangle outside the kitchen that told us to get our hides ready for dinner. We would congregate by the wash stand next to the Lodge. Somebody would say,

"Where's Freddy?"

"Rye-cheer," would come the reply. Jimmy Money would be closing the commissary while Jim Talley would be ambling over from the corral. Maybe Dimalanty was off on a vacation day, because that spluttering laugh of his was missing. Bob Dog was there, with his perpetual air of canine mischief. Had he had a good day? Could he ever have a bad day with the way he wagged his tail all of the time? One thing was sure, he was a tired doggy since he and Bobby had been to Black Mountain and Red Hills that day. And Paul—talking to Control, or maybe making the rounds of the campsites to be sure we had a Beaubien campfire full of happy campers.

My reverie was broken by Greg Acland who closed the evening meeting, and invited advisors to the crackerbarrel. The boys headed back to their tents in a campsite now dampened by the steady drizzle that had plagued us for most of the day. The crackerbarrel was a short-lived affair since most of us were tired from hiking around the Susquehanna highlands. I made my excuses, and headed back to the campsite. The "Sixers," Fletch Swanson's crew, had a roaring campfire going that attracted the Scouts from 4 and 21 alike.

It was fascinating to watch the interaction of the Crew Eleven boys because half were from West Chester, and the balance from Pottstown. We were the only crew containing two separate units—a situation that could easily lead to lack of cooperation if handled improperly. Although I had secured the eleventh crew, I decided that our expedition should be a fifty/fifty undertaking. For the first half the trip, 21 would lead, and 4 would lead for the second half until we got back to camping headquarters. Son Will had gotten himself elected crew chief from 21, but was decidedly under the weather with the flu during our shakedown weekend. His place was taken by Tom Hillhouse, who also was a troop ASPL.

Since the shakedown weekend was so programmed, there

wasn't much opportunity for Tom to exert his leadership. I suggested that he approach Aaron Smith, Troop Four's boy leader and work out a duty roster formed by mixed teams from the two troops. They did, but there was still no fraternization in the off-duty moments. I knew this was going to change, and looked forward to it. As it transpired, I would have to wait until we were on the trail to see comraderie between the two troops. Aaron was no rookie: he was already a Philmont veteran. Clearly the two groups would eventually mesh well since we apparently had no troublemakers on board. Still, they eyed each other warily just as they had done on the day of the big meeting for parents' orientation.

The parents' meeting was an interesting session for me since I had been press-ganged into a speaking role. We had around twenty advisors going, and needed five speakers to give a brief presentation to the assembly of Scouts and their parents. I had always laid back in the weeds, and not discussed my Ranch background unless asked. I was asked. Others would talk about transportation, discipline, and the shakedown weekend while I was asked to tell the parents what Philmont is. I began by thanking Greg for telling me to keep it down to ten minutes (we might have been there for days had he not been so prudent). My little talk was remarkably brief, but I was forced to wax poetic at the end. I recited the lyrics to the Philmont hymn, which I think captured the spirit of the trail. I concluded by telling the audience that I would close with the lyrics to a less frequently heard song, but one that would definitely recapture the spirit of the trail. It was the Ranger Song.

We had also gotten our first itinerary choice for that year: #3. It was only fifty-seven miles (on paper) but included the best of the south country, although Abreu was not part of it. We would try Trail Peak, Black Mountain (for the energetic), and would do Mount Phillips and the Tooth of Time. This "typical" trip involved more climbing (with pack) than many northern itineraries, which included a packless sidehike of Baldy. I was looking forward to itinerary #3 since it would allow me to fill some surprising gaps in my own Philmont experience. I had never done Tooth Ridge, never stood on top of Urraca Mesa, and never climbed Mount Phillips from the southwest. There were also several new trails, such as Apache Creek and down Comanche Peak. Could some of them have been laid out by Buster Simpson and Dave Taliaferro so long ago?

Had Vic been able to select his own itinerary, he would have opted for a northern route. I told him that he would become a south country "believer" when he came off the trail. Already I was thinking that Vic was going to be lucky in that he would see both of the major sections of the ranch after this, his second expedition. Again, I was dumfounded at how many crews in our expedition, who were embarking on repeat trips to the Ranch, had selected northern itineraries for the second time without ever having seen the south country.

I had toyed with the idea of going for a super strenuous itinerary, and doing Baldy again on a clear day. However, we had too many first timers and younger Scouts in our crew. Besides, trying to do a hundred and ten mile, north-south trip would be like trying to see Europe in ten days. Better to save the north country for another year.

We had more shakedown training planned. In May, we headed up to French Creek State Park in northern Chester County for our regular monthly camping weekend. It offered some nice trails over which we could get in some modest climbing, but again it was less than four hundred feet. Philmont Scouts would take a full pack on this hiking weekend, which was also the first camping weekend for the new Webelos Scouts who had just joined 21. The younger Scouts would take only a snack, a canteen, and growing enthusiasm for this hiking business. After a Friday night of thunderboomers so noisy that the owls kept quiet, we headed out for our midday hike. French Creek is a lovely park with lakes, wooded trails, and nice camp sites. Around one P.M. we got reacquainted with trail lunches, and their "spreadables." This was nothing new for the older boys who had been to the previous Jamboree. Because I had been doing my time on the stepper, I wasn't having a problem with the hike in spite of a slightly overloaded pack.

The years were rolling back as the afternoon progressed. The rich woods of northern Chester County gave way to some trails hiked so long ago, and to another Scouting company. Just ahead of me was "A.J." Zadrozny who, at fourteen, was sprouting some dark growth above his upper lip. He looked a lot like Bobby Rabuck, one of Philmont's Texas Rangers from that summer so long past. A.J. had the same heavy-duty legs, and a voice that was already nearly as deep as Bobby's. There was Tom Hillhouse, a bright, scientifically-oriented fellow whose wit might someday put him in a class with Giff Kessler. Tom's name badge said, "Tom Hillhouse, Guru At Large." It was something that the Braintrusters would have appreciated (but not worn in Mr. Dunn's presence). Josh Rea was having a little problem with his pack that went unnoticed at first. Something of a free spirit, Josh was showing the independence and determination that told me he was going to get a lot out of his Philmont experience. I was trying to keep a close eye on these Philmont campers without being overbearing, but missed Josh's problem with his pack. When he finally mentioned his problem I was appalled to find that he had been plugging away essentially without the benefit of his hipbelt. Yes, Josh had the pluck to make it through the Ranch.

Finally, there was Will, the "Young Scout," the other Cass on the trail. Could he make it to the top of Phillips? He was so much the young colt, all legs, and apt to ride off in four directions at once. Yet here was a kid who could kick back with a Stephen King thriller and read for hours on end. Could I thread my way through a couple of tough, lacrosse defensemen whose purpose in life was to make sure I, playing attack, did not have a good day?

Could I run my guts out for the better part of three quarters while playing midfield part of the time? Maybe I could have some years back, but Will had been doing it throughout the spring lacrosse season. Here was a kid who could hit seventy-five sit-ups and then start accelerating. I knew he didn't want "Old Scout" crowding him. I resolved to give him his rein, and let him set his own pace when we got to the Ranch. The real question was if the "Old Scout" could keep up with the "Young Scout."

By mid-afternoon, the serious hiking was over. We poked our way back to the campsite with two other Chester County troops who had taken the campsites below ours. There were a few visual cues that sent me back in time again. One of our new Scouts had insisted on hiking in uniform—polished cotton pants and the old style, Scouting garrison cap. This uniform said he was proud that his Dad had been a Scout. Then, slung around the shoulder of little Paul, also one of our new Scouts, I saw an old style canteen. Its BSA logo included a signature line that said New York City. Clearly, we were in good company.

As the weeks passed, I kept persevering on my infernal stepper machine. I found that as I set the countdown timer out further and further each week, I was ready to give up about three-quarters of the way through. Then that second breath came, and I could finish with no problems even with the pressure selector all the way out. The effect was the same that I had always felt on Philmont's mountains—about ready to call it quits when a surge of reserve power kicked into gear. The last bit of preparation was getting a tan. In recent years, I had decided that being a paleface was better for the skin than sporting a bronze tan. At the Ranch, I knew that either sun screen or a decent tan was essential to avoid the types of sunburns I had seen on so many young campers. Figuring that a natural tan was better than gooing myself up with sun screen, I left the office at noon, and got an hour of sun each day. Within two weeks, I figured I was safe. Taking a shower and looking at the tan line on my legs was like old times.

When on staff, especially my ranger year, I had gotten such a tan that its upper limits on my legs were visible well into the depths of winter.

Then, we were into late July, and fixing all of those last minute glitches that add to the urgency of getting to the Ranch as soon as possible. No, we couldn't go to Pike's Peak as originally planned. This was a real disappointment since I had so desperately wanted to stand on its summit. Should we go to the Royal Gorge? No, it didn't consume enough time. Would we like to go rafting on the Arkansas River before we went to the Koshare Kiva in La Junta? Yes, we would. Before I knew it, I was passing out T-shirts and neckerchiefs while asking parents to rendezvous in the church parking lot at 5:15 A.M. for the drive to Philadelphia International Airport.

A pre-departure shakedown hike.
A.J. Zadrozny, Tom Hillhouse, and Will Cass

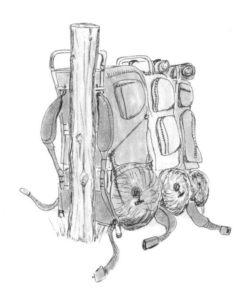

12

Lucky Eleven, 730E-11

Early on the morning of July 28, we all congregated, in Class A uniforms and unwrinkled expedition neckerchiefs, at Philadelphia International Airport's USAir counter. The weather in the east, lately, had been glorious which was not so where we were bound. Perhaps the weather gods would smile on us, and the Southern Rockies would be freed of the monsoonal rains that had been soaking the Sangre de Cristos over the previous weeks. Very shortly, our baggage was whisked away, loved ones departed, and we were waiting impatiently at the departure gate. We were slightly delayed, but at 8:15 were thundering down runway nine.

I never cease to be thrilled by takeoffs—even when somebody else is at the controls. I was no stranger to Philly's airport, and had flown from its runways on countless numbers of business trips. This was different; it was more than a vacation. We were taking off into adventure, and for me it was probably closer to something of a pilgrimage. Some of our Scouts were taking their first ride in an airplane, and the excitement showed in their faces. In Pittsburgh, we changed planes for the long haul to Denver. The edited journals of Lewis and Clark became my reading for the next several hours. The actual journals, replete with pages of scientific details, are more than the average reader can cope with. That is why Bernard DeVoto's edited version is such a delight, and is one of my frequent travel companions. How appropriate to be reading the record of the greatest scouting experience in American history as we passed over the Mississippi and the Missouri. The Lewis and Clark expedition arrived at the mouth of the Columbia River in late autumn where they remained until spring. The sun shone on them fully for only twelve days as they wintered at Fort Clatsop. Would we be so lucky to see that much sun in our twelve days or to avoid so much rain? Fortune, as fickle as mountain weather, would spare some crews, but abandon others on this Chester County Council expedition. Crew Eleven, in some ways the orphan of the contingent, would emerge as the luckiest of the lot, but that would not become apparent for quite a while. Unfortunately, the early signs were pointing to atmospherical disaster.

Concern for the weather was swept aside by our first sight of the Rockies—a jagged horizon containing a few splotches of white. Soon we were starting the maddening wait for our gear at the baggage claim area. Then it was onto the waiting buses of Long's Bus Service, those delightful shepherds of so many Philmont-bound crews. The first stop, however, was the nearest fast food emporium for a dose of cholesterol, salt, and preservatives.

A little over an hour later we rolled through the Air Force Academy's north visitor entrance for a look at "Diamond Lil," the veteran B-52. The next several hours were spent touring the

Academy. The view from within the chapel looking out was
every bit as spectacular as the more familiar, external view. The
sunny afternoon was winding down, and with it a little more of
the tan and high altitude acclimation that we would need. How
nice it was to feel the heat of the sun without the humidity that
accompanies eastern summers. A local Kings Table family
restaurant survived the descent of our 106 hungry souls. After
eating I spent a few moments in the parking lot wistfully looking
at the ramparts of Pike's Peak some twenty miles or more to the
west.

Fletcher Swanson had seen the mountain many years before
as a young camper at the Colorado Springs Jamboree, and I had
driven past it on vacations and business trips. We both had been
unable to get to the top on past occasions, but I had vowed that
I would come back and stand on its summit someday. The sun
was sinking however, and we still had miles to go before reaching
our evening's lodging, a place called "The Abbey" in Canon City.

We didn't have much information on the Abbey. I didn't
know if it was a canvas-topped feedlot or some old wooden, five
storied monastery scheduled for condemnation. It turned out to be
a junior college associated with a religious order whose church
evoked visions of a modest cathedral. We weren't put up in some
stifling crypt, but got the gymnasium floor instead which proved,
with our air mattresses and pads, to be reasonably comfortable.
There was a momentary flap before we could get into the gym,
however. It appeared the bus driver had misplaced a very
important part of my gear. My seatstick was lost. I was headed
for near panic until I found it on the bus' upper rack. Seemingly
a ridiculous piece of ironmongery fit only for use by eccentric
Englishmen, my seatstick would serve a variety of purposes other
than that for which it was originally intended. The seatstick is
essentially nothing more than a pointed walking stick whose twin
spade grip handles fold out to form a seat. Once plunked into the
earth, and held secure by a flange, one simply sits on the seat. I

wasn't planning on Philmont being a substitute for the races at Ascot, but thought the stick would be a handy camera unipod, water carrier, and at least one means of keeping my balance as I gasped for breath on some steep Philmont trail. I was not disappointed; that rather foppish accouterment proved to be an absolutely worthwhile addition to my equipment checklist. I'll never be without it on the trail again. It was a rather bizarre item—I painted it fluorescent orange to make sure I didn't leave it behind in any campsite.

The next day we had a choice of whitewater rafting on the Arkansas River or mountain biking, i.e., hypothermia or hemorrhoids. I chose the former figuring that forty pounds of pack and Fowler Pass would probably bring on the latter anyway. Fletcher had recently been at a sales meeting in Denver, and had scouted out the rafting outfitters. His recommendation of Colorado Whitewater Expeditions proved to be a good one. We selected an intermediate run that was something more than placid, but something less than the turbulence of Royal Gorge. After all, if we were going to break any bones, best to do it at the Ranch, not before we got there.

Our guide, an ebullient college lad named Jim, gave us a thorough briefing, and recounted his days as a Scout in Denver. He had attained the rank of Star, and regaled us with his recollections of his trip to Philmont seven summers before. All of us from Troop 21 had a modest amount of canoeing and rafting experience, but Jim's instruction in whitewater basics was eagerly received by the lot of us. With his calls of "forward two," "backpaddle," "left turn," and all of the other commands, we managed to hold our own. I had taken the liberty of bringing a modest little, baggy-wrapped 35mm camera in a fanny pack. With it, I would get the only action shots on the river. I even got Mike Basquill, one of Troop 55's advisors, as he floated by. Mike had been thrown out of his raft, and had quickly done as instructed—placed feet forward and face downriver. He had a remarkable air of calm on his face as he bobbled by us. He couldn't have looked more composed unless he had a book on his stomach, or maybe the chill in the water had something to do with his unexcited countenance. Jim bade us paddle as hard as possible. Troops 21 and 55 always enjoyed a friendly rivalry. Since Mike seemed delighted to become the eighth member of our crew, I told him we would send him the bill later. We stranded him on a gravel bar where he later rejoined his crew.

A.J. was the next to go. We hit a rock, and he flew out, but had the drill down perfectly. He already had his feet aimed downstream, as Jim yelled "forward." A.J. wasn't in the water more than fifteen seconds before Jim and Will dragged him out. The race wasn't over since A.J.'s paddle was still headed toward Kansas, but we got that after some hard paddling. At that point, we had learned to stroke as a team, and Jim's voice became less strident. While I hadn't been wildly anxious to do the whitewater program, I enjoyed myself immensely, especially since the boys were clearly in high spirits. We hit some more rapids, but with Jim's setting up the approach, we had few problems. Josh almost got tossed out, but Jim grabbed his life preserver just in time. After about an hour, we rounded a bend to see the big picnic spread that had been set up for us.

We got back on the river around 12:30 P.M., and floated into smoother water. That's where the inevitable splash fights erupted with adults giving and taking as though they were still Second Class Scouts. There were still a few minor rapids, but we encountered longer stretches of placid water, which was a good excuse for a little raft grandstanding. Jim had no problems with all of us standing up, and holding hands in a ring-around-the-rosy type formation. We had seen other rafts trying this. It usually ended with one or more people going for a backflopper a split second after some riffle buffeted the raft. I thought we were going to be the exception until Will's yelp was followed by a big splash. We were in calm water again, so his rescue was no where near as exciting as A.J.'s. Unfortunately, the end was in sight as we rounded a curve to see a few other rafts headed for shore where the buses were parked. It had been an exhilarating day, and another major attraction awaited us just a couple of hours down Route 50.

By late afternoon, we reached La Junta, home of the renowned Indian dance teams of the Koshare Kiva. I had never been there, but was aware of their reputation from campers whom I had served as a ranger. Everybody said it was a "must," and not just for Scouting audiences. We had dinner in the cafeteria of the adjacent junior college, and then passed the pre-show period by going through the museum and their hall of Eagles. I could have spent much more time in the museum since it contained so much western and Indian art and memorabilia, but we hastened to the Kiva to get a good seat (as it turned out, it is impossible to get a bad seat). The show was fascinating not only for the drama, humor, and costumes, but also for the dedication that it all represented. What fantastic ambassadors the Indian dancers are, both when they are on the road and when they are dancing in their Kiva. Greg Acland knew what he was doing when he insisted that we drive the extra distance to La Junta to visit the Kiva.

We spent the night on the Kiva floor and were on the road by eight A.M. the next morning. It was the big day—we would be at the Ranch by midmorning. I was wondering what was going through the minds of other expedition members. There were probably a dozen who had been to the Ranch in recent years. Chuck Kelly, Scoutmaster of Troop 22 and an erstwhile acquaintance of Steve Gregory, was going back for his sixth expedition. It was a return for Vic and two of his boys. It was a return for Fletcher too, since he had been a member of a three-day expedition that visited the Ranch after the Colorado Springs Jamboree. Probably nobody was approaching it in the same sense as I was. For me it was a sort of Rip Van Winklesque sojourn back to my youth.

I had quite recently talked to Ned Gold about the Ranch, and how it might have changed. I was prepared not to recognize much of camping headquarters with all of its new construction. The trails would be the same, the land, the mountains, creeks, ground squirrels—surely none of that had changed. Ned said that the only change I might notice could be in the staff. I knew that the ladies had become part of the staff, but Ned was talking about more subtle changes. But then, why shouldn't the staff evolve. After all, it had been well over two decades since Ned and I had last had a radio conversation between Abreu and Fish Camp. As I ruminated over what to expect, we reached the top of Raton Pass. Here we paused to stretch our legs and take pictures with the Spanish Peaks in the background. Then we descended into a very changed Raton that now had a bypass. As we passed the little airport south of Raton, my pulse quickened.

There in the distance was the backside of Tooth Ridge and Trail Peak. I said nothing, partially because I was enjoying the view, also because I wanted to see if anyone else would recognize the Ranch. Nobody called out when Baldy and Touch-Me-Not occasionally bobbed into view to the west. We descended around the curve into Cimarron, which looked as though the years had not changed it substantially. I looked to the south side of Route 64 for Miss Dee's Cafe and Lambert's but they were gone. The buildings were there but the businesses therein were different. We took the left turn onto the Ranch road, and within a few moments I saw that Vera's Casa de Colores had been rejuvenated, and given its original name, the Saint James Hotel. It was hard to believe I had come back as an advisor after all these years. We passed the commissary warehouse, Cito Road, Villa Philmonte, the Training Center, the health lodge, and the Director's residence. It didn't seem so long ago when I last saw the same view. Wally and I had closed out Cito, and came down to camping headquarters for our last night.

But it was that long ago. We made the right turn through a bigger, more impressive Philmont gateway. Earl Swope was not there to greet us, but many of the new buildings were. We knew what the drill would be. Pick out a post, and line up our crew packs in a line. This done, we stood by. Rangers were filing into and out of the Welcome Center. A couple of our crews had already been greeted by their rangers, who, after introductions, were taking their new charges off toward tent city. As I was gazing around at the familiar sights of Tooth Ridge, Urraca Mesa, and Trail Peak along with the unfamiliar headquarters buildings, an authoritative voice called, "730E-11."

"Right here," I said as I watched a tall young man confidently walk toward us with his hand extended. I could tell immediately that we were in the hands of an experienced ranger. Todd Johnson introduced himself, and I in turn introduced Will and Vic.

"Well, when y'all are ready, we'll just head up to your assigned tents, then start getting y'all checked in."

As we walked to tent city with our gear, small talk revealed that Todd was from Tulsa. He was a training ranger now in his third year at the Ranch. He also mentioned that the weather had been rotten until the day of our arrival. They had gone through a full week without sight of the sun. We then went through itinerary planning, registration, and security before heading to the new dining hall where Todd led us in the Philmont Grace. Lunch was just as I recalled food at headquarters.

I had decided not to tell Todd about my previous association with the Ranch. Just another old staffer coming back probably wasn't that unique, and I didn't want Todd to feel that somebody was second guessing him as he guided us through the first few days. I had previously told our crew that I was ancient history, and the Ranch had probably changed so much that they better pay attention to someone who was on top of things. I had planned to let Todd know about my past days as a ranger just before he left us on the last morning.

We had to wait briefly at the health lodge where a couple of other crews had arrived before us. We were all cleared for the trail, although I was surprised to see that my blood pressure had edged up slightly. I was told that this was not unusual, that it might increase with altitude. All of us were aware that we could easily suffer from symptoms of altitude sickness, especially during the first few days of the expedition. Sure enough, several of us did have a few symptoms during our second day on the trail. Fortunately, our problems lasted less than a day. Several other crews had some real difficulty adjusting to life more than a mile above sea level.

The most interesting stop on the early blur of rounds through headquarters was "Logistics." Here we were briefed on the details of our trip, where we would pick up food, and what programs we would take at which camp. Since we were on an "A&B" itinerary, this briefing was shared by Fletcher Swanson and Troop 6's Crew Leader, Abe Breslin. From this rapid distribution of facts, I hoped that Will and Abe had remembered that the water was questionable at Lookout Meadow, that the horse ride at Beaubien was at one P.M. or never, and that there was good water at Shaefers Pass. One thing for sure, if Will or Abe lost the crew leaders' copies, we were in for a good lesson in wilderness survival.

The briefing center was much more sophisticated than in my day. I had some doubts that the young lady who briefed us had ever backpacked along most of the trails over which each of us were about to haul life, limb, and forty pounds of pack. Although I could find no fault with her suggestions, my thoughts were of Jim Place. After years as a ranger, Jim could dispense first-hand advice about the trails over which his audiences were about to embark. Todd lingered over the water suitability briefing board for a few moments, then asked us to join him on the next stage of our orientation.

Todd then took us to our campsite for the shakedown. Checklists and weight control had been a big part of Troop 21 trail talks, so Todd's review indicated that we were pretty well prepared. The old ranger was the only one with some dubious gear. I had brought an extra pot, but learned that we wouldn't need it since the standard equipment issue included an extra pot. I had also brought a "bake-packer," an ingenious little device that we had used on our training weekends to bake biscuits and breads in a pot of boiling water. Since Philmont trail breakfasts and dinners didn't include muffins, biscuits, etc. the bake-packer stayed behind in the crew locker.

I had brought along an old "Philmont Guidebook for Leaders and Campers." The old and new versions were essentially similar, but there were a couple of interesting differences. No longer are campers advised to bring "official uniforms of longs and shorts for the trail." You don't need to bring your "official campaign hat" anymore either. There was one striking difference, though. Today, campers need canteen capacity totaling two quarts. Back then, it was only one quart. Clearly, health lodge tracking of dehydration cases had had some impact.

The last big stop was the services building for our trail equipment and food. Todd was the thirteenth member of the crew, so we were going to eat well since we would be carrying food for sixteen. Todd was, however, well worth the extra weight we would be carrying. As he led us through these rounds, I was thinking that things really hadn't changed that much. Sure, the buildings were more impressive, but rangers still did the same old things. Shortly, I was to learn that rangers had a few, new pieces of wisdom to share, especially in environmental matters.

In talking with Todd, I was thunderstruck to learn that we were only his sixth expedition of the summer! By early August of my ranger summer, I had already done nearly a dozen trips, and still had the busiest part of the summer ahead of me. Todd said that the policy was "four days on, and four off." I couldn't tell him then that an older generation of rangers was used to four on and one off, and sometimes the numbers ran to four and zero.

By late afternoon, we had finished with the check-in procedures. Most of us were now sorting out the nonessential items that would be left behind in our crew locker, making phone calls, or discovering the snack bar and trading post. I decided to take my own grand tour of headquarters. The Tent City, reminiscent of WWII Army camps, was gone: the tents were now segregated into incoming and outgoing camper groups. The arrangement was in U-shaped clusters for individual crews and expeditions. I wandered out to the west end of tent city and gazed out toward Stockade, which was just barely visible. Way back when, Stockade stood out like a sore thumb. To make its picture complete, there were usually a few of the fleet-footed pronghorn antelope prancing around just beyond tent city. There was still a broad expanse of prairie between headquarters and the young trees that were starting to obscure Stockade. I wondered where the antelope had gone. Anyway, the thirteen-lined ground squirrels were very visible as they skittered from tent platform to platform.

Ranger City, my ancestral home of sorts, had been relocated. No longer the horseshoe-shaped compound at the west end of tent city, it had been moved to the north side of headquarters, and was squared up to look like a small tent city. It also apparently was home to non-ranger H.Q. staff too. The square locker building was gone. It had been replaced by a ranger headquarters which, from a distance, could be mistaken for a small church with attached chapel.

While the facilities had changed, the look of a ranger had not, especially when seen returning from an expedition. The wind-blown hair, the suntan, maybe a little patina of trail dust, and the well broken-in boots completed the picture. The uniform had seen many miles and so had his pack. Even without a pack, the rangers were easily identifiable. Beyond the easy gait and lean frame, there was still something familiar in the gaze—something that after all these years I was unconsciously doing again. When rangers are in headquarters, they always seem to take a longer look out past the Tooth Ridge. Their eyes tend to be searching for something out there beyond Urraca Mesa and Trail Peak. It is probably a subliminal dissatisfaction with headquarters life, and suggests that the desire to be back on the trail has already set in.

The old camping headquarters office had become a meeting room for incoming advisors. It was just across the quad from the trading post/snack bar that was the dining hall in days past. Both the health lodge and the chapels had been expanded. The new ranger headquarters must have taken some heat off the staff lounge. Here rangers, fresh off the trail, used to do their laundry and ironing while watching what must have been the only television in headquarters. The old staff lounge was now part of the health lodge complex.

As usual, my mind was slipping back in time to a Philmont more than just a couple of decades older. Then there was just a single pay phone located near the dining hall. Now there were banks of them in the new services building (all in use while more anxious callers waited in line). The advisors' lounge, where Earl Swope regaled the tired and the eager alike, was gone, but had been replaced by a new facility. Was the new lounge the same old ranger office that had been spruced up with the addition of showers and other amenities? The nature center was gone, and with it Jerry Traut's interesting talks on the fauna of Philmont.

I then drifted past the advisors' lounge, half expecting to see Phil Yunker or Paul Felty with their packs slung over one shoulder, just getting back from the trail. Maybe I would turn a corner and run into one of the Hobbs brothers or possibly Don Carlson. That slender, dark haired guy with the crew cut—would he turn around and be recognized as Jack Crider? Was that laughing guy with the Texas accent, the one telling jokes—Bob Reeves? No, certainly not. I wouldn't see Joe Martos, Neil Karl,

Jerry Thatcher, or Dick Laudenslager on this trip either. Would I see their kind again? At this point in time, if I didn't see their kind, I might easily see some of their offspring working at the Ranch. I was coming out of this nostalgic reverie thinking about Mr. Dunn. Had he lived to see these new buildings or the new Ranger office? Yes or no, from what I could tell, rangers still were the same elite corps that I remembered which I am sure would have pleased Mr. Dunn. It was after five P.M., so I hustled back to our cluster of tents to make sure our gang was ready for dinner.

Todd joined us for dinner after which many of 730E-11 wandered off toward the trading post. Vic and I had to attend an advisors' meeting along with the other incoming leaders. Will was off to a similar meeting for the crew leaders. Doug Palmer led our meeting, which was essentially an overview of the ranch operations and safety procedures. This would have reassured all of the campers' mothers had they been privileged to be there. Through a show of hands, Doug learned who the veteran advisors were. Many hands went up for those on their second trip, and the number declined until our Chuck Kelly, a Vigil Honor, Silver Beaver Scouter on his sixth expedition, was identified as the veteran advisor in our group.

We had some more free time until we would rendezvous near the welcome center before walking down to the opening campfire. I was feeling like the odd man out. I was a veteran of quite a few Philmont expeditions (or at least the first four days of each), probably had been to the Ranch before any of the other advisors at the meeting, yet here I was headed for my very first opening campfire for campers! I enjoyed the campfire immensely, but sensed from the distant roars of laughter from across the road, that the closing campfire was going to be even more enjoyable. As it would transpire, I was overwhelmingly right in that conclusion.

The campfire, which was only my second "headquarters

campfire," set off another one of my treks back in time. The campfire in my memory occurred during my ranger summer. Ray Bryan, who was then General Manager of Phillips Properties, had been the guest speaker at the ranger opening campfire. I was not as impressed then, as I would have been this day, that Ray Bryan was a close link to Philmont's past. He had been on the National Office's engineering staff, and was appointed to oversee both the Ranch and the Philtower Building in Tulsa. The latter property provided income that helped support the ranch operations. After he was introduced, he stood before us, and in a measured gaze, sized up the company assembled before him.

"My, but you're a good-looking bunch," he said enthusiastically. I was overwhelmed and underwhelmed at the same time. I'm sure he used the line on other occasions. He didn't have to tell that to us rangers, since we, in our youthful enthusiasm, already knew that we were at Scouting's leading edge. Still, he had taken the time to come to *our* campfire. Here was a man who had not only known Waite Phillips very well but probably knew the Ranch almost as intimately. Perhaps he was here because it was Mr. Dunn's fervent wish that every ranger "know Philmont."

The opening ranger campfire was not the only campfire I revisited through the dim recesses of time. Thoughts of Jim Talley's mastery of Beaubien's campfire swirled around in my memory, as did the regrets of not having been to some other campfires. Where was Joe Martos, my old ranger tentmate? I had never been to the Cito or Clarks Fork campfires when Joe was singing there, and I'm sure I missed something special.

However, the campfire I was at now was quite lively. We were regaled with stories of the early Cimarron days and the southwest. But it had been a long, very busy day, and when it came time to sing "Silver on the Sage," I was more than ready.

I was anxious to "rack out" as we used to say. Two nights on gym floors hadn't exactly provided me with a full night's sleep in either case. The day we flew out had been preceded by an abbreviated night's sleep as well. Will went off patch trading leaving the Old Scout to hit the sack early. It must have been sometime between three and four A.M. when I stirred, and woke. Suddenly I was wide awake, and had a good idea why the antelope had departed the flats for greener pastures. Coyotes! There weren't just a couple, but it sounded like tryouts for the Cimarron Coyote Chorus.

I had seen the occasional coyote at the Ranch before, but this nocturnal, canine serenade was completely new. There must have been at least a dozen or more howling, baying, yipping, and yodeling at the moon between Tent City and Stockade. They wouldn't shut up—they just kept pouring it on. After about twenty minutes of the noise, I managed to doze off again, but was awake by 5:30 A.M. That was it. The big day! Unfortunately, however, we would be off to a slow start since our bus would not depart until 2:30 P.M.

Todd joined us, and after breakfast gave us a few more briefings. The boys were rapt, of course. I paid attention also—he was getting into a few departures from the sessions I had conducted so many years ago. Todd stressed the importance of crew integrity, and how to handle emergencies on the trail. We went through first aid, and then got into personal care.

The map and compass session proved to be routine, and by midmorning, Todd had taken us through everything that could best be accomplished while still in camping headquarters. This left us time for an important stop—the Seton Library and Museum. Scouting memorabilia has always fascinated me. I was especially interested in learning more about Ernest Thompson Seton since he had been an important part of my "Scouting Art" presentation done for Wood Badge.

Lord Baden-Powell was a gifted amateur artist whose water colors and line drawings showed considerable talent. Dan Beard, American Scouting's first Commissioner, had been a student at the Art Student's League, the same school through which Norman

Rockwell later passed. Beard, a writer early in his career, had also worked as a professional illustrator. But it was Seton who had the truly professional training. Educated at art schools in London and Paris, he brought an added dimension to his many books. I was not disappointed when I found many of his originals in the museum. I was fascinated with the many exhibits and the treasure trove of Phillips and Scouting memorabilia. Steve Zimmer, curator of the museum and author of *Philmont: An Illustrated History,* happened to be in his office. I introduced myself, mentioned how much I enjoyed his book, and asked about the exact details of the demise of the Old Abreu Lodge. We talked about the fire that destroyed that charming old cabin, and discovered a surprisingly large number of mutual friends.

Steve had been a member of the summer staff a few years after my time, and had served as camp director of Porcupine one summer. After a few more minutes of conversation about old camps, trails, and personalities, it occurred to me that Steve probably had more important things to do than talking to one more old ranger. I thanked him for the information, and said that I had best absorb as much as I could while in the museum. We were scheduled for another input session from Todd at eleven. As I was glancing at some of the art, including the striking portrait of Seton by Winfred Scott, I was startled to see that Todd had shown up at the museum. He had also been taking in the Seton memorabilia.

On the way back to our next session, I started asking Todd about rangers and the impact of the young ladies on the staff. I was interested in his interpretation of any changes that might have come over the ranch in the three years since he first arrived. I wasn't playing it entirely straight with Todd. I had purposely neglected to tell him of my three years service on the staff, including the one year as a "lean, green hiking machine" as they were now called.

Todd thought the ladies were a very positive influence. Like many old line, traditional Scouters, I had some questions about these distaff Scouters. However, looking back to my college days, it was clear that when there was just a bunch of guys together, things could get out of hand. The presence of young women tended to be a stabilizing influence. Despite one's view, it was a reality at the Ranch.

I asked Todd where he was headed after working at the Ranch. His response suggested that he was off to a good start. He had just gotten a B.S.E.E. from the University of Tulsa, and had signed on with Westinghouse as an instructor in nuclear engineering. His job would start at the end of the camping season, and take him to Idaho where his students would be naval personnel. He thought he would be living in Idaho Falls or maybe Pocatello. Since he liked to hike and climb mountains on his days off, it sounded like he had made some wise career decisions. When I asked him if he had played sports in college, since he did look like an athlete, he said no. On the other hand, I suppose few college athletes struggle as long and hard as Philmont rangers do in the summer.

I didn't remember that many engineering students when I rangered—pre-law, business, and political science were the big majors then. Todd said that the most popular major now was environmental science, and that seemed quite appropriate for an employer like Philmont. Then Todd led us through our last headquarters meal for a while.

"See you down at the loading dock at two, Todd." I wondered if he had caught the "loading dock" slip instead of "Welcome Center." Long before two P.M., we had crammed all of the extra gear into our lockers, and headed across the parking lot with our packs. Todd was there a little early, so I continued to ask him questions about the ranch and contemporary rangers.

When I asked him what part of the ranch was his favorite—where he preferred to hike on his days off, the response was immediate—the southwest corner. Here was a young man after my own heart, and for the same reasons too. That is where most of the mountains are, and for Todd it had the added attraction of being lush country. Had I come from Oklahoma, I probably would have been more attracted to the greenery of the South Country as well. I favored it because it reminded me so much of the Appalachians (beyond the fact that the eastern mountains are only about half as high).

All members of our crew had arrived, so we started weighing packs. Most packs weighed in right around forty pounds. I was disappointed to see that the old feed scales had been replaced by one of those spring scales from which the weight is suspended. I had been looking forward to weighing myself before and after the expedition. Perhaps the old scales had been removed when crews realized that trail food wasn't so high in calories after all.

After weigh-in, Will made a last minute presentation on the rules of the trail, and just as he was wrapping that up, the bus arrived. Emblazoned on the side was, "Swope Land and Cattle Co." It certainly seemed appropriate for that jovial old gent, Earl Swope, to still be casting his shadow over the Ranch.

In the Tooth's Shadow

All packs were heaved into the back of the bus, headcounts of
730E-1 and -11 were made, and then we were off for the great
adventure. The ride was a bit anticlimactic since we were dropped
off after riding for what seemed like only a few minutes. We
unloaded just past Rocky Mountain Scout Camp, which was new
to me. Perhaps it was used for JLT purposes or for guests from
the Training Center. We did not linger, and, with the great Tooth
over our right shoulders, set out for Lovers Leap Camp.

Will placed our chubbiest hiker at the front of the crew to
maintain a pace that would be comfortable for everybody. During
our Shakedown weekend we learned to place the slowest in the
front of the pack. If the hiker was located in the middle, we
rapidly got strung out to a point where we were out of sight and

earshot. As it turned out, our pace setter was not very slow in flat country. Within a few minutes we arrived at Lovers Leap. Here Todd told us the story of the ill-fated young Indian couple who leaped to their deaths from the great stone formation rather than live their lives apart from each other.

As we had approached Lovers Leap, the sky was changing. Where there had been just a few scattered clouds as we got off the bus, sky conditions were now moving from broken cloud to overcast. While the sun had been out, the flats below the Tooth had been awash in color. Any of the impressionist painters would have had problems getting it all onto one canvas. In my first Philmont life, I had been much more tuned into the fauna instead of the flora. If some camper asked me to identify any flower except Indian paintbrush, he was likely to get something short of an accurate answer. There had been a standing joke that if somebody asked you what a flower was, and you didn't know the proper name, just say, "That's the Rocky Mountain blueflower." Or it could be the New Mexico Red, or the Rocky Mountain Pink, or New Mexico Yellow Flower. Campers rarely asked, which is probably why we forgot the names of the more common flowers. Yet all of us had attended training sessions that included a brief review of flowers typically found at the Ranch.

While my knowledge of flowers during my staff service placed me somewhere between moron and imbecile, my awareness as an advisor had improved somewhat. Sarah had always had a burning interest in wildflowers, and shortly after we were married, we began flower hunting on weekends. We would be out hiking around at six A.M. nearly every weekend. My growing interest in photography found an outlet in closeup photography of wildflowers although identifying every new find was Sarah's department. But, through osmosis I had absorbed some knowledge of eastern wildflowers.

The recent rains had obviously done wonders for Philmont's flowers. There were so many different varieties. I could pick out a few, but much beyond Indian paintbrush, I was still in trouble. So, when in doubt, ask your ranger. Todd proved equal to the task, and quickly identified the vervains, shooting stars, scarlet beard's tongue, poppies, and several others. As I would discover in the days ahead, Philmont's burst of color extended from the prairie all the way to mountaintops. There, there were delicate little alpine flowers growing amid the rocks above timberline.

Shortly, we reached Lovers Leap camp. The ceiling had come down dramatically, and since rain looked imminent, we covered our packs and had our raingear ready. We set about looking for a suitable campsite, and finally found one atop the ledge that overlooks the jeep trail. Todd's real work with us was now about to start. Getting the tents up was the first order of business since it still looked like rain, and plenty of it, was headed our way. Having rangered, I was not prone to the resentment that some advisors feel when somebody else starts teaching their Scouts. In a very real sense, I had taught these five boys from Troop 21 much of what they knew about the outdoors, teamwork, and the other disciplines of successful patrol living. The Ranch would provide some valuable graduate education for all of us. As we put up our tents, another transition was taking place. I was very proud of the way "my" boys were setting up camp, and approaching their duties.

But, I wasn't the advisor anymore, Todd was. I was becoming an observer. I hoped that I could stay in that mode for the rest of the trip, although I knew Vic and I would have to relax our detached approach to things and be the occasional consultants.

As I was pinning down the corners of my tent, somebody tapped my shoulder. He had a silencing finger over his mouth, and was pointing to a clearing about twenty feet away. Since he looked like he had seen a ghost, I couldn't imagine what Will had seen until I saw it myself. Strutting toward us was one of the largest wild turkeys I had ever seen. He was out gathering in a little dinner, and headed right our way. He finally hauled up, looked at us, and scurried off up the ridge. I had only seen a few turkeys on the Ranch before, so this was a real treat. Either there had been a turkey explosion, or they had become accustomed to seeing campers, since we would see turkeys nearly every day. For some reason, ground squirrels had abandoned our Lovers Leap campsite. They just weren't there. It seemed completely implausible—a Philmont campsite and not a ground squirrel in sight. We would be compensated in spades soon enough.

"Will, let's get all of the food out of your packs. Then get a couple of bear bags and your rope, and have the guys gather 'round."

Todd was about to instruct us on how to save our bacon. This was going to be interesting since what Todd had taught us so far was pretty much what I recalled teaching groups so many years before. We had three bear bags with us, but for the instruction, we would only run two bags up. With the demise of commissaries at all staffed camps, the bruins could have had a field day with the trail food groups now carried on the trail. Therefore, every camp, from unstaffed trail camps to big centers like Cito, sprouted cables strung in high places. Todd took us through the knots, and we quickly hoisted our food to safety. Any garbage, unused food, and our "smellables" (personal hygiene items) would go up later. Todd reintroduced me to another Philmont smellable when he led us over to a stately Ponderosa pine. Anytime a camper wanted to imagine he was in an ice cream parlor, all he had to do was go over and sniff the piñe bark. It was a long forgotten scent—vanilla laced with butterscotch.

As we hoisted the next three days' worth of food skyward, I was delighted to see that the solid overcast was rapidly breaking up. Our campsite was soon bright and sunny. It was almost as though the stage lights had come on for Todd's next performance, the one I was looking forward to most of all. Todd was about to take us through dinner preparation including peach cobbler. Like many crews, we had already had some experience with trail food, but nothing our council had provided prepared us for the notorious cheese enchilada dinner. We had been trained on the more bland turkey and chicken menus. Tom Hillhouse and Wes Heidel were pressed into service as the cooks. Will had belatedly sat down with Aaron Smith to draw up the duty roster for the trip. My only instruction was that there be one Scout from each of our troops assigned to those tasks where more than one body was required.

Tom and Wes were just getting the water started when Todd got a wood fire underway in the metal-ringed firepit. Here was another change—pre-set, sunken firepits complete with a couple of metal bars running across the top. In the days ahead, we would be hard-pressed to find a traditional stone ringed, surface firelay. A Dutch oven seemed to appear from nowhere. It was heated over the fire until Todd judged the moment just right for a liberal squirt of cooking oil. Gone were the ubiquitous, oil-stained gray cardboard boxes containing a bar of margarine, salt, sugar packets, and pepper. From his pack, Todd then produced two cans of peaches and two boxes of biscuit mix. One can of peaches and juice was soon hissing in the oven. The hissing was silenced by one box of biscuit mix to which some sugar and spice had been added. The sequence was repeated, and the lid was clanged onto the top. Todd then removed the oven from the fire, and placed the appropriate amount of coals atop the oven. That was the part I recalled as the toughest, since my most recent Dutch oven cooking was done with charcoal, whose temperature was so predictable.

Tom and Wes were then the centers of attention, but not so much for the soup, lime drink, peas, or chocolate pudding. The enchilada dinner, enough for sixteen souls, had not looked all that inviting when it went into the big pot. We weren't very hungry since the hike into camp wasn't that demanding. There were quite a few leftovers (enchilada that is, not the pudding or peas). Todd's cobbler turned out to be the *piece de resistance a la rangere.* When I was in my cobbler-making prime, I would have been hard-pressed to do it any better. Todd shrugged off the rave reviews with his "Aw, it wasn't anything, really," understatements. One thing for sure, cleaning the oven was going to be easy compared to the enchilada pot.

Packets of tetrox soap had long since become history. Cleanup was a whole new program as Todd was about to demonstrate. We learned all about camp suds, crunching disinfectant tablets, and "spatulating" garbage into the "yum-yum" bag. We became adept at getting even more goodies out of the sump frisbee and into the yum-yum bag. Best of all, we got to carry the yum-yum bag to the next camp. Disposing of garbage in the fire was no longer part of the program. Even the waterlogged ashes now had their own special destiny. We all became members of the black hand society as we crumpled up the ashes, and distributed them far and wide at some distance from the campsite. Todd then demonstrated wilderness dental hygiene by taking a carbonized ash core and running it around his pearly whites. I am sure it was highly effective, but decided to rely on my dental floss instead. Evening was upon us as a chill in the air now signaled. Todd again gathered us in a circle by the fire, and suggested that we have a little debriefing session each night. We batted around what went right, what went wrong, and set the stage for what we hoped to accomplish the next day. The morrow would bring a moderate day of hiking—only four miles of gradual, uphill trails starting in the meadow below our campsite. Lovers Leap must have been one of Todd's favorite jump off points. A deepening smile came over his face as he suggested that we get up early to see sunrise from atop Lovers Leap. It sounded like a good idea to us.

"What time should we get up?"

"Oh, about 4:30," came the reply. It was spoken deliberately, and followed with that gentle nodding of his head and closed lips. I was tempted to repeat Todd's way of saying "right" by drawing it out and nodding. Though I was definitely a morning person, I rarely got up that early even to go duck hunting. But the Scouts were keen, including Will, who never had been a morning person. There was a little light left, so we sat around the fire ring and talked some more about the day's events. I soon drifted out of the conversation as I had a stream of thoughts going through my mind. These ruminations would occasionally be punctuated by the sounds of jets passing overhead. They were so much in contrast to the gentle babbling of Urraca Creek's South Fork, which was just a stone's throw from our campsite. How often had I been a passenger in trucks or jeeps as they sped along the road by the creek's edge? In all of those times, I had never really taken a close look at Lovers Leap.

I was wondering how the boys from these two different troops would interact. Would we be two separate troops hiking in close proximity, or would we bond together as Crew 11 instead of Troop 21 and Troop 4? The early signs were encouraging. Will had asked for Aaron's help in pulling together a duty roster, and the other boys were talking together. Wes and Tom had done a fine job on dinner. Still, there were some differences. My boys averaged a year or two younger than Vic's. The older boys were talking about pickup trucks and cars. The latest movie or music video was the most likely topic of conversation for the younger Scouts. Except for Will's lacrosse playing, we were not especially athletic. On the other hand, Vic had some outstanding soccer players in his troop. Two of his boys, Aaron Smith and Jeff Mann, had talent that was of college scholarship level. Aaron and Jeff could keep a soccer ball aloft so well that they could be mistaken for jugglers.

We had a lot of common ground though. All save one were members of our extremely active OA lodge, and all had plenty of camping experience. Our little gathering was now lit by moonlight. The stars were brilliant. I suspected that if we waited long enough, we might see some shooting stars especially since our expedition nearly coincided with a summer meteor shower. But with the trees, the view was not especially conducive to sky watching. Besides, we had a pre-pre-dawn takeoff scheduled for the morning.

My internal clock went off shortly after four A.M. I crawled out into the chill and was greeted by the Seven Sisters riding high in the night sky. After I shook a few tents, more figures emerged into the darkness. I had forgotten who was on bear bag duty, so Vic and I went down, lowered the bags, and gathered up the breakfast we would take to Lovers Leap. By then the rest of Crew 11 had gotten itself together. We gathered up our canteens and threaded our way through several campsites full of sleeping people who were about to miss a glorious sunrise. I hoped it was going to be good because I needed something to take my mind off what was turning into a splitting headache. Figuring it was probably an altitude adjustment problem, I took some aspirin, and headed down the trail.

We hurried up the switchbacks thinking that we might be late for the sunrise that was obviously going to be spectacular. There were just a few clouds in the sky, but they would make the sunrise even more colorful. Perched on the rocks, we passed around the granola, beef jerky, and banana chips. It was light enough to make out all of the prominent features surrounding us. Dominating the panorama was the eternal Tooth of Time, and to the rear was Trail Peak. I wasn't the only one who was surprised at how quickly we had gotten to Lovers Leap. The meadows of Lovers Leap camp and the road leading thereto looked small, far away, and so much below us. How easy it was to forget what a forty-five-pound burden on one's back could do to groundspeed. Then it happened.

The fluorescent ball, nothing more than a pinprick at first, broke over the edge of Urraca Mesa. It grew and marched steadily upward. It was hard to resist looking directly at the golden orb, but it wouldn't do my eyesight any good so I stole only a few more indirect glances. After the sun had started climbing, the more interesting view was behind us—the shadows fleeing, and the forest's colors shifting from dark to light, bright hues of green. After the sun had climbed a few degrees, the realization sank in that we had a big day ahead of us, so we headed back toward camp. We spent about half an hour striking camp, and then the real adventure began. We decided that the navigator's role would shift daily, but no serious decisions would be made until we came down to the signs at the bottom of the meadow.

In our pre-trip planning, I had outlined what each day would bring, and pointed out all possible trails between camps. Todd had told us that we ought to take the trail signs as only a general indication, and we should consult the map at every junction. Vic and I had long since decided to play dumb about navigation, so we said nothing as we were led up a trail that we were told looked like the sure bet to Stonewall Pass. Todd wasn't saying anything either. As we poked around the tents of some trail development crew, it dawned on our navigator and crew chief that this might not be the best way to get started for Urraca Camp. A hastily called conference was held. No, we were not headed the right way. We should be traversing a meadow now, and not barging through somebody else's campsite.

Back at the weathered, wooden sign that seemed to point in several directions for Stonewall Pass, we took new bearings. It was firmly established that we should head diagonally across the big meadow using the well-trodden path in its middle. In a few minutes, we were across the meadow, and starting to climb the four or five hundred feet up to the top of Stonewell Pass. So many years ago, Jerry Thatcher, then Olympia's director, and I had come over this pass, and I had a headache then, as well.

Back home, I had suggested that the boys consider the scenic route to Urraca, keeping the Tooth on their left shoulders. However, their conversation suggested the wisdom of getting to Urraca as fast as possible, i.e., pushing on to the top of the pass, climbing up to the top of the Mesa, and then finishing the day with an easy descent into Urraca.

"Do what you want to. Vic and I are here just to take pictures. If you want to avoid a lot of climbing, we won't argue with you."

We took a few quick swigs from our canteens, and were led away on what seemed the wrong trail. I looked at Vic, and then our eyes met Todd's. We formed a silent conspiracy as we read each others' thoughts, "I won't tell if you won't tell," we seemed to be saying to each other. So onward we went. We delighted in the knowledge that we would be enjoying one of the Ranch's most spectacular panoramas and that our crew would be learning something important soon (hopefully). After about fifteen minutes, the error was discovered, but by then Tooth Ridge and the view to the north were working their magic. I was like a hog in slop—this trail was new to me, there was hardly a cloud in the sky, and the trail wasn't all that demanding (yet). And the vistas were "awesome" (to use a favorite, but overworked expression of the boys in our crew).

At one of our watering stops, Todd suggested that the time for some practical map and compass work had come. With all of the flying I had done over the years, land navigation was almost second nature for me. Even with slide shows and flip charts to liven things up, I found that younger Scouts seemed to shy away from map and compass work (probably because it was too much like schoolwork). With scenery like this, it was hard not to find it a pleasant diversion. Suggesting the use of the Tooth, Shaefers Peak, and Camping Headquarters as triangulation points, Todd soon had the boys pinpoint our location. It turned out to be pretty much due south of where we had been dropped the day before, above Rocky Mountain Scout Camp.

Although we hadn't done any serious climbing, I was surprised at how much water I was guzzling, and we were really only half way to Urraca Camp. Granted, it was late morning and it was warm, but there was a nice breeze. As easterners, we were used to August temperatures in the nineties along with similar humidity levels. As we cruised past the scrub oaks, the temperature was probably ninety plus, but the humidity was deceptively low. We *were* sweating, but it was evaporating so quickly that we didn't notice it. Fortunately, we didn't have to wear the dark green, old vintage Explorer shirts that absorbed sunlight and made sweat run that much faster.

We came to a fork in the road. The view demanded a picture, so I shot our guests first, then had Todd shoot the whole gang, and then just East Goshen 21. We were all impressed with the view, but I was adrift in waves of nostalgia. The Tooth, its ridge, the prairie sweeping up to Colorado and its mountains, and the camping headquarters of my ranger summer were all there. It was like taking vows with my mate of many years, Sarah: something old (my trusty Kelty), something blue (the sky), something borrowed (my 35 to 105mm lens), and something new (maybe it was the confidence that I could get through seventy miles and thousands of feet worth of climbing and still talk about it).

One thing about this fork appealed. It led downward. After another half hour, we were out of the scrub oaks, and among the ponds and meadows of cow country. I silently mused that maybe somebody ought to publish a "Smells of Philmont Book" much like the "Smells of Christmas" that my kids had enjoyed so much. Pine was in the breeze, and so was the unmistakable scent of cows. It was so familiar—not so much the cows of the Bonita Valley, but the same scents I knew so well when I chased the cows home with my grandfather. We had hills to climb then too, but not with forty-five pounds on our backs. Shade was a scare commodity here, but we did find a little stand of trees that provided some shade as we pulled off the trail for a snack. We were all ravenously hungry.

Breakfast had been a while ago, and the morning had involved more exertion than driving to the office or getting on the school bus. Just as we were shedding our burdens, three high powered young men with packs roared past—rangers on their way back for the noon deadline at camping headquarters. I was wondering to myself if I really exuded that much energy when I rangered. Lord, here I was about to crash trail side hoping there was enough sugar and calories in our trail snack to get my bones up the road to Urraca Camp.

The snack, mainly leftovers from breakfast consisting of granola and banana chips, disappeared quickly, washed down with iodine-neutralized lemon-lime drink. The effect was almost like plugging in a battery chargeable device. I could literally feel the inner hiking man coming back to life. Granted, I might have taken a rain check on an invitation to climb Black Mountain immediately, but I felt energized. This little repast galvanized all of us—especially those who experimented with taking cocoa powder straight. A good thing too, since the last half mile into Urraca from the east is not a piece of cake.

Most of us were somewhere between taking a pull at nearly empty canteens and wiping sweat off our brows when we saw it. The unmistakable sign of civilization, black piping running from a well, said we were within a few minutes of making camp. Sure enough, we rounded the last climbing turn in the road to emerge at the head of a meadow. At the far side was a cabin. Clusters of tents told us that we were not the first to arrive.

"Ah yes, the presidential suite, and please have room service send up twelve pitchers of iced lemonade," I intoned to our hosts.

The young lady gazed up accommodatingly, and invited Will, Vic, and me onto the porch. She probably thought we had nervous tics as we dodged the hummingbirds that were making high speed passes around the porch corners. There must have been half a dozen of the exquisite little creatures punching in at the special feeders suspended from the porch roof. Now and then, one of them would disengage, roll out, and buzz off. They had no intention of skewering our foreheads, but it sure looked that way. Anticipation of some real bug juice helped calm our nerves as we signed in.

"We're going to need an early checkout. What time will somebody be available to come down and inspect our campsite?"

"Oh, you just check yourself out whenever you want to. And please don't make too much noise when you leave."

Yes, there had been some changes at Philmont. Most crews were, to be sure, mature enough to leave a campsite in better condition than they had found it, but the sleeping in came as a surprise. Our hostess then cooed her regrets at having given the presidential suite to some North Carolinians. She had the next best thing, and hoped we wouldn't mind having to put up with its "Pilot-Bombardier" (whatever that was). The campsite was lovely, but it was Siberian—well over a quarter mile distant and way, way downhill. We topped off our canteens and descended into a campsite that was reminiscent of the pine needled-carpeted campsites of Abreu.

At Inspiration Point with Training Ranger Todd Johnson

The cumulus was starting to build, so we got our tents up as soon as we got to the campsite (better safe than sorry). Lunch came in a plain, brown-gray wrapper. It was the same old peanut butter, only the packaging was different. Todd sat next to me, and I started asking him more about his Scouting experience. His three years on staff had been preceded by a Jamboree and four expeditions to the Ranch. He asked me if I had been a camper before I went on staff.

"Who ever said I worked here at Philmont?"

"You did, down at the museum with Steve Zimmer." The cat was out of the bag. It probably didn't make any difference anyway since I had an idea that Todd might be interested in what rangering was like in a different era. As most of his instruction with us had been completed, it was time to quit playing games. I started slowly, talked of the similarities, and then of the differences. When I said that there had been only seventy rangers in my summer, and that we served around fifteen thousand campers, he was surprised. Apparently none of the current rangers faced the prospect of taking a group out the same day they got back to camping headquarters. It happened more than just occasionally "way back when."

I asked if there were any pictures of Mr. Dunn in the Ranger Office. He said he thought there were, but I sensed that the long shadow cast by Mr. Dunn had started to fade. Another foremost question to Todd was why he decided to become a ranger in the first place. He made his decision on Mt. Phillips as a result of seeing sunset and then sunrise. I told him my decision was a bit less spectacular—that the only way I could really experience the Ranch was through rangering. As in any ranger get-together, we talked about the tough trails, the thrill of meeting crews after their return to headquarters, the characters we encountered, and what we did on days off. We got around to talking about fishing in Wyoming when Wally and I drove back from the last season. Todd told me that his new job after the summer season was going to take him close to some of the best backpacking country in America. I talked about fishing the Snake and how the raccoons made off with our breakfast. I also described how my air mattress went flat on our last night of camping above the Snake. Unfortunately, the last story proved to be prophetic.

With our batteries recharged (or at least most of the *young* batteries recharged), we went back to the cabin to meet Dave Hill. He would take 730E-11 through the Urraca Challenge. The Challenge is designed to develop teamwork. In our case, it was very important since we were the only crew from Expedition 730E containing leaders and Scouts from two different troops. Dave was the ideal program counselor for administering the challenges. His manner was a blend of think tank strategist, psychologist, and some submarine commander thrown in for good measure.

"What is your objective? How are you going to accomplish your goal? Do you have a plan? What is your plan? How will you measure the effectiveness of your strategy? Who is your leader?"

Dave's steel-blue eyes, soft voice, and measured speech created an air of melodrama. That he assigned time limits introduced more tension into the situation. I was surprised at how well Crew 11 was doing, and very glad that we had the services of our stronger, taller associates from Troop 4. The first few challenges went well, especially when they decided to "shoot the moon" on the pole touching challenge. They actually went one notch higher than their goal. The confidence was soaring, especially after everybody got through the suspended tire in record time. Wildly overconfident at this point, they all perished in the acid pit challenge—those that weren't picked off by the imaginary laser cannons. A swinging rope dangled from a high tree branch above a rectangular "acid pit" clearing. The objective was to get the crew over the pit one at a time via the rope. Crews not acting quickly enough would perish by cannon fire.

The problem was poor communication and weak strategy. It was obvious, from the look in their eyes, that they were going to get it together as they went to what is probably the toughest challenge of all—the wall. The wall doesn't require much in the way of strategy. The goal is to get everybody over the top of a high wall that has a ledge and stairway attached to the backside. No more than three persons may stand on the ledge from which it is possible to lean over and help haul others over the top. The strategy was so simple that little needed to be said. Our two tallest Scouts, Wes Heidel and Jeff Mann, were the key players. Getting all of the other players over the top wasn't difficult after forming human pyramids from which the topmost was hauled over the top. Then it came to our three strongest Scouts with hands hanging down the wall's edge ready to clasp Jeff's hand as he leaped up against the wall. Jeff ran, leaped up at the edge, and there was a momentary meeting of fingers. It wasn't good enough, but it was a start. Jeff knew the next try had to be better, and while he got more altitude, the hands just missed getting a good lock.

The scene was almost reminiscent of Michelangelo's painting, "The Creation of Adam," where the two hands' fingertips are almost touching—so near yet so far. The next go was much better; with their right hands gripped, they tried to lock left hands, but in the strain and commotion, they lost it, and Jeff dropped back to the dusty ground. I saw the look in his eyes each time he walked back for the running start. When he came back for the sixth time, there was almost a detached air of calm on his face. The pre-game jitters were over, and he'd loosened up some. The secret wasn't in gripping with hands. It had to be hands on wrists, and a quick roll with the shoulder so both hands and wrists could lock. Getting just a few more inches of height into the jump was the bottom line. It worked.

There was a little scrabbling of feet on the wall, but Jeff's associates had gotten him up far enough so he could swing one ankle over the top. Once there, there was no doubt about the conclusion. Even the stoic Dave Hill was applauding. In nearly all cases, crews could get all save one over the top. With the advantage of height and good physical conditioning, our crew had made it. They had taken some basic steps toward becoming a crew, and not just two patrols hiking in close formation.

There was no victory dinner awaiting us as we descended into our Siberian suite. Through some cruel twist of fate, we were to have a repeat menu of the previous night. This curve was thrown to us through some quirk in rotation of meals on our itinerary calendar. Or at least so we were told. Surely Todd couldn't have any enemies in the headquarters commissary, or could he? However hungry we were, we were also learning some tricks of the trade. Why bother with separate cooking pots for soup and peas when we could throw them into the main pot? Besides, it might dilute the taste of the cheese enchilada dinner. It did not dilute the impact of the spicy concoction that soon drove us to discover what a "pilot-bombardier" really was. Accustomed to the traditional Scout camp latrines with their L-shaped entry way, I found the pilot-bombardier a bit primitive, but then when one is in a hurry, any port in a storm would suffice. This contrivance at least offered its user the opportunity to commune with nature while answering its call.

We were starting to see more ground squirrels, or "Mini-bears" as they were now called. There was a pair of them that would not avoid our dining fly from the time we started cooking dinner until the time the bear bags went up.

As soon as we would shoo them away, they would be back. Just before Josh and Aaron were to serve dinner, the persistent ground squirrels brought one of their big cousins down to help with the pilferage. Will saw it first, and the stare on his face matched his look when he first saw the turkey at Lovers Leap. Before us was a remarkable squirrel. I had never seen one like it before, or if I had seen one at the Ranch, I had forgotten about it.

This fellow was a monster of a squirrel—even bigger than the Delmarva fox squirrels in Maryland. It was a tassel-eared squirrel, also known as the devil's squirrel because the ear tufts looked like horns. With a pale belly, and a deep gray back, it was a handsome specimen. Although he had his eye on the dining fly, he was more easily frightened than his more aggressive, smaller cousins. Considering the fact that cheese enchilada was for dinner, maybe we should have let the squirrels get it all. Perhaps we could then plead with the Urraca staff for an emergency replacement dinner. It was said that each camp had a supply of trail food for use in cases where crews had met with disaster. I wonder if the emergency dinners consisted of a more enjoyable chicken dinner. Or, with some irony, might the emergency rations consist solely of cheese enchilada dinners?

The coffee hour then beckoned several of us uphill where we compared notes with other advisors. I hadn't seen much of our sister crew from Troop Six since they were just arriving from Lovers Leap as we were starting out for the challenge program. At the coffee hour, I found Fletcher Swanson, Tom Breslin, and Jack Spangler looking none the worse for wear for their day's exertions that were, apparently, more rigorous than our own. Starting later than we did, they had opted for the shorter but harder route that went to the top of Stonewall Pass, and then up the southwest side of Urraca Mesa.

Fletcher asked some question about what Urraca was like when I had been on staff, and the question had been overheard. Urraca Camp had not existed then, and for that matter, the Urraca Camp staff was probably nothing more than a sparkle in their parents' eyes. Dave Hill and a couple other staffers seemed interested in my old codger tales. It was nice that these college kids were out on the porch with us listening to our tales of hard hiking and sharing their insights on the Ranch. It was as I remembered coffee hours at Beaubien.

Vic, Fletcher, and I then started talking about the next day that would take us to Lookout Meadow. The water was reported to be marginal there, but there was supposed to a good spring at Lower Bonita trail camp. There was also the Bonita Creek itself, but based on the cattle and horses upstream, I viewed the creek as a last resort. I had been in the area of Lookout Meadow before, and my lingering impression was of an alpine pasture tucked up on the side of Rayado Peak. I wasn't convinced that it was worth the climb to get there.

Urraca Camp's hummingbirds again mesmerized me. These little aerial wonders were busy at the feeders again. As an easterner, I was familiar with our iridescent green, ruby throated hummingbird, but none of the other hummers. On vacations out west, I was always amazed by the greater variety of humming-birds (and irritated that I had never brought a western bird guide along with me). How easy it was to slip into my time warp again. I went back to those August evenings on the porch of Old Abreu Lodge where Wayne, Bob, Light and I would marvel at the little hummingbirds. Unlike Urraca's aerialists among the porch feeders, Abreu's hummers hovered among smaller flowers practically at ground level. The hummingbirds that I remembered were much darker in color, and looked more like big bumblebees in loose formation.

Some other advisors must have wondered if I might be a bit barmy as watching the hummers seemed to ease me out of the conversation. Fletcher started talking about the next day, which brought me back into focus right away. He had covered the trail that we would take, and it was new territory for me, or at least the better part of the first half was. Fletcher's Sixers had a tough choice. Take the scenic route that we had covered, or backtrack over the shorter trail they had covered that day. Soon, the advisors' hour was over, and we started walking toward the campfire. Urraca's campfire was another version of the opening campfire at headquarters. At the end, Dave Hill asked if there were any old staffers present, and two hands went up. There was another alum from three years after my last year, but in the confusion after the campfire, I lost sight of the other old ranger. Unfortunately, I could not track him down the next day or later when we returned to headquarters.

We drifted back to our campsite where Todd suggested that we have our daily debriefing. After some grumbling about the double doses of cheese enchilada dinner, we found that the upside was a great deal of satisfaction. We saw many grand vistas of the Tooth and the crew was pleased that they had done so well in the challenge program. The daily duties, in which Scouts from Troops 4 and 21 were paired, had worked out well. Several of Vic's boys expressed some unhappiness at what they felt was a slower than necessary pace on the trail. I reminded them that crews should adjust to the pace that was most comfortable for the slowest hiker. The slowest hiker should not dawdle, but set a pace that was not physically threatening. Todd noted that we had made it from Lovers Leap to Urraca in exactly the average time almost to the minute. That included some cartographic hesitation at first, two extended photo ops, and a very leisurely break for a snack. Why anybody would want to focus ten feet in front, and pour on the coals on a day like that was beyond me. One thing we all agreed upon was the fact that Philmont weather couldn't have been better that day. Maybe Todd had been our weather good luck charm. He was leaving in the morning, and we all would be sorry to see him go.

Leave he must, but only after taking us up to Inspiration Point. He had mentioned that he had several days leave coming, and that he would be Colorado-bound. We both sensed that Crew Eleven was pretty well prepared for the trails (or trials) that lay ahead. I couldn't help but think back to another ranger era, and compare my handling of groups with how Todd had guided us. It was probably not a fair comparison. I was among a handful of rangers who got the quantum promotion to a camp directorship so my work couldn't have been all that bad.

On the other hand, I could have hung in there as a training ranger the way Todd had done, but I hadn't. My goals were different, but then maybe I didn't have enough of the right stuff either. However, Todd had done only six trips so far, and he didn't have to dine on trail food as much as we did. Our packs were heavier. He taught much more than we did. I was getting bogged down in a sea of reminiscences, and I was also bone tired. My headache had long since faded, but my shoulders and neck were sore. I was asleep within minutes of hitting the sack.

I slept soundly, but woke early—just a few minutes before sunrise. Something was wrong. There was a heavy presence about my kneecaps. My lower ribs, while they weren't hurting, were feeling almost out of place or as though they were being pushed by something. Then it dawned on me. I should not have told Todd about my air mattress going flat above the Snake River. This was just what I needed—a slow leak with the possibility of replacement being several days away. I had brought repair materials, but could tell that this was one of those slow leaks that is next to impossible to diagnose. Well, if the Lewis & Clark people could hack it, I guess I could also (but then I had a tent and sleeping bag).

After helping to get the bear bags down, I found another disappointment. My foot powder container had opened and all of my personal care items were now covered in white dust that was also much more smellable. Well, Urraca was not a dry camp, and the mess could be washed off.

After getting up at five, we got through breakfast and cleanup quickly. This, our fourth day, was going to be our first real trial. Within the nine miles that lay ahead were the ascent of one mesa, a traverse of another, and climbing a high pass. We topped off our canteens, and dropped our packs at the cabin. We treaded on silent cat feet so as not to wake the slumbering staff. Todd led us upward and northward for about a tenth of a mile until we arrived at a rock outcropping called Inspiration Point. I was glad to find out where it was since its name and location had driven me crazy after seeing it in Steve Zimmer's book. I couldn't remember any Inspiration Point, and recent maps didn't show it.

Well named, it offered a panoramic view that was so appropriate for Todd's departure. Todd's leave-taking was in some ways like a peptalk. Its more serious undertone was an admonition to take care of the land we were about to enjoy on our own. Not surprisingly, he asked us to take the Philmont Wilderness Pledge, and then distributed the pledge cards. We all signed right on the spot. What a place to sign off from! I had to think back to my many less-dramatic departures—about the best leave-taking I had managed was after a morning flag ceremony at the Crags. No wonder Todd had said that itinerary three was one of his favorites—talk about going out in a blaze of glory.

We took a few pictures of Todd and the crew, and then with crew chiefs, and advisors. He mentioned that he was scheduled to be in headquarters when we got off the trail. It was already understood that we would look him up and let him know how we had made out. Then he went one way, and we another.

14

Adventure, Be Our Companion

It became abundantly clear how advantageous it was to have had a previous expedition under one's belt. Knowing the little things about Philmont made the trip much simpler, but it took some of the expectation out of each day. So far, all of us had really covered familiar territory since we had been able to see the side of Urraca Mesa from headquarters. I was the only one who knew what our fourth day would be like. Yet, there were to be some new wrinkles. Ironically, I had never been on top of Urraca Mesa before, and had never climbed along the side of Fowler Mesa. Generous switchbacks made the first part of our day less taxing than I had anticipated. When we reached the top of Urraca Mesa I was in for a real surprise.

Somehow, I had gotten it into my mind that the top of Urraca Mesa had to be covered with short prairie grass. How I ever conjured up such a preconceived notion is a mystery. I was thunderstruck to find trees on top, and a jeep trail too. It was a level trail, and we quickly crossed the mesa to emerge on its south side to a view which brought back so many memories. About three miles below, the Rayado came out of its canyon and flowed past Abreu. Down there too was Zastro, and a now quiet Olympia. Never the most scenic of camps, Olympia nonetheless compensated for the lack of natural charm with its extraordinarily enthusiastic staff members. It was all silent now, but maybe there was somebody up at Abreu who greeted crews the way Bill Benner did, or had a welcoming smile like Jerry Thatcher's.

The crew was kind enough to leave me alone with my thoughts for a few minutes, but we had to be up, up and away. We wouldn't want the Sixers to overtake us. Shortly, we were descending the trail they had ascended the day before. The look in Will and Tom's eyes said volumes about what a wonderful mistake our crew had made yesterday. It was some grade, and there were no switchbacks. Although I had been over Stonewall Pass before, I had never noticed the stone wall. Here it was, and it looked just like the stone fences so common around the highland pastures of Bradford County. We were no longer enjoying a casual downhill glide. We were now going uphill without the benefit of switchbacks. It was a tough, mean little trail that must turn into a mudslide during rainshowers. Fortunately, this grind only lasted for half a mile at which point the fork in the trail spelled relief. We were all sweating like pigs, breathing heavily, and more than just a few backs were aching.

It was time for a breather, a leisurely swig from the canteen, and maybe one of those energy bars. As the sugar reached the inner man, I felt refreshed, and decided to take stock of things.

We had a good crew, we were covering ground at an average speed, and I hadn't had my heart attack yet. I had pretty well concluded that I probably wasn't going to have it on this expedition anyway. Still, we were going to have a rough go after leaving Crater. Also, there was still the specter of doing Mount Phillips from what was supposed to be the hard, switchbackless side.

The boys in the crew were not aware of it, but we were passing through some of Philmont's geologically most interesting terrain. Only a few minutes before, we had looked down at Abreu, which had at once been an ocean floor. Now, its sedimentary rocks yield many of the most interesting fossils found on the Ranch, including the shark's teeth that so fascinate campers.

The more likely finds at Abreu would be fossils of clams, oysters, and snails. The black shales in this area contain a variety of plant fossils, but the most interesting aspect of the terrain was the effect of Philmont's most recent volcano. Crater Peak, now out of view behind Rayado Peak, had been the volcano whose flows had produced not only Rayado Peak, but both Fowler and Urraca Mesas. Philmont's geologic history had been a rich one. Nearly every common rock throughout America can also be found within Philmont's boundaries.

After a crew of power hikers from Phoenix passed us, we were up again, and on our way to Crater. We passed through varied topography—rich woods, then open meadows, and back to the forest again, then into meadows and little glens with brooks pouring forth. Had Sarah been along, we never would have made any progress due to the rich variety of wildflowers. I couldn't remember seeing so many flowers, even in the spring back east. We passed Bear Caves, but the bears had clearly lit out for richer pickings elsewhere, so we pushed on up the trail to Crater.

I was looking forward to Crater Lake since it had always been one of my favorite camps. Crater "Pond" might have been more apt since the body of water had never been the great sheet that the term "lake" implies. It was just minutes past noon when we rounded a bend in the trail to emerge at what was obviously the pole climbing part of Crater's Continental Tie and Lumber Company program. Within a couple of minutes, the trail emerged at the far side of the Lake that, thanks to the wet summer, looked more like what it was supposed to be.

I had never really thought much about Waite Phillips in my previous Philmont life. Now, I was thinking about the man more and more. We were passing through Crater where he had stopped so often on his way to Fish Camp. It was eerie to think that we were treading on ground that he had walked over so often. As would happen constantly on this expedition, my mind was drifting back. Now it was to another Crater—long after the Phillips' fishing parties passed through. It was the Crater of Tom Whiting, his telescopes, and of the mellow-voiced camp director, Frank Estes. But, that was of the past, and now I had a back that was just aching to be rid of its burden.

We plunked ourselves down, and hastened to unpack lunch. Program would have to wait. The clouds, however, had not. We had wakened that morning to a high overcast that had broken by midmorning to produce a clear sky and unlimited visibility. But now, the trend had reversed itself, and only the eastern sky was clear.

Fletcher and the Sixers were also having lunch on the other side of the "lake." I had been mulling over the possibility of changing our itinerary to stay at Lower Bonita instead of Lookout Meadow. I didn't recall the view as being any more spectacular than the vistas we were now enjoying, and I wanted a faster start to Webster Pass. As the clouds built, I was also thinking that being positioned for a faster march to Beaubien made sense if any rain turned into the day-long variety.

Fletcher had some "press-on" kids in his crew—most notably his son and their very capable crew leader, Abe Breslin. I had served as a merit badge counselor for all of those boys. Therefore, I knew that they would just as soon pack over any obstacle in the rain as slosh around in the flats. However, the last chance to change our itinerary was through Crater's radio. I finally decided not to decide, at least until later that day. Knowing that Logistics wanted to know where we were, I took some relief in knowing that the Sixers would be at Lookout, and they would know we were at Lower Bonita.

"We're probably going to spend the night at Lower Bonita, Fletcher. Why don't we rendezvous there later today since you're going to have to pass there to get water. I'll let you know what our gang decides."

Fletcher nodded in agreement just as we caught sight of Al Rundle who was advisor to one of Troop 22's crews. His gang had just come down from sidehiking Trail Peak. They had done it from the more difficult side, but had no problems with it. It was a just a warmup for them since Al's crew was on a super-strenuous itinerary.

Our crew took a very brief tour through Crater's program, but I excused myself, and wandered over to the Lodge. I had never been inside it, and introduced myself to a guitar player who obviously was in charge of Crater's campfire. He gave me the brief tour of the two-room lodge. Although I had passed Crater often on the way to Beaubien, I had not then been aware then that Crater was a genuine Phillips lodge. It had originally been a "half way house" of sorts for trips to Fish Camp. The road ended at Crater, and the horse trail started. The road still looked mighty rough to me. Driving a truck on some of these trails is definitely not for the lighthearted.

Crater's ground squirrels compensated for the absence of their Lovers Leap-based cousins. Crater's mini-bears rapidly went from curiosity to nuisance as they tried to inspect our packs for some little morsel. The brazen little blighters tried to squirm into even the slightest opening in pack pockets. It almost seemed as though there was at least one squirrel working over each of our packs.

Time was a-wasting, and we still had a tough hike in front of us. With a final swig from our canteens, we shouldered our packs, and asked Al Rundle to take a few pictures of our gang in front of the Lodge. Then we were at it again. This was a new trail for me, and it was no pushover. I had always done Fowler Pass in the back of a truck or riding shotgun on a jeep. Fletcher's gang was right behind us when we left Crater, but we must have gotten a second wind, since they were soon out of earshot.

The inner hiking man started responding to the call of the trail again. "Push, push, keep going, wipe the sweat off, pull up on the pack a little, keep putting one foot in front of the other, keep planting that stick, if the other guy can do it so can I, hang in there old boy, just keep going, you'll make it." At last our point hiker sighed, "Stop."

We had it down to a ritual. We would pull up beside each other, and get canteens out of each others' pack sidepockets. After a few swallows of "yellow," "red" or whatever the color of the day was, we replaced each other's canteens, and stood there panting for a couple of minutes. And so it would go for six or seven more switchbacks until the procedure was repeated.

"Is anybody not ready?" the voice would sing out. After nobody answered, the sounds would start up—creaking, squeaking packs, gentle ringing of metal pots clanking against pack frames, the slosh of canteen water, pebbles flying, soft footfalls, heavy breathing, and the occasional grunt. What I couldn't hear were their thoughts.

Mine were probably a little different. "Lord, let me have my first heart attack back in West Chester, and not here on the side of Fowler Pass. How can that son of mine look like he's not at all tired by this? When are we going to hit that jeep trail? When is our point man going to run out of steam and call a stop? Walking stick is the best piece of equipment I've brought except when it gets caught between stones or in a rut. I'd really be in trouble if I hadn't spent all that time on the stair climber. Maybe I shoulddda bought a new pack, this thing is killin' me. Come on somebody, call a stop, call it. I'm ready man."

Then the magic word would come, "Stop." My early concerns about Josh were totally unfounded. He could eat up real estate right along with the best of them. He would take pity on the slimy oldster behind him, and offer the use of his kerchief to soak up some of the sweat. I had also been worried about A.J. and Will's knees. These worries also proved groundless. When we would arrive at the top of a pitch, A.J. would just hang his hands on his packframe, look around, and give the impression that what we had just been through was just a warmup for the real thing. Will's right knee and heel had taken some abuse in the spring lacrosse season, but all of the running and conditioning had obviously paid off. Will and Tom always seemed so maddeningly unaffected by the climbing we had experienced so far. I knew that there were tougher times ahead, but was comforted by the knowledge that if we were going to have any medical problems, they would probably have surfaced by this point.

We finally broke out onto the jeep trail, and this was familiar ground. Just a few more switchbacks, and we would be on top of Fowler Pass. Sure enough, we rounded the last curve, and I knew it was downhill to Lower Bonita.

I had pretty well decided that we ought to pull up short of Lookout Meadow. I posed the pros and cons of it to the boys, who would make the final decision. While it was clear to the east, things were not so rosy in the other quadrants. I figured we would get down to the creek, and then let the crew decide where they wanted to put up for the night. If the ceiling kept coming down, and the breeze picked up much more, it would probably be a unanimous decision.

We walked along the road in loose formation knowing that we would shear off and head down into the Bonita Valley. We were now in Philmont's prime cattle country, and the anticipation of seeing Beaubien soon was really building. We turned at the

Webster Pass sign, and dropped down to find the Bonita Creek swollen by all of the recent rain. The first time I had been here, the creek was practically dry (although I would subsequently get soaked by a sudden storm at the bottom of the valley). It was time for a serious, pack-off type break as we considered whether to stay at our alternate camp. In either case, we were going to have to cross the creek, and that didn't look like it was going to be easy. After saddling up again, we moved down the valley and found a shallow spot over which some logs had been thrown. Will, Aaron, and Jeff tippy-toed across, and went up the meadow to see if we were where we thought. It didn't take long to confirm our position, and that the spring was spouting clear, cold water in quantity. When it came to crossing the creek, I had visions of some of us losing our balance and going for a splash, if not in the creek, then in the waterlogged, grassy edge of the creek. We all made it though, and set up camp on the edge of the meadow just above the spring. Normally, we set up tents right away, but I threw caution to the wind (which was picking up), and walked back to the creek. The Sixers were coming down the trail, and a brief chat with Fletcher seemed in order. As I thought, Fletcher's crew planned on going to Lookout.

Crew One's very determined campers started to fill their water bags in the creek. I suggested that the spring in our campsite might be a better option than the creek, which was downstream from more than just a few cattle and Beaubien's horses. They were so enthusiastic about the Ranch that they said they were going to "pack over Trail Peak on their way to Fish Camp tomorrow."

"More power to'em," I was thinking as I assumed that they might take a good look at their maps before heading off in the wrong direction. We just didn't have that much steam, and we also were not planning any serious diversions until reaching Beaubien. While the rest of the crew topped off their canteens, I talked to Fletcher about plans for the next day. He was planning on taking the ridge trail to Webster Pass, down to Fish Camp, and thence to Beaubien via Phillips Junction.

"I don't know just what we're going to do. Maybe let the weather decide. Webster Pass is nice, but we'll probably go directly to Beaubien, and see who wants to volunteer to go to P.J. for food after lunch. Maybe we'll all sidehike Fish Camp on the day we go to Crooked Creek, which looks like an easy day. See you 'round, Fletch."

"See you at Beaubien however you get there, Bill," Fletcher said as they hoisted packs and shoved off. The ceiling was really starting to come down as I hastened my way through the flower-dotted meadow to our campsite. As I was unpacking my tent, the frisbee started flying. Where did these kids get the energy? Two of our bear bags were already up. I was ready to crash, and what better place to catch a few "Zs" than Lower Bonita late in the afternoon. A curse of my life, however, is an almost complete inability to catnap. On those rare occasions when I do snooze in midday, it usually means that I am coming down with something.

This day was no exception. Besides, there were so many nice recollections surrounding this valley. I just sat in the grass and looked out at Trail Peak. Its base was right across the way, and the scent of wildflowers was in the air. We had a level meadow in which to pitch our tents, and the nearby ridges would probably shield us from the heavy weather that I was expecting. The breeze had died down, and the last patches of blue to the east had vanished. I looked at my trusty old pack, with the miniaturized thermometer hanging from a zipper pull. All I needed was a matching barometer to become the complete weather guesser.

Our cooks were now preparing another link with the past. Its number wasn't "One" but the contents were the same. Dinner that evening consisted of orange drink, spaghetti, and apple sauce. While I was thinking about the passage of years, I was now losing track of the calendar. I was unsure of the day of the week, and the date was lost to me. We were starting to measure time by geography. This must be the fourth day since here we were along the Bonita Creek, or was it the fifth? We shared the campsite with two other crews. There were some Californians just above us in the upper campsite by the bearline, and then some Georgians were further up the meadow. Lower Bonita was not a Grand Central like Beaubien or Cito, and that was the way we liked it. We were about halfway through dinner when a small crew from North Jersey came panting up the trail.

They looked like they had been through the wringer, and many of them probably should have shed a few pounds before leaving home. They had come from Miners Park, and had packed over Trail Peak. Conventional wisdom said find a convenient place, drop your packs, and have at the Peak. These chaps had done it from the hard side after taking program at Crater, and probably hadn't left Crater until mid-afternoon. It was another case of putting the show on the road much too late, and not using common sense.

We finished dinner on the edge of darkness. Cleanup was simple since ravenous appetites ensured the lack of garbage. Our debrief was short, as we were all pretty well played out. We decided that we could sleep in since the morrow's hike would not be difficult even if we joined the Sixers on the Webster Pass route. We broke up, and within a few minutes the plastic zippers on tent flaps and sleeping bags soon started their nightly chorus, followed by the occasional "rrriiip" of separating velcro. When I had gotten back into Scouting, those sounds always got to me. Turning in for the night had always been so quiet when I rangered. There was no velcro, no plastic zippers, no nylon—just a quiet rustling from each tent.

As soon as we zipped up our tent flaps, the gentle "pitter patter" of raindrops started. I knew we'd had our run of good luck, and just hoped this wasn't going to turn into several days' worth of precipitation. It was steady rain, but, fortunately, not heavy. The even rhythm of the drops hastened my departure into sleep even with the prospects of my mattress going flat. How ironic it was to be rained upon this night—the night before returning to Beaubien. I had an extraordinary ranger career in terms of rain. There was a misty night at Clarks Fork, intermittent, light rain once at Abreu, and a storm the night I visited Steve and Ned at Lost Cabin. To be rained on only three nights during an intensive summer of camping was extraordinary.

As a rule, I fell asleep reasonably quickly as a ranger, and had always slept very soundly. In the intervening years, the pattern remained except those nights spent camping with Will's troop. I had become a light sleeper in the great out-of-doors. I was never a coffee-drinker when camping, but still sleep came slowly. This was much in contrast to being in my bed at home where it would take an earthquake to stir me. But, my return to the Ranch restored my old sleeping habits. That night at Bonita, I was so beat that I was gone within ten minutes of going horizontal.

The rain, unfortunately, was still with us when I woke up sometime around 6:30 A.M. It wasn't a downpour, but just a steady rain. Sighing, I figured wet feet were going to be part of this day. There was no way the not-so-little Bonita Creek was going to be as tame as it was the day before—not after eight or nine hours of steady precipitation. The rain dampened crew spirits, mine included. I had wanted this day above all to be bright, shining, and glorious. On the other hand, if we had to have a rotten day, this was the best day for it since it was an easy hike. I hoped the Sixers were going to enjoy seeing the deep, wet woods on their way to Fish Camp. We had decided a straight shot to Beaubien was the best way to go. Besides, we had a conservation project to do, there was program, and if nothing else, maybe a crackling fire to help get us dried out.

We were on the trail by 8:30. We got across a swollen Bonita Creek without any mishaps, although the water level was several inches higher than the day before. Considering what we were in for, we might just as well have waded right through it. The trail was waterlogged, and the grass transferred its wet load to our boots immediately. No longer were there the soft footfalls of vibram meeting pebbles. We were "squish-squishing" our way to Beaubien. Adverse weather is part of life in the mountains. At elevations over nine thousand feet, there is some form of precipitation, rain or snow, an average of one hundred days a year at Philmont. This year was proving to be an excessive exception to the rule. We must have been a sight. Here we were slopping along with our ponchos on, packs covered with brightly colored covers, and our heads hung low. We looked like neon monks put out to rainy pastures.

Spirits brightened somewhat when the path reached the jeep trail, but even here the going was slow. The mud, dotted with little pebbles, loaded up our boots making the hike even more difficult. In some sections, the road was completely flooded.

We passed Bonita Cow camp and the bend in the road below Trail Peak, so I knew we were getting close to Beaubien. We came upon some extensive corrals that must have been built as part of Beaubien's riding program.

Then we rounded a bend, and out there was Trappers Lodge. My reaction was something between a double-take and a squint.

Yes, it was clearly Trappers Lodge, but what had they done to hide it? I could hardly see the front of the Lodge. Somebody had put up another one of those tacky gateways, but that wasn't the real problem. There were trees, right there in front of the porch! It took a while to realize that those little, shoulder high bushes from my day had now grown into mature, tall spruce trees.

Still, it was a breathtaking sight. The rest of the crew was probably wondering if this sight was really worth standing in the rain for, so after the obligatory pictures, we were off to squish-squishing the rest of the way to the lodge. The bunkhouse by the corral had improved with age. New siding, new roof, and a new porch graced Dick Gertler's old home. We turned the corner, and headed up that trail that I had walked hundreds of times before. The perpetual see-saw battle for real estate between the pines and aspens had not been completely resolved, but the Ponderosas were winning by a wide margin. When I had last wielded a crosscut with Dimalanty and Freddy, the aspens were dying out, and the pines were not very tall. Now, the gray, dead aspens were gone, and the towering pines dominated Beaubien's southern border. However, the aspens were very much holding their own up at the head of the valley and on the ridge overlooking Black Mountain.

Vern Fails, a program counselor, met us at the porch that I saw now sported a roof. At this point, I broke with my usual laid-back tradition, and told Vern that I had been a staffer at Beaubien, that the crew was cold, wet, and wanted the closest campsite. The staff shower now occupied what had been the best campsite, but Vern obliged us by giving us some prime real estate next to the campfire. Things were looking up. It seemed almost providential, but the rain had stopped, and the sky was much lighter. The ceiling had improved dramatically, but still there were no breaks in the overcast.

"Get your tents and the flies up, and then let's meet back here when that's done."

I had just chucked the last of my gear into my tent, and was walking back to the firepit when there was piercing thunder. In a flash, a Navy jet screamed by. He was really down in the weeds, hauling buckets, and I hoped not on a course that would take him into the side of Black Mountain. He certainly seemed headed that way. As I looked down from the sky, my eyes met those of Jeff Mann. We spoke simultaneously.

"A-4."

Jeff knew his planes, and was considering applying to the Air Force Academy. Being a bright young man, and an athlete, he would probably do well as a cadet. His Scout training would help, and coping with the rigors of Philmont was proving to be a test of what he had learned so far. I was impressed that he called it correctly as an A-4 since it had been barely visible above the treetops.

The aviator was warm and dry, which was more than could be said for Crew Eleven. What little wood that had been left at our campsite was soaked through, but we had to have some dry wood. I hauled Will off to the side and told him that when lunch was over, we needed to accomplish two things: get some volunteers to go down to Phillips Junction (P.J.) for food, and get a good fire going so we could get socks and boots dried out. I knew that they could find dry wood if they fanned out on the ridge above us and looked hard enough.

Will then called for three volunteers to go to P.J. Wes was the first to speak up, and was followed by Aaron and Tom. Everybody else would scour the countryside and have a fire going upon our return. As they were cleaning up from lunch and running the bearbags up, I walked down to Trappers Lodge to ask about our conservation project since we wanted to get that out of the way as soon as possible.

The conservation counselor was dubious about our prospects due to the rains. She thought it was too wet to accomplish much.

"No mud to be moved? No stones to be shifted? Surely there is something to do when we get back from P.J. You want us to move a latrine, we'll do that. Clear some trail? Maybe repair the benches at the chapel? Whatever we do, we have to do it today, since we have a full schedule tomorrow."

"Let's see what the weather is like when you get back from P.J."

Vic and our three volunteers had shown up, so we headed down the trail. We passed the old commissary that was now a staff bunkhouse. It looked the same, but was obviously no longer the center of activity from which Jimmy Money had dispensed humor and trail food. In many ways, the old Beaubien was gone. I resented the big aerial on the lodge, the cardboard signs on the porch, and the solar power panels in the meadow. I wasn't very happy about being told we couldn't do any conservation because it was too wet. Had I been camp director, the gateway would have created plenty of warmth—in the evening campfire.

Yet, for all of my grumbling, clearly Beaubien was, in many ways, even better. The program was obviously superior, and the facilities had definitely been improved. The bottom line, of course, was how much adventure the campers were having, and I suspected that when the weather improved, the excitement level would pick up again. As we came to the cattle guard at the end of the meadow, I turned to look back, and saw blue sky beyond the top of Black Mountain. Here and there a shaft of sunlight was piercing the gloaming, so maybe the day would turn around after all.

Still, I couldn't quite shake a faint sense of disappointment. After thinking about it for a while, I realized that it was no different from going back to some old haunt alone. Looking down a runway, maybe, and thinking about the guys I had flown with. Or maybe the reunion of a ship's company—perhaps a college class reunion. I had been back to Washington College for a niece and nephew's graduations, and had come away feeling the place wasn't the same in spite of all the activity. Maybe a Philmont Staff Association Trek would recapture it, but except for a few ranger acquaintances, most of my old staff friends had been scattered to the four corners of the earth. So, I resolved to put the past in place, and enjoy what I was doing as a crew advisor right then. I had been having a ball for the last five days, and the best was yet to come.

We passed through the cattle guard beside the sign that discouraged use of the jeep trail. The Apache Creek Trail we were now on was familiar, but it seemed much improved. The lower end was all new, and it was much more scenic than the last time I had been through. Sounds of civilization heralded the approach of P.J. and we switchbacked down to a large commissary building where Porky-Ado Junction used to be. We hadn't timed our ETA too well, and wound up sitting on the porch while the staff was finishing lunch.

Joining us on the porch was a downtrodden Illinois advisor who was waiting for a ride back to the health lodge. The poor guy had acquired such a remarkable collection of blisters that he had no other choice but to throw in the towel. We felt sorry for him, but couldn't understand how anybody could lose it on such a basic point as foot care. We were still hiking about with soggy dogs, and would be good candidates for blisters if we didn't take some measures soon. Fortunately, a hazy sun was casting enough of its rays to at least get a start on drying our footwear.

So we sat on the porch, barefoot. My boots were the same pair I had rangered in (with a new pair of soles), and it was sheer pleasure pulling them off. I promptly added the removal of wet, confining boots to the list of life's top ten feelings. Even taking off ski boots didn't feel this good. After about fifteen minutes of enjoying the sun, signs of life were audible in the commissary whose Dutch door promptly opened. We drew our provisions, divided them up, and headed back up the trail. We took more time on the return trip since the weather looked as though it would be clearing. The profusion and variety of flowers along the trail was striking, but most interesting of all was a Spanish moss that clung to many of the trees. The moss was reminiscent of the type one might find in a damp, Pacific Northwest rain forest. Apparently, staffers weren't kidding when they said this had been the wettest year at the Ranch since the flood years of 1965 and '68. We saw several tassel-eared squirrels on the way back. Their demonic countenance earned for them the nickname of "satan squirrel" or "devil squirrel." One squirrel followed and scolded Tom Hillhouse for nearly a hundred yards. Tom thought the devil squirrel had marked him for some cruel fate. I told him that the squirrel knew who was carrying the nut-laced Waga-Roo chews, and was just looking for a handout.

More quickly than I anticipated, we were back at the top of the Apache Creek Trail, and crossing the cattle guard. Black Mountain was no longer highlighted by the occasional golden ray. In fact, Black Mountain wasn't visible at all. At least it wasn't raining—yet. When Vic and I got back to our campsite, it was obvious that Crew Eleven's dry wood scavengers had been successful. Is there anything so uniting and uplifting as a warm, crackling fire on a dreary day?

Adversity always tightens the bonds, and Crew Eleven was no exception as we dried boots and socks together. The warming fire was surrounded by a dozen pairs of liner socks and outer socks. Many socks had taken on a variety of colors not intended by their manufacturers. My boots, in concert with the "waterproofing" fluid, had stained my socks a dull orange. I was impressed, however, that these old technology boots, combined with new technology polypropylene liners, had carried me through seven or eight miles of wet hiking without a hint of blistering.

The rain had started again, but was light and intermittent. It wasn't heavy enough for the boys to miss the western lore program, and soon they were sporting brands on boots, hats, and shirts. I had walked over to the western lore program area to take a few pictures. Watching the brands burn into boot leather, it occurred to me that these young program counselors and all staff alumni had been branded too. Although our skins weren't marked with a "/8" we had been branded in so many less obvious, sometimes humorous ways. Shaving in cold water was never a problem for me since it would be hard to find water as cold as that bracing fluid that flowed from the Beaubien washstand every morning. Our grocery shopping list at home never contained toilet paper, it had always been written simply as "AP" (All Purpose Paper).

The boys headed back for the campsite after the branding session, but I hung around the corral thinking about some warmer, drier days of Beaubien's yesteryears. Will, Tom, and

Josh had interrupted their journey back to the campsite to get out of the drizzle and sit on the normally camper-free Lodge porch. One program counselor, a young man from the upper Midwest with a deep Texas drawl, happened by. The disapproval in his eyes said that verbal instructions for the boys' departure were imminent. Tom Hillhouse, ever the young iconoclast, was carrying on.

"Well, I'm a brand anything, step in anything, do anything, spit anywhere kind of guy," Tom said in an accent that started as derisively southern but ended in Philadelphian-west/suburban.

This was met by the staffer's cold stare.

"That's OK, we're Yankees!" Tom announced standing up, and leading a hasty retreat from the staff haven. I wonder what Tom's Confederate ancestors would have thought.

The rain was not heavy enough to interfere with another of life's top ten feelings: getting clean in a nice warm shower. After shedding several days' worth of accumulated trail grime, I headed down to the lodge to ask about our ill-fated conservation project. As I approached the lodge, our friends, the Sixers, arrived and were led up the trail by a program counselor. True to form, Abe Breslin had led his crew on the high road. From Lookout Meadow they had taken the trail along the ridge to Webster Pass, and dropped down to Fish Camp where they had caught several trout. The prospects of a trout dinner were obviously brightening what had probably been a dreary day for them.

As it would turn out, we were not to be favored by improved weather. The conservation project was again scrubbed, as was the evening's campfire. Will got the crew started on an early dinner that was topped off by a peach cobbler. It may not have been quite the *tour de force* Todd had prepared for us at Lovers Leap, but it certainly hit the spot. The boys were obviously in the mood for early retirement as Vic and I rounded up our cups and headed for the advisors' hour at the lodge. I found that the coffee hour was no longer held inside the lodge as was the custom in bygone days, but was now held on the porch. The light went on in my mind, "Aha, that's why there's a roof over the porch nowadays."

While there were no staffers about, the porch was filled with advisors who were keeping at least one Philmont tradition alive: talking about how tough their trails had been.

"You a farmer?"

The question was directed to me by a grizzled old campaigner whose red jacket carried the name of some council in Iowa.

"No, but I grew up on a farm." At first I couldn't fathom why he asked me that question. A quick look at my hands would reveal that they had been engaged in work other than mending fence, pitching hay, or putting corn heads on combines.

My hat was the giveaway. "DeKalb T1100," read the big seed company patch on my yellow hat. I had taken to wearing farm supply and equipment hats a long time ago, and saw no reason to change just because I was headed to the Ranch. The cornbelt advisor and I talked a little bit about farming and Scouting. Small town Iowa probably wasn't that different from small town, northern Pennsylvania, except in corn production. In Bradford County, corn played second fiddle to milk as the source of farm income.

I was mildly surprised to find a farmer at the Ranch, since I assumed that 4-H and FFA probably had the corner on the rural youth market. It set me to thinking about farm community Scout troops, and one in particular. During my brief service as a Scoutmaster, I had taken our troop camping over to Gettysburg where we had encountered no shortage of other Scout troops. As we were walking through the national cemetery, I noticed there was a troop from General Sullivan Council, but we didn't have time to stop and chat. That was the council I would have joined had I remained in Bradford County. That evening, I wandered around the youth camping area, and found the troop from Millerton, Pennsylvania, on the edge of Bradford County. The advisor had been a farmer, and like so many Scout units from the mountains, it was obviously a good one. I had never traded patches in my life, but thought it might be nice to have his OA lodge patch. He seemed agreeable, so we sat on a log, took our shirts off, and cut the patches away right on the spot. His Winingus #30 became one of my prized patches.

Farm talk on Beaubien's damp porch set me to thinking about other country boys who had been on staff with me. Wasn't Jerry Thatcher who rangered with me and then was camp director at Olympia from small town Iowa? I made it a point in these gatherings not to bring up my past unless somebody else leaked it or asked for which only somebody with a historical perspective could properly respond. I started the evening being all ears since I did have a couple of questions. I was interested in what the trail was like from Clear Creek to the top of Mount Phillips since I had done it every way except that one. I had since forgotten how long the round trip to the top of Trail Peak was other than recalling it was roughly a half day side hike.

The consensus was that the southwestern approach to Phillips was tougher than doing it from the other side due to the scarcity of switchbacks. Of more immediate interest was the Trail Peak round trip since we had a one P.M. horse ride. Four hours seemed to be the average including lunch on top. The conversation drifted to the crash itself, and somebody said it had happened in '44, which I corrected with the proper date and year. Vic and I were sitting with some Minnesot'ns, and my past staff service surfaced. Those gents seemed quite interested, and asked which year I had spent at Beaubien.

"Golly, isn't that the year that Jim was out here? He's got a picture of himself down by the sign at Trail Peak. You ought to go talk to him. He's the one with the beard down at the other end of the porch."

Our conversation continued for a while. I got up for some more hot chocolate, and made my way down to the end of the porch. Here I introduced myself to Jim DeWeerde who had almost certainly gone through my hunter safety course. The conversation was most enjoyable, and was one of the day's higher points. After about an hour, we donned ponchos again, and headed back to our tents. Although not as tired as the night before, I was ready for the sack. We had an early takeoff scheduled, and many boys were already asleep.

As I curled into my sleeping bag, hoping that the mattress would hold up for at least half the night, I took stock of this day that I had looked forward to for so long. I concluded it was a draw since taking a little ration of rotten weather is part of the game at the Ranch. "Better having poor weather today than yesterday, eh, Old Scout?" Sure, I missed the acquaintances of my Beaubien summer, but at least I had made it back. Perhaps each of my fellow staffers had as well in other summers. I hoped they had, because even with the evening's rain, I was having all of the high adventure I had hoped for. Best of all, Philmont was starting to work its magic on my son and his friends.

15

Over the Top

The Trail Peak climb accentuated the bittersweetness of returning to Beaubien. The panorama from the top was disappointing because the views to north and east were obscured, although the vistas off to Phillips and La Grulla Ridge were breathtaking. However, I knew that having a southern itinerary would provide us with at least three more major opportunities for views from mountain tops, so the law of averages was on our side. The climb itself seemed steeper than I recalled (but in early middle age, most climbs do). The crash site appeared more forested and overgrown, but that was only to be expected. The crash, with its seeping fuel in the absence of a fire, would have delayed regrowth, but after the passing years, nature would regain control. With Baldy being the big attraction, Trail Peak wasn't getting as much traffic. In truth of matter, I was happy just to make it to the top.

Before returning to the Ranch, I had obtained the B-24 Liberator crash report from the Air Force Air Safety Directorate. Unfortunately, its contents did not pinpoint the cause of the crash. It was a time when young men were flying very high performance airplanes with only a minimum of flight training. Pilot error was not an infrequent cause of crashes. There is no single reason for the Trail Peak crash—to my mind it was a series of weather, mechanical, and shortcomings in airmanship that came together at once.

Since all of my flying was of a later generation, I turned the report over to a business acquaintance and senior pilot, Bill Newberry. He was a Scouter in his day, and a B-24 aircraft commander while I was in diapers. Bill came to much the same conclusions that I had. He too was puzzled by the circumstances of the crash, especially since the aircraft commander was an experienced pilot.

Bill also couldn't understand the easterly heading at the time of the crash. They may have given up on the storm, headed for an alternate field to the east, and then ran into a downburst with fatal windshear. Also, they had lost an engine. Maybe they were carrying some ice. The crew probably could have survived any one of the problems, but taken together it was too much.

It seemed that except for the plaque in memory of Lt. Roland Jeffries, time had also abandoned the Liberator crew. When I had previously climbed Trail Peak, there had been a heavy, cylindrical container mounted on a post in the middle of the crash site. Inside there was a standard issue American flag and a printed record of the crash that contained the names of the crew. There was also a stern warning not to remove any fragments of the wreckage.

The canister was still there, but instead of a reminder to respect the memory of the crew, there were little shreds of paper containing expedition numbers. As we turned to leave the peak, we became aware of somebody coming up from the Crater Lake side. Sure enough, it was a ranger on a day off. He said that the season was slipping by too quickly, and that he was going to do a little sightseeing before he ran out of days off. Trail Peak was just a warmup since he was going to pop over and do Black Mountain and Bear Mountain for good measure. That restored my spirits—rangers never die, they just keep on hiking up and down and away into sunsets.

We arrived back at the Beaubien corral in time for the horseback ride. My short term infatuation with the horse world had long since cooled so I appointed myself as horse photographer. Our Sixer friends were gathering at the corral. I was surprised that they had not done the Trail Peak climb. Earlier in the morning, I occasionally looked over my shoulder to see how quickly Fletcher and his crew might be gaining on us, but they weren't there. Instead, they had opted for the conservation project. I had hoped that we could put the project behind us at Beaubien to leave more time for program at Cimarroncito. Unfortunately, it looked like we had no choice but to do the work later.

After a brief tutorial from the lady wrangler, Crews One and Eleven were off for an hour or more of riding, or walking as the case might be. I wondered if they would ever get up to a full trot. Only Josh had any significant, recent riding experience, but I doubted they would be gone long enough to wake up the next day with aching bones. I spent the next half hour talking with Fletcher and the other Troop Six advisors, Tom Breslin and John Spangler. Each had left his razor at home, and was now starting to look like he really belonged in the mountains. They were an interesting trio with Fletcher checking in at six foot, four inches, almost a foot taller than John. Of the group, John was the hiking machine, and appeared to be having no problem with the trail at all. Tom Breslin looked most like the Philmont "advisor" type with his bush hat, a week's growth of beard, swirling moustache, and well-muscled legs. Had the Ranch needed an adult to play a part in the mountain man rendezvous program, Tom would have fit the part perfectly.

The Sixers were a bit down at the mouth though, and in that respect were just like every other advisor that day at Beaubien. The weather for most of the past thirty-six hours had been the pits.

At the back of our minds was the knowledge that for a full week before we arrived the weather had been dismal. Had we been able to peek into the future, we would have been gladdened to know that our fortunes would change dramatically the following morning. Unfortunately, the same good fortune would not visit our Chester County brethren who were hiking Philmont's north country.

Squeeze cheese and lemonade near the crest of Trail Peak.
Will Cass, A.J. Zadrozny, Josh Rea, and Tom Hillhouse

I spent the rest of the afternoon wandering around the meadow, exploring the chapel, and walking around the jeep trail, awash in a sea of nostalgia. I had already decided that Beaubien wasn't the same, but that I ought to enjoy it for what it was and what I was—an advisor along to serve as a consultant for nearly a dozen kids. Beaubien probably wouldn't even be the same if Jim Talley started singing or Dick Gertler appeared on the porch to ring the triangle for lunch.

The next morning, though, there was something decidedly familiar in the air. A real chill permeated the woods. There was the scent of pine blown along by a steady breeze. A deep blue sky above was without so much as a hint of cloud. This was the way I remembered Beaubien. The symphony of zippers and velcro music started, followed by the appearance of sleepy-eyed lads. I had slept remarkably well considering how quickly my air mattress went flat. I had heard that the commissary at Phillips Junction sold roll-up foam mattresses, so there was some relief in sight.

This morning would not start with an old-fashioned, crackling wood fire. We were now in the white gas and backpacker stove era, which was fine with me (though it did add some unwelcome pounds to my pack). Our little Coleman stoves performed marvelously, and got hot chocolate water ready much faster than the wood fire. Although we were impatient for anything hot on this cold morning, we were in no great hurry to break camp. We were bound for Crooked Creek, which would make this one of our shortest days.

By 8:30 we went down to Trappers Lodge where we took some group pictures. A few minutes later we were at the cattle guard at the head of the Apache Creek trail. Black Mountain, with its great rockslide, beckoned just over Bonita Ridge. Unfortunately, we did not have time to climb it or even to go over to the picturesque Black Mountain Camp. Perhaps Will and I would get to see Black Mountain on another expedition. That always struck me as a great appeal of Philmont—an advisor could go to Philmont for twenty summers in a row and still have plenty of new trails to hike. If I couldn't make it back, maybe Will would climb Black Mountain someday. Perhaps he would even become Director at the Camp that had been my first choice for my last Philmont staff year.

"No horsin' around on this trail, and make sure you're well spaced apart. Mess it up here, and it's a long tumble down to Apache Creek."

It was a lovely trail, even more enjoyable than the two days before, when several of us had gone down to P.J. for food. While we were hiking on the shadowed side of the canyon, its western walls were glowing in the sunlight. I was somewhere in the front third of the line, and was followed immediately by Will and Tom Hillhouse. Their conversation showed what five days of trail food could do to growing boys' attitudes about home cookin'. They started talking about what they were going to eat when they got home. This was a long, long conversation, and lasted for what must have been well over a mile. I hadn't heard who started it, but knew that Will's first choice would have been a steak of epic proportions.

Cheesesteaks, "hoagies" (Philadelphian for a submarine sandwich), a really good pepperoni pizza, homemade vegetable beef soup, grandmother's apple pie, grandmother's cherry pie, the other grandmother's crabcakes, roast wild duck, and on, and on. I almost thought I heard a few foods over which Will was not normally so enthusiastic, but compared to a trail food cheese enchilada dinner, maybe items like cauliflower or brussels sprouts might seem appealing after all.

When Will finished reeling off a few favorites, Tom chimed in with his preferences. Where Will's list was reflective of the typical suburban Philadelphia teenager, Tom's was much more diversified. His mother was from Arkansas, and his father from Mississippi. Tom has lived in Australia, England, and several places in the United States including the south, so his tastes were eclectic. Beef Wellington was mentioned in one breath, and butter beans in the next. Grits with gravy was just one of the many dearly missed foods that would be consumed within the first few days of getting back to civilization. Their chatter continued, and was broken only when we stopped to admire the view to the west.

We paused by an interesting rock formation for pictures. This was a nicer trail than the old Apache Creek Trail. The Apache Creek Trail was essentially a creekside trail before it got to Phillips Junction, or, as I would have called it, PorkyAdo Junction.

The sounds of civilization became audible several hundred yards above the red-topped commissary building. Our pace quickened as the boys sensed how close they were to a trading post with its many goodies. Vic and I had to buy a replacement water bag since one of ours had sprung a hopeless leak. I invested in a mattress pad that did not look like it would provide much comfort, but it had to be better than hard ground.

A young lady in the trading post saw the "Chester County Council" on our T-shirts. She mentioned that a P.J. staffer was from Malvern, a Philadelphia suburb on the eastern edge of Chester County. None of us knew Trevor Chabinsky since he was in a different district. He was in his first year on the Philmont staff, and said that he was thinking about returning the following year as either a ranger or wrangler. Needless to say, he got the full treatment on the importance of rangering.

We had a split in opinion about how to spend the rest of the morning. Some wanted to enjoy the good life at P.J. with its hot showers and easy living. I was tempted, but had advertised Fish Camp as well worth the few miles required by the round-trip. With my little Voyageur fishing rod in my day pack, and some #14 black gnat flies, Will, Tom, Josh, A.J. and I headed down the trail. It turned out to be some of the most pleasant hiking of the entire trip. Here we were surrounded by the Rayado Canyon's high walls, a rushing stream, and an archetypical Philmont morning sky. The wind in the pines seemed stronger than ever, and the sky couldn't have been more blue. It was a much more scenic hike than I remembered, especially the red rock palisades towering above the Rayado.

We crossed the Rayado several times before reaching some of Fish Camp's outermost campsites. The Phillips Lodge at Fish Camp had not changed. The staff offered us fly rods but we were more interested in the lodge tour. One of my favorite pictures of Fish Camp was taken of Ned Gold and me on the porch. We recreated that scene with Will playing Ned's part. It was no costume from the wardrobe department for me. I was wearing the same boots, pants, and old Explorer shirt with its Minqua Lodge patch that I had worn when the original picture was taken.

We all learned something in the tour of the lodge. Dimalanty, Freddy Blair, and Ned with his staff had all lived in the lodge. I had been an occasional guest on days off so the rooms of the lodge were not new to me. But the tour brought out much of Fish Camp's history of which I was rather ignorant. As I looked over the young faces seated around me during the lecture, it was obvious that they were increasingly impressed with the magnitude of Waite Phillips' gift to Scouting. They were fascinated with the stories of hunting, fishing, and of the Phillips' many prominent guests. The tour wound down, and we left the lodge. As was happening all too often, time was running short. We didn't have time to look at the rest of Fish Camp, so we headed back toward P.J.

When we had hiked down to Fish Camp, I kept my eyes peeled for likely fishing holes. When we came to the first such spot, I let the four Scouts head on up the trail. I knew they were eager to do the trading post and get a shower at P.J.'s propane heated showerhouse. I had never fished this section of the Rayado before, and had always regarded it as poor fishing compared to its lower sections between Fish Camp and Abreu. However, the

P.J. commissary clerk said it was excellent between Fish Camp and Porcupine. She was right.

On the first cast, I saw a flash of silver roll in the clear water, but nothing came to the surface for my fly. The second cast produced nothing, but the third did. It was a rainbow that would not set any records, but would fit nicely into a frying pan. It was an unusual looking rainbow with dark splotches running the length of the lateral line, and there were yellow highlights here and there. It must have been a hybrid. Now confident I could bring back a full string of fish, I missed four strikes in a row. After that display, things got mighty quiet. Since these fish were thoroughly scared, the next hole up the creek beckoned. It produced one nine-inch trout, and more incompetence on my part. I had clearly lost my touch. I was having so much trouble setting the hook, that I wondered if I had ever had any touch at all. Granted, some of these were very small trout, but they were still legal, and certainly more appealing than spreadables for lunch.

The third trout struck almost the instant the fly hit the water, but the pool ceased to be productive after that. Time was running out. I told Will that I would be back by one P.M., and it was almost 12:45 now. Hustling back to P.J., it was hard to resist stopping at a couple more holes where I seemed to regain some of my reflexes by catching more fish. As I was about to cross a single-log bridge, a garter snake abruptly ended his sunbath, and slithered away in the grass at the water's edge. He would probably spend his entire life within sight of that log. Beneath the log, the rushing water of the Rayado was just starting its fifteen hundred mile journey from the side of Mount Phillips to the Gulf of Mexico via the Arkansas and Mississippi Rivers.

I could have spent the rest of the day fishing the Rayado. The lack of time was proving most vexing. The thoughts of a Rayado Trek next time were entering my mind when P.J. came into view. Crew Eleven looked clean, relaxed, and almost anxious to hit the trail again. However, Will, Tom, A.J., Josh, and I were going to

have something better than squeeze cheese for lunch. Borrowing
A.J.'s Buck knife, I cleaned the fish, and soon had our little
Coleman stove stoked up. Will said he never tasted fish so
delicious. It took us only a minute or two to turn the golden fried
trout into little skeletons.

Vic's boys, always eager to burn up a trail as fast as they
could, were anxious to head for Crooked Creek. I was in no hurry
since it was a short haul. We heard the scream of a jet, but it was
out of view beyond the canyon's east wall—probably the same
Skyhawk jockey that overflew Beaubien the other day. The roar
disappeared in a moment, and was followed by an encore not of
the A-4 type. It was a sharp roll of thunder. How could this be?

Here we were, cleaning up our frying pan in the brilliance of
the midday sun, and were about to suffer a thunderstorm. That
thunder had been unique since it was much sharper and more
brilliant. Maybe there was something in the acoustics of the
Rayado Canyon, the humidity, or the barometric pressure. One
thing was for sure, there was an impressive wall of cumulus now
headed in our direction from the east.

I suddenly became as eager as Vic's boys to get underway. I
wasn't anxious to repeat our Beaubien march in the rain. We left
the thunder behind, and moved up the Rayado where we came
across more of Philmont's finest looking cattle.

Then we passed a visual cue that set me off on a philosophical track in contrast to the sea of nostalgia that I had been
wallowing in for most of the day. The cue was a simple trail sign
that pointed to Brownsea Camp. How appropriate it was that
Philmont, as Scouting's greatest "camp," has a tie to Scouting's
first camp.

The name Brownsea always initially strikes me as a bit out of
the mainstream of Philmont's magic place names. Brownsea has
none of the excitement of names like Midnight Mesa, Black
Mountain, Lovers Leap, Black Jack's Hideout, and many of
Philmont's other intriguing place names.

Yet Philmont has, along with most council camps in the country, a Dan Beard Camp that recalls the early days of American Scouting. This realization brought my Wood Badge ticket counselor to mind as we glided along below the Rayado Canyon walls. "Counselor" Jim Smith, as a youngster in the 1930s, had known Dan Beard. That senior statesman of American Scouting was "Uncle Dan" to Jim and his fellow Scouts from the Scranton, Pennsylvania area. Dan Beard's own private camp was located not far from the local Scout council camp, and Jim would frequently hike over to see Dan Beard.

It had been Jim's grandfather, a Scranton photographer, who had taken the very familiar, 1930s photo of Dan Beard and Lord Baden-Powell seated on a camp bench. The picture shows the retired British general and the frequently buckskin-clad American Scouter in relaxed, friendly poses. They were obviously pleased with the development of the international Scouting movement.

As time would tell, the world would be turned upside down within a decade, but Scouting would emerge from the war stronger than ever. I wondered how Scouting's fathers would react to the environment in which Scouting would find itself a half century later.

They, along with the rest of us, would probably conclude that Scouting is more relevant than ever considering the size of society's problems. Fortunately, Philmont's trails are not beset with the quicksands of society's shifting values, rampant litigiousness, or any of the other forces that have buffeted organizations that foster traditional values.

Within about fifteen minutes, we pulled up at Porcupine, or maybe more appropriately, Porky Ruins. Porky, where Steve Radford used to teach program, where Fred Denton brewed coffee with character, and where Steve Gregory held court, had been downgraded to unstaffed, trail camp status. We paused only long enough for a picture since we heard more thunder to both the east and north. The sky immediately above us was still blue which in reality meant that we weren't going to get rained on—at least not for another two or three minutes anyway.

The inevitable sprinkle did come our way, so we halted, and hurriedly put on ponchos and pack covers in anticipation of the worst. Fortunately, it never came. Our protective patch of blue sky returned and seemed to set up a holding pattern right above us. The falling drops went away, and our ponchos went back into our packs. We continued, moving an occasional stone out of the trail, and keeping a watchful eye on the sky, which now held a wall of clouds to the south. Still, we had our own little patch of blue above which was following our every turn in the trail. We came to a fork in the trail that was marked with the usual arrowed sign, so we turned up the glen for Crooked Creek.

I was looking forward to Crooked Creek since I had never been there. Between rangering, sidehikes, riding with Jim Talley, and poking around Lost Cabin, Crooked Creek was one of few south country camps I had not seen. It was well worth waiting for since Crooked Creek proved to be one of the most pleasant surprises of our entire expedition. After a brief climb, we encountered the dead giveaway of civilization, a spring with many footprints. We were at the edge of a highland meadow upon whose western slope was a rustic cabin.

After the introductions, we set up camp in a little clearing just inside the rich woods a hundred yards or so from the cabin. The little cabin brought back memories of Black Mountain. After settling in, we learned that there were several conservation projects available. Our crew decided to take the homesteading program first, and to get in a couple of hours worth of work before getting dinner ready.

The Sixers arrived just as we were filing into the cabin for the program. Brad Hoopes was pulling double duty as Program Counselor and Assistant Camp Director. He filled us in on what it was like to be a real homesteader in the 1870s. The history lesson was just an arm's reach away throughout Crooked Creek.

Their costumes were realistic looking along with all of the other trappings of frontier life. Crew 11 learned just how tough it really was to spend years on the land until one could call it his own. Nicole Crawford was the pioneer lady at this camp. Despite how some of us with "old fashioned" attitudes on the distaff role in Scouting may feel, I had to admire these young women who served on Philmont's summer staff.

Seeing her sent me on another one of my daydreaming trips to the past. I wasn't seeing Nicole, but my wife, Sarah. She would have been perfect for the part of frontierswoman. At the end of the summer when I was closing down Abreu, Sarah was getting ready for her first job—teaching social studies on Maryland's Eastern Shore. The following year, she would spend two semesters at the University of Maryland where she got her M.A. in Diplomatic History. Her true interest was the history of the westward expansion in America.

Will Cass, saddled up and ready to head for Clear Creek Camp

In later years, she would add dimension to her classes by appearing in frontier garb singing the folk songs associated with the old west and the pioneer days. She would have been a natural at Crooked Creek (and I would have been the camp director for sure!).

As we were engaged in the first of two conservation projects, I met the camp director, Dave Liebman, four times a ranger. We were clearly in good hands at Crooked Creek since Brad had also spent a summer rangering. They said that more work would await us in the morning since the trail down by the spring was getting muddy, and could do with some reinforcement. In truth of matter, I was ready for a little fortification myself: my stomach was growling and there was a definite chill in the air. I shouldn't have been surprised by the chill—Crooked Creek is at a slightly higher elevation than Beaubien.

Even trail food was welcome that evening. We were now at the point where meals were starting to taste the same. No matter if it was chicken, turkey, beef, or whatever, the sauce and noodles were so constant that we were accepting it for its true value: enough calories to fuel our exertions up the next trail. At this point, Vic and I were becoming almost completely detached from advising the crew. We merely showed up for dinner that had been cooked with new efficiency. Even the cleanup was going much faster.

In the adjoining campsite was another crew from our expedition. They had taken essentially the reverse itinerary from ours, and had just come down Mount Phillips the day before. They looked as though the going had been a bit rough. Rick Creitz, their advisor, said that hiking up Phillips on their fourth day out had been rough. They spent the night on top of Phillips in the same rain that had dampened our night at Lower Bonita. We were two thousand feet lower, and in a protected glen, where they were caught between a rock and a hard, cold wet wind. Fletcher and I had talked about doing that itinerary, and how fantastic sunrise and sunset must be from Phillips. However, I wasn't willing to take the risk due to the possibility of bad weather. Rick wished us well on our Phillips climb, which he noted was essentially without switchbacks.

We had more time to poke around Crooked Creek, talk with the staff, and meet the various animals. There was Dale, the mule; Cora, the cow with her calf, Sunday; Tolby the lamb who was also known as "the dog"; and Smokey the cat. As I was walking to the cabin, my path was crossed by a weasel that had a ground squirrel in his mouth. The little weasel seemed remarkably at ease with so many humans about. The staffers probably were glad that the pint-sized powerhouse preferred rodents over the half dozen chickens that were dotting the grounds.

The staff was building a barn, but the real center of activity was the corral. Here Nicole was about to enlist the help of some city slickers in milking Cora. The cow tolerated all of this attention with serene, bovine resignation. The Scouts learned more about life on the farm, and the staff got some ultra-fresh cream for their morning coffee.

When Brad got a campfire going, the advisors' hour began. Here was a staff that put on a friendly coffee hour with the type of warmth that matched that of their fire. As usual, I didn't volunteer my background until somebody else let it slip. Dave and Brad were as interested in old time rangering as I was in their more contemporary experience. Both must have made excellent rangers. Dave was a teacher, and Brad was in the management seminar business, and had returned to the Ranch for the summer before accepting a new position in the autumn. I would like to have carried on the conversation longer, but even with the fire we were all starting to shiver, and it was late.

My new roll-up foam pad was an improvement over sleeping on the bare ground, but not by a whole lot. Still, I slept very well, and was greeted with a sunrise that seemed to say that we were going to have another fantastic day. We also had a marvelous breakfast of pancakes and bacon. This meal was so good that it was hard to believe that it was trail food. The bacon had been pre-fried, preserved in a foil pouch, and required only a relatively greaseless reheating in a pan. We took our time since our next camp, Clear Creek, was not that far away.

We also had more conservation work to do. It was close to 10:30 A.M. when we finished improving the trail below the spring. The boys had to decide which trail to take to Clear Creek since there were three options. We could have traveled by way of the Rayado, taken the jeep trail, or the southern trail near Garcia Peak. I would have preferred the Garcia Peak route, but the boys voted for the middle road. Crew One, the Sixers, took the high trail, and we were into Clear Creek before'em.

Crooked Creek had been the high point of our trip so far. Dave and Brad really recaptured the flavor of the settlers, especially in their lecture inside the cabin. The only dead giveaway was the handheld VHF transceiver they used to check in with Control Center. Dale the mule was their only other link with civilization. Much like the Black Mountain staff when Paul Dinsmore directed it, the Crooked Creekers would lead Dale over to a jeep trail where the commissary truck offloaded their supplies twice a week. It was this trail that we took after completing our conservation project. When we reached the jeep road, it was nearly 11:30 A.M. Between shifting stones at Crooked Creek and the little climb just before the trail, we were hungry—even for squeeze cheese.

As we guzzled "lemonade" and munched on crackers and jerky, the pristine blue sky started to wear edges of billowing white cumulus. We hadn't covered that much ground at all, and had a good four miles ahead of us. Off to the northwest, Mount Phillips reared its bulk skyward. What memories that place had. If I could just get my hide over that one, the rest of the expedition would be smooth sailing. Would I be up to the task? I thought probably so, but knew that no records would be set. What was upsetting was the thunder, and the way clouds were starting to spread across the sky, which was now about four-tenths covered. The stretch from Crooked Creek to Clear Creek on the jeep trail is not difficult, but would be no piece of cake in the rain. Still, our luck was holding as the miles ticked by.

I enjoyed the trail to Clear Creek immensely, and probably with more satisfaction than the average expedition advisor. At this point, Vic and I were just along for the ride. Crew 11 had its act together, and was enjoying the hike. There never was any conversation when the climbing got difficult, but on this afternoon there was constant chatter about sports, videos, cars, movies, food, and occasionally young ladies. As usual, I was drifting back in the canyons of my mind to another Philmont. This trail really epitomized the entire trip for me: a blend of the old and the new. Always off to our right was the soaring mass of Mount Phillips, which I was looking at from a trail which didn't even exist when I was a staffer. I had to check myself every time I thought about that mountain, Mount Phillips. It would always be Clear Creek Mountain to me.

It was *the* mountain of my Philmont era. Granted, Baldy was a bit higher, and Black Mountain steeper to climb, but Clear Creek was the capstone of any itinerary in the "old days." Fletcher and his Sixers were probably getting a better view of it from the side of Garcia Peak, but they were also probably catching some weather over there as well. The wind had come up, and it was noticeably cooler as we reached the sign that called for the descent off the jeep trail into Clear Creek Camp. We hadn't gotten off completely Scot free since a chilling drizzle set in. At least we were in camp. The boys had the drill down, and tents were up within a few minutes after getting our campsite assignment.

A good thing too—our little protective patch of clear blue sky had drifted off to protect some other lucky campers. The drizzle continued as we headed to take in Clear Creek's program. The mist wasn't heavy enough to really be a problem, but combined with Clear Creek's elevation, it created a chill. We ran into a couple of Fletcher's Scouts, Dave Benson and Willie Scott. Both of them had impressed me as promising Eagle candidates when I had worked with them as a merit badge counselor. Dave was wearing a remarkable hat. It looked like an Inca Indian cap with its dangling ear muffs. Considering the chill in the air, I nearly considered making him an offer for it.

We walked up to the black powder rifle range, and took in the lecture about cap and ball procedures. I could see that Will was anxious not only to use a muzzleloader for the first time, but to hit the mark squarely. Oddly enough, after being around firearms for most of my life, I never had shot one of those old muzzle loaders.

Whether we hit the target was uncertain. That we did create a lot of smoke was, however, quite definite. There was practically no recoil, but the clouds of smoke created with the discharge obscured the target (somebody's well-ventilated hat). Next stop was the axe throw. The results were much more obvious. The drizzle had stopped by then, but the chill remained. Clear Creek, at something exceeding 10,200 feet above sea level, is Philmont's highest staffed camp. The heavy frost in the meadow the next morning came as no surprise.

Clear Creek's program, based on the fur trapping aspect of Philmont's heritage, fascinated our boys much as Crooked Creek's homesteading had. Sample pelts of the various furbearers were exhibited throughout the lodge, which accentuated the realism of the program.

Our cooks made their apologies after a couple of axe throws, and headed back to our not-so-flat campsite to get dinner underway. Vic and I hung around the cabin to talk with other advisors, especially those who had descended Mt. Phillips' southwestern side. With the modifications to our itinerary, the Phillips climb would be one of our two longest days. It would also include the most up and down. I was more concerned about the down part with its blister potential, but the presence of switchbacks would probably mitigate that problem.

As usual, Vic and I kept our plastic cups out of the bear bag, and headed down to the advisors' hour after dinner. Fortunately, there was a fire going just outside the cabin, and we took places as close to it as we could get. I had been looking for Beaubien's stuffed bobcat and nasty, toothed bear trap since not finding them back at Trappers Lodge. They weren't at Clear Creek either, although there was an impressive Oneida trap whose dimensions suggested that it could have trapped a bear. With the fire crackling away, we found the Clear Creek staff to be as warm as their fellow staffers at Crooked Creek. The staff live-wire was a black powder rifle instructor called "Cajun."

He regaled the assembled advisors with stories of hot trucks, girl friends, college antics, past summer jobs, and his aspirations for Philmont summers yet to come. He was so unlike the only other Louisianian that I knew during my ranger summer. Bill Hogg had come from Baton Rouge, and was as calm as Cajun was animated. On that evening, the advisors could have used the warmth of the Hudson Bay coats worn by the Clear Creek staff. I was wearing a turtleneck sweater over a heavy undershirt and my old red BSA jacket, but wasn't overheating even next to the fire.

The fire was the scene for an evening tradition at Clear Creek—cleaning the black powder rifles. Several advisors' jaws dropped as the staff started to clean the rifles in what, to some, would be an unconventional manner. The metal parts were washed in soap and water. Naturally, they were dried and oiled, but it was clear from the looks in some eyes that several advisors disapproved. I was chuckling silently since it was a technique my brother-in-law had used often when we came back from duck hunting. Sonny Malkus would simply disassemble his weather-beaten Model 1100 Remington, and drop the receiver, action, and magazine in a large pot of boiling soapy water.

"Only way I can keep it from jammin'. Believe me, it works." He was right.

There was a heavy layer of frost in the meadow as we emerged from our tents the next morning. Luckily, another brilliantly blue sky replaced the overcast of the previous night. "CAVU" (ceiling and visibility unlimited), I was thinking to myself. We hoped it would stay that way until we could find an Adirondak shelter at Cyphers. We had a good breakfast, and put extra energy bars in our pockets before leaving for Phillips. As they used to say in the movies, "This is the big one, the one we've all been waiting for."

At the edge of Clear Creek camp, we passed through a meadow that contained a solar generator. It was the only level, sunny place at the camp, and would have made a good campsite. A little sun would have been welcome. It was still cold, and only a few minutes after 7:15 A.M. when we started up the mountain. The climb turned into a grind within minutes after passing the meadow, but it was a familiar routine. Keep pushing on until our point man called a halt. We would catch our breaths, and then have another go. We fell into a routine of picking out some tree up the trail, reaching it, taking a break, and then continuing again. Rick Creitz had been right—no switchbacks. We just kept on grunting our way, and soon pulled up to make way for a Michigan group that was descending. Their good word was that we still had a long, long way to go.

This trail was heavily wooded, so the views off to the west were rare. But it was obvious that we were making progress when we came to the occasional break in the treetops. We had been gone for about an hour and a quarter when we heard the Sixers below us. They passed us within fifteen minutes as we were taking a break. The grade on this trail didn't seem quite as steep as Trail Peak, but we were now carrying burdens heavier than just a camera, lunch, and canteen. We were obviously making progress in this high, cold air because the horizon was changing. We all seemed to catch that second breath when we could see more blue sky above and to the sides.

For Will, the climbs of the Tooth would be the summits of this Philmont adventure. He would do the Tooth twice on this trip, but his old man, the "Old Scout," had only enough steam for one show up the solar molar. For me, the Ranch has only three summits. Although I had done Baldy, the Tooth is the traditional summit, while Phillips, or Clear Creek, is my sentimental favorite along with Black Mountain. The last time I had been on Phillips' summit was nearly three decades before. A lot of water had passed beneath the bridge since then. My son, who in the wisdom of his fifteen years was keeping an eye on the old boy, had only been a sparkle in his parents' eyes when I last approached these heights. Yet, the climb was unchanged in so many respects, including the thoughts of the inner hiking man on this clear, cold day.

"When is this going to end? This is the last rock heap I will ever climb. Is there a really good reason I am here instead of Nags Head? Why doesn't that kid up in front call a break? I'm ready to blow a gut. If it's so bloomin' cold, why am I sweatin' so much? If somebody offered me an hour in the dentist's chair instead of this, I think I'd take it. If that point man doesn't call it in another twenty-five steps, I'm goin' to. It's 9:15 here, and Sarah is either swimming at the pool or down at church playing music. Or maybe she's tending to all of the flowers in our yard. Holly is busy at her summer job in an air-conditioned office, or maybe on a coffee break. Those raspy voiced ravens are lookin' at me like Dave Bates is going to have to get some helicopter to haul me off the mountain and take me to the cardiac care unit in Raton. Well, I was the one who asked for it, and flamed if I'm going to hang up my spikes on the side of this mountain. Last time I was here I didn't get clobbered like this."

As we got closer to the top, I was again slipping into the

backward time warp to my first climbs of Clear Creek Mountain. I had sidehiked it from Beaubien, and then climbed it on my birthday with a group from Houston when I was a ranger. I worried about the advisor because he was old—ancient even. He must have been all of forty, maybe even forty-five! Well, here we were at full circle, but at least Todd Johnson wasn't around to listen to my heavy breathing. I was having a good time, especially with Will at my side. I was very pleased that he was keeping an eye on the old man just in case I took a misstep or suddenly became prone to altitude sickness. But that was not to be. I felt quite good, and was about to experience that extra spurt of energy that comes when the goal is within sight.

After some more plugging away, we broke out at the timberline. We coasted the last several hundred yards to the top where the Sixers had just shed their packs before taking pictures. This was a special summit served by a new trail—the same path that had been illustrated in *High Country* (the staff association newsletter) and the two coffee table books on the Ranch.

Vic stoked up our stove to get some water heated for hot chocolate—a real treat. Even the beef jerky strips were welcome. It couldn't have been a more beautiful day. The air temperature of fifty-five degrees Fahrenheit felt even colder with the steady breeze. We got out our cameras, and took the inevitable shots of the group, and fathers and sons shaking hands at 11,711 feet. We panned the horizon for shots of Wheeler, Baldy, Touch-Me-Not, and the remaining windswept vistas. I played the role of tour guide since I was the only one who had seen these peaks before.

It is only from Philmont's great peaks that one can sense the great majesty of these Cimarron Mountains. It seems hard to believe that the rugged mountains we were enjoying started as an ocean bed. With the passage of time, the land had been forced upward but was only a prairie, a mere thousand feet above sea level.

The upward thrust of metamorphic rocks many millions of

years ago shaped the Sangre de Cristo Range as we know it today. Volcanic activity and the inexorable effects of weather further defined the face of Philmont. That definition continues. Geologists bet that forces deep within the earth will prevail over the rounding effects of weather, and that Philmont's great peaks will continue to rise. Wouldn't that be something if Mt. Phillips grew a little bit faster than Baldy?

After half an hour of enjoying the view, we swung our packs back on, and hiked through Mount Phillips Camp, and then down to Comanche Peak. Here Troop 21 got in some more map and compass work for the backpacking merit badge. The sun had climbed to the point where the wool jacket was no longer necessary. As I was changing, a gray jay flew past with his head turned as if to size us up for the possibility of a few snacks. We did spare him a few morsels for which he proudly posed, not in our hands, but still within a few feet. These moments were the highlight of the trip since so many of the Ranch's great peaks were in view—including the back side of the Tooth.

For the first time, I think, the boys in Crew Eleven were sensing the importance of what they had accomplished in the previous week. Vic and I were looking at it somewhat differently. One part of us was still the youth, always the young Scout looking for the adventure that the Ranch delivers in spades. The other half was viewed from the Scouter perspective. Here were our kids, who just a few short years ago couldn't tie a bowline or start a fire. Back then, they might hesitatingly try to put up a tent, but secretly would be happy if an older boy came by and showed them how to do it again. Their attention spans had been limited then. Now they could look at a map in confidence, and say just how far they had to go, through what they had to hike, what the change in elevation would be, and roughly how long it would take to reach their goal. These accomplishments illustrated the higher purpose of the Scouting program. The B.S.A. provided these kids, and hundreds of thousands of others, with the skills to approach problems somewhat greater than reading a map correctly.

People like Vic and I might take some modest credit for this transformation, but we were only instruments in the larger process. Philmont is, of course, a real test of that process. My philosophical meandering was interrupted by a growling stomach. At Comanche Camp, we found a few logs on which to sit for lunch. Could a vacation be any finer? The sun was warm, the spreadables tolerable, the orange drink quenching, and the gray jays up to their ingratiating best. And it was downhill from here on in. Actually it wasn't, but we knew that Shaefers Peak wouldn't be as difficult as what we had been over this day.

16

Ridgerunners

We shouldered our packs, secure in the knowledge that Cyphers was easy switchbacking downhill. There was no real need to pause for frequent breaks, but all of the flowers beckoned. I would not be rushed this afternoon, so I stopped at every new flower for a closeup shot. As I was pausing over some unknown jewel that would fascinate Sarah, the silence of the moment was shattered by a pair of F-111s. The Aardvarks were out of Cannon AFB, which is located along the Texas/New Mexico border. Their wings were not swept back on this flight. The pilots needed all the maneuverability they could get at low airspeeds since they were down in the weeds where they were playing hide and seek in the mountain passes. They hugged Bear Mountain in a turn, then rolled out on a northerly heading that took them to the east of Cimarroncito Peak, where we lost sight of them. How times change. The last time I had been approaching Cyphers, it had been B-52s that were skimming the ridges.

There were new trails in this area. I wondered if they were legacies from Buster Simpson and Dave Talliaferro. Comanche Peak's eastern ridges had also changed. I remembered them as not so heavily forested. The view then was so unobstructed that it was easy to see the groups below us struggling on their way up. Today, it was wooded, and in some places littered with fallen trees. Fortunately, our sky conditions were still holding. More so than any other day on our expedition, this special day was providing us with that archetypical southwestern sun and low humidity. There was a light breeze that carried the warm scent of pine across this section of remarkably smooth trail. The trail was a broad path without the usual large stones that sometimes seemed more numerous than the legions of ground squirrels. The trail was so pleasant that I might have assumed that it had been put in by golf course contractors.

As we neared Cyphers, my frequent pauses to photograph flowers had the effect of splitting Crew Eleven into two groups. Vic and his faster hikers were out of earshot before we could do much about it. They arrived at Cyphers well before Troop 21's more leisurely hiking gang showed up. Cyphers' camp director was on the ball, and politely reamed us out for breaking the cardinal rule of compromising crew integrity. After taking our medicine, we were shown our evening's accommodations, an Adirondack shelter of generous proportions. The twelve of us could easily fit in the shelter, but I decided that one of us wouldn't. The Adirondacks were built on the supposition that there is not a level, stoneless spot to be found at Cyphers. But find a small spot I did—right on the edge of Cimarroncito Creek. My little Cirrus Two tent doesn't require much space, and the ground I selected was both level and soft.

I was beat. My mind was racing but the old "bod" was nearly

spent. With my pack braced at the base of a tree, I sat on the soft earth, and then sprawled out. The sky was still blue, and I still had not answered that question I had posed to Ned Gold some months before. Was Phillips tougher from Cyphers or Clear Creek Camp? There was, of course, no answer to the question. The asking and ruminating over a logical response were the only purposes. Clever Ned the lawyer had hedged his arguments. He thought it was a "bear" from Clear Creek, but noted that many thought the trail from Cyphers was tougher. It was a comparison of shorter and straight up on one hand and switchbacked and longer on the other. I had no answer, but was glad that both were within my experience. As I enjoyed the reflection, it occurred to me that maybe doing Comanche Pass from Cyphers had the measure of either.

Cyphers held two attractions for us: the mine tour and showers. Of the two, the latter was most appealing, especially since I had passed up a shower opportunity at Phillips Junction in favor of fishing the Rayado. My sleeping bag, while not smelling quite as obnoxious as a municipal garbage dump, was starting to ripen. The shower and subsequent shave worked wonders. I was a new man again. That shower renewed my conviction that getting clean is, indeed, one of life's top ten feelings.

For good measure, I treated my clothes to the same wonderful sensation in one of Cyphers' great galvanized tubs. The mine tour followed, and was as I remembered it from my ranger days. Cyphers had changed a little. The shower house was new, and the little miners' shack had more than doubled in size.

As dinner was being cooked, I located the Sixers and Fletcher with whom I discussed our plans for an itinerary change. Vic had done the Cito to Tooth Ridge Camp trail three years before, and was anxious to shorten it. We were scheduled for Webster Park the next night. I knew nothing of the camp except that water had to be carried to it, and we had heard the place made for pleasant camping. Fletcher thought his crew would probably make a decision after they got to Cimarroncito the next day. I was mulling around the possibility of staying at Upper Clarks Fork, but decided to ask the crew after we did the rock climbing program at Cito. Our subsequent decision to stay at Upper Clarks Fork would prove to be one of the wisest choices of the entire expedition.

I hadn't paid much attention to what was being cooked for dinner, but it certainly had caught the attention of everybody else. We hit the peak and trough in dinner that night. Pinto beans, which dominated camp swap boxes from Dan Beard to Abreu, proved to be the low point. Even our most adventurous gourmet, Tom Hillhouse, decided that the beans were not up to par. Offsetting the leguminous disaster was a monster lemon crumb pie that was cooling in the creek shallows. As we consumed the last of the pie crumbs, we had our evening debriefing session. There was clearly quite an air of accomplishment and gratitude in our assembly that evening. We had all come over the top in fine shape, and had been blessed with weather that matched our first full day on the trail. Only after the passage of another hour would we realize just how lucky Crews One and Eleven had been. Overlaying our gathering was the bittersweet realization that in two more days the great adventure would come to a halt. On the other hand, when we reached the end of the trail there would be real food, hot showers, and no more forty pound packs.

I knew that the boys would probably retire early that evening considering the day's exertions. Before heading for the advisors' hour with Vic, we moved our drying clothes from lines among the trees to the ceiling of the Adirondack. Then it was off to the miners' line shack for coffee and conversation. Unexpectedly, we ran into Mike Basquill and Roger Hoppe from Troop 55, which comprised Crew 7. We had seen only two of our Chester County crews before, and that was still early in the expedition. Mike regaled the other advisors with a narrative of his encounter with a rattlesnake at Pueblano. It was hard to tell which was more frightened, but Mike had not remained on the rattler's turf long enough to find out.

What we did learn was that the weather had been quite bad up north. With our council elders promoting Baldy country itineraries, most of our crews had headed north. While Mike and Roger hadn't rendezvoused with every Chester County crew on the trail, he said that his crew and all the others he had met were unable to climb Baldy due to weather problems. That word came as something of a surprise since we had naturally assumed that their expedition was having the same good weather we were enjoying. Sure, we had one day of rain, and some sprinkles, but all of our big days had been bright and sunny. On the other hand, we all knew that mountain weather could be capricious. To compensate, our Troop 55 friends were hoping to sidehike Mt. Phillips to make up for having put all of their big mountain eggs in one basket.

It was said that the Cyphers staff could put on a good advisors' hour, and that for those who wanted to stay, the singing and guitar pickin' were worth waiting for. It was another case of the mind being willing, but not the flesh. With the last light of day going and the hot chocolate having a relaxing effect, I was running out of energy. Others too were drifting away, so I made my apologies, and headed down the trail. I was looking forward to sleep, but it didn't come immediately since I was busy reviewing the day's activities. What a great day this had been—it had lived up to everything I had hoped for over the past few months. What I didn't know then was that in another thirty-six hours we would be embarking on another winner that, in most ways, was even better than our Mt. Phillips climb.

The crew had decided to sleep in which was fine with me. I had taken longer than usual to fall asleep, but the steady murmur of Cito Creek had finally done its job. I awoke only once when something was scratching at the edge of my tent. Whatever it was, it was smaller than a bear, and therefore not worth much worry. How different it would have been in the days of open, unfloored tents. Of all the good things in the "good old days," tents were not among them.

It looked like we had another jewel of a day as we emerged from tent and shelter, and it would be an easy hiking day—essentially all downhill. The crew had voted for breakfast on the trail, so our pre-breakfast consisted of a couple of swigs of bug juice and perhaps a chew on a leftover energy bar. As I was pulling my canteen out its pack pocket, I realized that I had inadvertently committed two grave errors. I left my canteen and part of a chocolate bar in the pocket overnight. It was a "first and last time" type mistake. Well, it was probably nothing to worry about since that pack hadn't been disturbed. After all, it was a small pocket in which the canteen made a very snug fit. WRONG! The pack hadn't been disturbed, but the chocolate bar certainly had. Nothing was left but hundreds of tiny paper shreds. Served me right.

Cito bound, we were advised to take the middle fork trail since the north fork was closed to all but jeeps and commissary trucks. That suited us fine until we realized how often we would be crossing the creek. Still, the creek trail would be more enjoyable. Here was another trail full of happy memories. This was the trail of my first ranger trip with the South Carolinians. From nearby Lamberts Mine and its chocolate pudding disaster, I had climbed Clear Creek with the Houston group. The trail was much more lush than I remembered—the recent rains had made the whole Ranch more green. Sarah would have enjoyed this stretch, which held a tremendous number of flowers, several of which I paused to photograph. Never could I resist catching a butterfly on a flower with my camera. It was so lush that it was easy to assume that one was in some damp creek valley back east. The creek was running high. From what I could tell by the number of wet hikers in other crews, it had claimed a few of the less-than-agile Scouts.

We pulled up for breakfast half way down to Cito Hunting Lodge. Breakfast consisted of dried fruit, granola, and for the observant, some wild raspberries. I had been picking them along the trail for the last half mile or so. Todd had said that the bear troubles had not been as severe this year since the wild berries had been so abundant. The pickin's were indeed good. Had we come down this trail in another couple of weeks, we could have had blueberries as well. Still under a blue sky, we shouldered our burdens again, and emerged from the valley at Cito Hunting Lodge, which was sporting a newly painted roof.

Deciding to check out the lodge later, the crew pushed on up the trail to Cito through the meadow. Here Bob Warner had directed the rifle and shotgun ranges in another era. All traces of the ranges were gone. Now, it was just a meadow where any activity was created by mule deer and the occasional strutting of wild turkeys.

Cito was perhaps the most changed camp of all. Once the hub of all activity at the Ranch, Cito almost looked like a ghost town. They were expecting a big night though—sixteen groups were scheduled in. That was probably about a quarter of Cito's old capacity. Still, there was one very pleasant surprise waiting at Cito, a young staffer in a class B uniform. I hardly disapproved of the new green activity shirts worn by the staff, but it was refreshing to see the poise and polish alive and well on this young man. I think he was impressed when I told him I thought he was the sharpest looking staffer I had seen so far.

Conservation and rock climbing were Cito's program activities, and therefore the reason for its large staff. We made our appointment for the last morning rock climbing session, and just kicked back until it was our turn. After the rock climbing warm up jollies and program explanation in the meadow, we all single filed it up to Hogback Ridge, or "Steamboat," as some now call it.

There was more rock climbing orientation on the long shelf

just below Hogback's eastern ridgeline. After getting acquainted with the harness, hardhat, and ropes, each Scout took his turn at the base of the wall. To break the ice, a young lady who worked the rock climbing program would yell down to the young climber whose pulse and blood pressure had probably edged up a few notches.

"Hey wild man, what's your name?" she would yell to each novice. Usually, a quick answer of a first name or maybe a nickname followed. However, when she yelled down to Will there was some negotiation between my son and the harness checking counselor. It appeared that the "Will" as one of several diminutives for "William" was not satisfactory. Perhaps there had been a surplus of Wills attempting the wall, and it was time for a change.

"What's your middle name, kid?"

"Don't ask."

"You wanna climb this wall or not? 'Will' just won't work. Now what's your middle name?"

"Which middle name do you want, the first or last one?"

"Huh?"

"I have two middle names, 'Briton' and 'Parks' after my great-grandfather."

"You're 'Briton' kid," the counselor said just as the, "Hey, wild man, what's your name?" routine came down the wall again.

"Briton!"

"Hey Briton, where you from?"

"West Chester."

"Where's that?"

"Near Philadelphia."

"Hey, wild man what do you do?"

"Play lacrosse."

Will had proven to be an adept climber, and had already eaten up most of the pitch. The young lady's repertoire didn't transcend her young charges' extracurricular activities or include further interrogation. I was a little surprised that she didn't ask what lacrosse was since I doubt that it was popular or maybe even known in her native Texas. The Ranch had, of course, changed since I had tried to teach lacrosse to the Beaubien staff so many summers before. I was not to know it on that sunny midday as our backs were to Deer Lake Mesa, but lacrosse was indeed being practiced with a vengeance back in Staff City. With all of our boys safely rapelled from the heights, we started our return journey back to greater metropolitan Cito and lunch.

Yes, spreadables, orange drink, and Cito's two orange kittens. It may not have been lunch with clients at Bookbinders in Philadelphia, but it hit the spot. The boys had some decisions to make. Which Scouts would volunteer to buzz off to Ute Gulch Commissary for our last food pickup, and where would we spend the night? The ultra-reliable Wes Heidel volunteered, and was joined by our two-man soccer team of Aaron and Jeff. The unanimous choice for a next destination was Upper Clarks Fork. Vic had been past it three years before, but it had not made a big impression. What had impressed Vic was that it shaved a couple of miles off the following day's march. We had only been rained on seriously once in our adventure so far. I figured that we were undoubtedly fugitives from the law of averages, and were going to catch our due soon enough. It made sense to be off the heights, in camp, and under nylon when the deluge came.

The request for a change in itinerary was handled expeditiously by Cito's talker. Control Center asked if we were aware that Upper Clarks Fork was a dry camp. This would mean two dry camps in a row, but I figured that nearby Bear Creek was by now probably much more than trickle. We also knew that the spring near Shaefers Pass was running well as of the previous week. After informing him that we were quite aware of the double dryness, we were approved for a night in Upper Clarks Fork. It proved to be a remarkably propitious decision. Our associates, the Sixers, had not yet chosen to amend their itinerary. They later decided to stay in Aspen Springs, a lovely camp between Cito and Ute Gulch.

We decided to meet our food gatherers later in the afternoon down at Cito Hunting Lodge so we had some time on our hands before shoving off. For some this meant catching a snooze at the base of a shady pine. Will had befriended one of Cito's cats, and was engaged in amusing the feline. The cats must have had some impact on the ground squirrel population. There were very few of the rodents in sight. Secretly, I hoped that any of Chubs' descendants had been blessed with the wisdom to spend the summer elsewhere. Dear old Chubs, he was most assuredly enjoying his afterlife in that great granary up in the sky. Maybe he was even looking down at us now in hopes that somebody would drop a cracker crumb for one of his many descendants to enjoy.

We still had some time to kill, so I decided that I would trudge around Cito for the next half hour. The once bustling commissary, probably the largest of any main camp commissaries, was now boarded up, drifting like a ghost ship in the meadow. The camp sites to the north of Cito's staff area were also quiet. The high grass spoke much about how few campers Cito was hosting which, after thinking about it, seemed quite apropos.

Cito had its charms, but the best way to enjoy the Ranch was in the smaller, out of the way trail camps. Clearly, the computerized itineraries made sense. By now, I was poking along the edges of Cito—out where the bears' antics would keep the kids chattering until late at night when I, as a ranger, was desperately interested in sleep. There had been one major improvement at Cito—the wall tents for campers were gone.

After wandering around for about twenty minutes, I rejoined our crew. The hikers were starting to shoulder packs for our downhill hike to Clarks Fork via Cito Hunting Lodge. We had about thirty minutes to wait at the hunting lodge before our commissary hikers arrived. We spent that time looking at the lodge, an original Phillips hunting retreat. As we sat around, it was obvious that the lodge would still be useful as a hunting retreat. The signs of deer were everywhere, and five turkeys were scratching around the meadow at Hogback's base. However, the greatest show of fauna, by far, was put on by the "mini-bears."

I had heard the term "chipmunk cheeks" before as it related to overdeveloped salivary glands. The ground squirrel before us put a new dimension into that term. This ground squirrel had to be a descendant of Chubs; he was built like a buffalo, and had his little cheeks packed almost to the bursting point with food. The effect was comical—the little creature's face was so swollen and heavy that he could barely keep his head off the ground. He had obviously found a nice source of nuts, and wasn't going to be caught wanting when winter came.

Nor would we be found wanting for food on the end of our journey. Jeff, Wes, and Aaron showed up, and we redistributed the two-days worth of food knowing that we probably wouldn't use the last dinner. We planned on substituting lunch for dinner on our last night, and just having a quick, cold breakfast on the last morning since the hike from Tooth Ridge into headquarters was so short. However, for the rest of this day, we would hike at a leisurely pace, and spend some time on the spillway by Cathedral Rock and Cito reservoir. That lake was even more beautiful than I remembered it since all of the recent rains had filled it to capacity.

Overhead, clouds were drifting by, and they issued a few sprinkles that were so gentle that we didn't even think to put on our ponchos. It was clearly just a passing shower since the sky contained only a few scattered clouds. Here and there in the reservoir, a fish would jump. As several ducks alighted on the water, it occurred to me that our adventure was really winding down. Just two more nights on the trail, and it would be over. We kept having such great fortune with the weather. It was almost too good to be true, and our luck would hold for the rest of the trip.

Will Cass after reaching the top of the Tooth of Time

We had left our packs under a tree by a bend in the jeep trail, and would now go through the routine of shouldering the freight. I had taught the boys how much easier it was to help one another with their packs, but we had fallen into a routine of swinging them on by ourselves. With a few grunts, clatters and clangs, creaks and pops, we were ready for the trail again. Clarks Fork was little over a mile away, and it promised to be easy hiking. It turned out to be not so simple due to the wet weather of late. The first half mile was easy hiking through green meadows, but when we turned south, the trail turned into a quagmire. If we'd had any brains we should have bushwhacked it, but instead stuck to the edges of the goo, and made the most of the stepping stones and ruts.

That we had reached Clarks Fork was obvious before seeing any signs of civilization such as a campsite or trail marker. The bear trap was a dead giveaway. The Ranch had changed in some ways, but Clarks Fork and its ursine problems hadn't. Within a few minutes we arrived at the camp. Here I introduced myself as a former near-Director of Clarks Fork, and asked if we could have squatters' rights for a while. We had no intention of cooking dinner at Upper Clarks Fork, but thought it made more sense to cook dinner and clean up at a vacant Clarks Fork campsite. We were welcomed, and told that we could have the first campsite opposite the jeep trail. We had already dropped our packs at the site, so it couldn't have been more convenient. Almost simultaneously, a Lancaster crew drifted in, followed by a horse cavalcade. Oddly enough, I had never seen a horse cavalcade before, and had long since retrenched to my ambivalence toward things equine. However, the idea that one could see as much of the Ranch on horseback in a week as it took us ten days on foot to see was appealing. The best part was that the horse got to enjoy carrying the forty pound pack! Our Lancaster County friends looked none the worse for wear although they confirmed Roger Hoppe's fears that nobody from our expedition had been able to do Baldy.

Dinner was just about done, and it proved to be one of the more appealing creations. The cooks had thrown everything but the pudding into one pot. The result was a combination of turkey noodle something with vegetable beef soup overtones. The pudding and lemon-lime drink neutralized the salt level of the main course, but left us enviously sniffing the aromas from the Clarks Fork chuckwagon dinner program. We were in no real hurry since our final destination for the day could not be much more than a mile away. After dinner, several of us were sitting on a log checking out tired feet, me included.

There had been a few blisters, but luckily, none were debilitating. I had several incipient hot spots, but was pleased that my ancient boots were still up to the task (along with their new Vibram soles). It was so easy to slip back in time as I was soothing my tired dogs at Clarks Fork. This had been Dick Pate's camp in my last year on staff. It was Dick to whom we shipped our surplus food when we heard that Clarks Fork was short on rations. My closest encounter of the bear kind had taken place at Clarks Fork, and it was the Clarks Fork staff that had been so cordial toward itinerant rangers.

The sounds of packs being shouldered broke my daydreams. With the grunt of a sumo wrestler, I swung the aging Kelty aboard, and headed up the trail. The sky was now completely overcast, and a very light rain was starting to fall.

Decisions, decisions—was this going to let up or was it going to be serious enough to require a poncho. Preferring safe to sorry, we put the ponchos on, and then, naturally, the rain stopped. Within twenty minutes we arrived at Upper Clarks Fork, which was a very pleasant camp. Nearby Bear Creek, little more than a trickle in a dry season, was babbling away. There were also several other crews camped along the edges of Upper Clarks Fork's meadow.

Upper Clarks Fork was Philmont camping at its best. There was the gurgle of a nearby creek, soft ground, and a view of tomorrow's climb. While Shaefers Pass was not a piece of cake, we had covered more difficult real estate in our journey, and were not really concerned about the next day's climb. The bear bags were run up, then Vic and I drifted around to the other campsites. We spoke with other advisors in what amounted to a makeshift, traveling coffee hour. We were among Midwesterners that evening since the other groups were from Michigan, Indiana, and Illinois. They had all started their expeditions in the north, had been rained out of their Baldy sidehike, and were fervently hoping for good weather to accompany them to the top of Shaefers and the Tooth. They were not alone in their aspirations.

A review of the map suggested that getting to the top of Shaefers Pass and Peak wouldn't be too difficult. However, as I looked at the Peak that evening from our lovely meadow, I could not help but notice the angle at which my neck was craned

skyward. "Not to worry," I thought, "we've been through worse."
We were up early the next day, and had a hot breakfast. The
sky was burning blue again, and it looked like we were going to
have another good day. With the purified waters of Bear Creek
in our canteens, we were out of Upper Clarks Fork at eight A.M.,
before the other crews had even started breakfast. Within minutes,
we discovered an error. We had spent the night in Lower Upper
Clarks Fork. Just below our trail was another, equally appealing
meadow that had not been used by any crew. I made a mental
note that if I came this way again, we would camp at Upper
Upper Clarks Fork.

Over Bear Creek we hopped, and then got into the ascent of
Shaefers Pass. It was not especially difficult going, and was
simplified by long switchbacks. We paused at the end of one
switchback to watch the antics of some young mule deer. They
were playing some sort of a prancing game. They bounded about
in an almost antelope-like pronking, but had limited their antics
to a small, squared off area. We were so struck by the display
that we started to look for a fence in which we thought they
might have been enclosed. But, there was no fence, and it must
have been a case of some yearlings stretching their legs.

I now became aware of something that was happening to most
of us. I knew it was inevitable, and had often talked to groups
about it when I was a ranger. We were becoming acclimated to
the elevation. While we still needed an occasional breather, we
were stopping less frequently. The irony of it was, the acclimation
usually took place just about the time crews came off the trial,
i.e., just when they didn't really need it anymore. While our
pulmonary capacity was improving, our waistlines were not. Vic
was tough and well muscled, and I weighed less than I did at the
beginning of my ranger summer, and most of the boys were in
good shape if not athletic. Yet we all had lost weight. It was most
obvious when we tightened our pack hip belts. Although we had
lost weight, the loss certainly hadn't slowed us down.

We decided to take a break after reaching the top of the pass. Several of us searched out the spring where the water was running as advertised. Two rows of packs in the campsite atop the pass showed that other groups were in the area. They were obviously crews bound from Crater or Miners Park who were sidehiking the Tooth before heading north. We ran into them on the way up Shaefers Peak. Just once, I'd like to run into somebody coming down a trail I'm ascending and hear those magic words, "It gets real easy," or "You're almost there." This time, we were told how much more we had in front of us, and how torturous the path was. Without many switchbacks, it was hard going, but mercifully short.

We had a leisurely lunch at 11:30 A.M. on the rock slab that marks the top of Shaefers Peak. I never had dwelt much upon Shaefers, and considered it one of the Ranch's lesser heights. The pass was a major north-south corridor, but the peak had clearly been underrated. The views from its summit were spectacular. It provided us with a panorama of the entire south country, Philmont's midlands, and the Baldy country. We relaxed after the morning's exertions knowing that the only climbing ahead was a packless sidehike up the Tooth. This was a wonderful way to end the expedition, especially since we could easily see the trails below us where we had hiked our first two days. The grand views were changing though, and not for the better. The sky immediately above us was still cloudless, but all four quadrants of the horizon were now bordered with cumulonimbus that was rapidly moving toward us. It looked like Beaubien was getting drenched again, and a stormy, grey curtain had descended from Cito Peak to north of Antelope Mesa. Then the thunderclaps came.

"Let's get offa this rock, now!"

We rapidly chugged the last mouthfuls of bug juice, and quickly filled the garbage bags with peanut butter, cracker, and jerky wrappers. The rain hadn't started yet, but we all had our ponchos ready. The trail we were on would take us to a little meadow from which we could climb up the backside of the Tooth. In one sense, this trail was among the most difficult we had encountered due to the many large rocks in the trail. Climbing and then descending, these rocks were beating up more knees than just mine. By now, the rain had become steady, but fortunately was still light. It didn't look like it was going to go away, so we donned the ponchos. It was maddening since we could look off both sides of the big ridge to see some areas of the Ranch that were still awash in sunlight. We could also see other areas getting hit much worse than we were. The trail tracked along the northern edge of the ridge where we could look off toward Cito. Then it would wend along the top where we could look down at Nairn Place and the jeep trail which leads toward Lovers Leap.

At one lookout, the western edge of the massive Tooth became visible. I couldn't agree more when the boys described the Tooth from this angle as "awesome." I wasn't prepared for the gargantuan proportions. Granted, the Tooth isn't exactly in the same league as Yosemite's Half Dome, but it is still overpowering, and even more so from close up. Yet we weren't really close up yet. After a couple more views of the Tooth's western buttress, the trail dipped down, and favored the north side of the ridge. Although the rain had almost ceased, the trail was tougher due to the small boulders. We were, in effect, rock hopping, which was starting to get to my knees. Any concerns about cardiovascular problems had been proven unfounded. The knee-high rocks along this trail were proving to be an orthopedic calamity, however.

My trusty seatstick was worth its weight in gold among these large rocks. It was my security blanket. We now hiked below the ridgeline with a great view to the north toward Webster Lake. It seemed that we'd been hiking for a long time, but we had yet to encounter a trail marker for the sidehike to the top of the Tooth. I was starting to have an overpowering feeling that we had passed the turnoff. Fortunately, we rounded a curve in the trail to find ourselves at a clearing where the sign clearly pointed the way.

It was obvious that my notion of the Tooth sidehike being just a short walk across a ridge was hopelessly naive. The crest looked like a long way up there. The trail, or what passed for a path, led through a field of large boulders to the top, which was less than half a mile away. By now, the sun was burning brightly again, but it was obvious that it wasn't going to stay clear for the rest of the day. We peeled off our packs, and started climbing. The trail was clear for a couple hundred yards, but then it became a matter of each man for himself, picking his way among the boulders. Maybe it was because we had just gotten rid of our packs, but Will and I were really feeling our oats.

The fact that we were really becoming acclimated, and had just chewed down an energy bar, put a new spring into our steps. I was surprised at what a head of steam we had built up. These were mighty boulders we were clambering over—some of them were much taller than my six feet, so care had to be exercised. In what seemed like only minutes, but was probably closer to half an hour, we arrived.

Ned Gold had said there was no better way to finish an expedition than to cap the trip with a climb to the Tooth. We were indeed on the "Summit of Scouting." We had it all to ourselves, and it was obvious that we could have it in fine weather for another half hour at least. We took the obligatory pictures, one of each Scout, and then of the entire crew, and then a special picture of Cass & Son. Hab Butler, our former council president, had been right when he said that going through Philmont with your son was a summit of Scouting. It was especially true on this summit. Each of us then claimed a little perch where we sat alone with our thoughts. Our eyes were sweeping the horizon. Most were thinking about the past ten days, but for me it was a passage of many years.

The years had hardly dimmed the memories of those long ago summers. The Tooth of Time could not have been named more appropriately. Time was the commodity out of which we were running, yet it was the dimension that held so many treasured memories. Seen from the Tooth, there was hardly a feature on the landscape that wouldn't hold a memory for an old ranger. Black Mountain, Trail Peak, the Stockade, Webster Lake, Lovers Leap, Rayado, Stone Wall Pass, Cathedral Rock, and, of course, Staff City, all were out there. Each brought back images of "happy campers" and happy days on staff. While I had been looking backward in time for the past ten days, the Tooth was also a focal point for looking into the future. Would I come back again? Probably. But the interval wouldn't be quite so long next time. More important, I had a growing belief that another Cass would be coming back to the Ranch. Son Will had been talking about returning as a camper, and then maybe as a staff member someday. It was the sort of torch passing that makes Scouting's summits so special, and this one the most exceptional of all.

Epilogue

Sky conditions jolted me back into reality. It looked rough over toward Urraca Mesa, and the wall of clouds to the north was moving ominously closer. We decided to give up the heights, and head for Tooth Ridge Camp. We had now truly reached the top of descent, and our expedition was going to go downhill, quite literally, from here on in. As usual, the descent was not easy, especially through this rockfall, which was not showing any mercy on my already aching knees. Less than a quarter of a mile from where we had dropped our packs, Tooth Ridge Camp was a total surprise. I had been imagining some stony outcropping just big enough to hold three or four crews. What we found was a sprawling area that could easily have held a complete Chester County Council Camporee. Interspersed between the pines and great rock formations were several dozen generously proportioned campsites.

We didn't tarry to admire the real estate. A strong, cold wind came up almost as we pushed the last tent pin into the ground, and the rain hit a few minutes later. There wasn't much thunder, but plenty of water. We had been the first group into camp, which meant that the Sixers, groups from Upper Clarks Fork, and probably other crews bound from Cito and Clarks Fork were really catching it. Being the first onto the trail was paying real dividends. There was nothing to do but hole up in our tents, so I decided to stretch out. Within a few minutes, something unusual happened: I fell asleep. For me to feel drowsy in the day is almost unheard of, but here I was around 3:30 in the afternoon, asleep like a napping cat. Only once did I stir, and that was at some laughter and angry shouting.

Will, Tom, and A.J. were sharing a Timberline Four next to me. They had poked some fun at our Sixer friends who were arriving in the rain after having wisely decided to postpone their Tooth climb until the morning. Crew Eleven's humor, aimed at Crew One's decision to hike in the rain, was not well received. One defiant Sixer marched up to the tent in the downpour and vociferously informed its inhabitants of shortcomings in their characters. I had been the communications merit badge counselor for this young man, and derived some satisfaction in knowing that his verbal skills were utilized to the fullest extent.

The rain passed within a half hour, and the sky went broken which allowed the occasional shaft of sunlight to reach this beautiful campsite. Few camps can match Tooth Ridge for grandeur. The only drawback is that it is a dry camp. That is a minor inconvenience since most crews have lunch for dinner, and then a cold meal for breakfast. The ground at Tooth Ridge is level, the trees are widely spaced, the great rock formations intriguing, and the views from the southern sites are almost as breathtaking as those offered by the Tooth itself.

After the rain stopped, the boys decided it was time to burn off more energy by climbing rocks and playing frisbee. At times like this, I often reflect on the Scouting movement. Here were these kids from suburban Philadelphia grinding their way through mountains when they could have easily stayed at home like some of their couch potato contemporaries. I have always been mildly aggravated by those who poke fun at Boy Scouting. However, I revive my spirits by reminding myself that those who chide Scouts are the ones who are really being short-changed. Here were our Scouts experiencing some real adventure when so many youth back home were limiting their exertions to walking to the nearest video store. Where these kids in Crew Eleven were getting the energy was a mystery to me. I was content to sit on a log and watch the remarkably tame deer that inhabited Tooth Ridge Camp. Eventually tiring of this, I decided it was time to check out this extraordinary camp, tired as I was.

My left knee was showing the effects of the beating it had taken that day, but my trusty seatstick was offsetting the problem nicely. My seatstick was showing definite signs of wear too. Here and there were patches bare of paint, and the toe had been dulled by the constant "clack-clack-clack" as I planted it down on the rocky trails. This day had been a tough one on both the stick and those of us whose knees had any weakness.

The shapes of the rock formations on Tooth Ridge are as fascinating as the stuff of which they are made: dacite porphyry, an igneous volcanic rock that cools on or near the earth's surface. As rangers, we bandied the term "dacite porphyry" about as though we were graduate geologists when we talked to our crews about Philmont's natural history. Most of us, including me, would simply have called it granite had we not been instructed otherwise. To the casual observer, the stuff looks like granite with which it is related only because they are both of igneous origin. Yet of the many rock types at the Ranch, dacite porphyry is the one alone which comprises the Ranch's most popular and enduring formations. It forms the Tooth, Cathedral Rock, Lovers Leap, and the Cimarron Palisades. It would not wear as quickly as many other rocks found on the Ranch, and, that day, the dacite porphyry was responsible for wearing me out, or at least my left knee.

We had all reached that point where the creature comforts of base camp beckoned. I was ready for a shower, hadn't shaved since Cyphers, and was eager for a meal that offered some "mouthability." Our last dinner on the trail would be spreadables, which do not require cooking. We held our debriefing over the cookies that were dessert. Will, Tom, Jeff, Wes and Aaron talked about seeing sunrise from the top of the Tooth. Way back when, I would have been eager to do a sunrise show. This time, I figured that I would watch it from an outcropping at the edge of Tooth Ridge Camp. Anyway, Will didn't need the old man along on every adventure. What he didn't know was that climbing the Tooth in the cold darkness was not my cup of tea. To say that I was completely unconcerned about Will and his friends would be inaccurate. But, they were all fifteen or sixteen years old, Life Scouts closing in on Eagle, and needed the sense of achievement that comes from such an unorthodox climb. Also, they knew their way, having been on the Tooth only a few hours before.

Stirred in my sleep, I awoke around 4:30 A.M. to hear hushed voices and see the flickering of flashlights in the chilly darkness. Our nocturnal climbers were on their way, and I found it difficult to get back to sleep. After catnapping for another hour, I finally crawled out. I found the rest of our crew also emerging from their tents to go down to the camp's southern edge to watch the sunrise. The Sixers joined us. They planned to sidehike the Tooth later in the day after having been rained out the day before. We all took our positions on a jagged rock formation just to the east of the Tooth, which was still cloaked in darkness.

Down below, Nairn Place and Camping Headquarters were well lit up, but completely silent. There were lights in Cimarron, and a faint light off to the southeast that I assumed was Springer. Shortly, Fletcher, Tom Breslin, and John Spangler joined us.

Clever John had enough foresight to bring along his unzipped sleeping bag to use as a comforter for the group. The rock ledge was hard, and the wind cold, but due to John's generosity, the "old Scouts" waited for the sunrise in warm comfort.

Vic had been on the Tooth only once before, and that was a sunrise climb. As day broke, they found that they were above the cloud banks looking down at the undercast. Here and there, Philmont's great peaks gathered shape as they were lit by the spreading light. That sight must have been beautiful in an eerie sort of way, but today Vic would see the more conventional sunrise. It was clear, however, that we had arrived at the rocks a bit early, since it would be another half hour before the sun climbed above the eastern horizon. We were quite unprepared for what was emerging between our position and the horizon. Little glimmers of silver were forming on the prairie as lakes reflected the first rays of light.

One doesn't normally think of the New Mexico prairie as having many lakes, but there they were. This had been a wet year, so the "lakes" (intermittent ponds in reality) were larger than usual. We had passed by only one of Philmont's several permanent, natural lakes on our fourth day. Crater Lake, whose campers and staff were asleep to the southwest, had not been formed by an asteroid, but was the result of water filling in a landslide. Someday, as the result of being filled with silt, it too will become intermittent, and eventually disappear. It was now only a few more minutes before official sunrise, and Camping Headquarters, about two thousand feet below us, was clearly defined.

The few clouds off to the east were putting on quite a show as they went through a series of color shifts. The hues of blue, silver, pink, gold, copper, and red were all parading along the horizon until the first pinprick of burning sunlight climbed over the horizon. It was moving quickly, and its ascent signaled the beginning of another good day. We watched as the sun climbed a few more degrees. We were about to clamber off the rocks when the owner of this piece of real estate showed up. As if to ask what we were doing there, a weasel scampered back and forth, obviously showing some impatience with what we had done to his prospects of a ground squirrel breakfast.

Our breakfast was somewhat leaner and cold. Just as we were opening the breakfast bags, our Tooth climbers arrived. They had clearly had a significant experience that morning. It would be hard to imagine a more quintessential Philmont sunrise than from the Tooth, where the whistling wind was pierced by the call of coyotes a half mile below. Crew Eleven, however, was overtaken by another urge: to get back to civilization. Headquarters wasn't much more than forty-five minutes away. Camp was struck, packs packed, garbage distributed, and we were out of there. Normally, Will and I would have hiked somewhere in the first third of the line, but today we brought up the rear. As we moved out of the pine woods, Will and I purposely slowed our pace to have a few minutes together at the end of this adventure. It had been just as much adventure for me as it had been for him.

Most people view Philmont as a camping experience for youth, which it certainly is. The longer view is that the Ranch is a continuum, a pyramidal, three-tiered experience of which the camper stage is the foundation. I had enjoyed the second stage, that of the staffer. Now I was experiencing what was probably the most rewarding experience, that of being along for the ride as an advisor.

We chatted about Will's first days in Scouting as we hiked along the trail. The past ten days had been almost a carbon copy of his four years in the Boy Scout program as, I suppose, it is for most fifteen year olds. He had some preparation for both experiences, and some confusion laced with a little disappointment in the first days of each.

Overcoming some adversity, whether it was a march in the rain to Beaubien or earning an especially tough merit badge, provided the seed of confidence that grew into enthusiasm. Will and his friends obviously weren't interested in immediately going back on the trail after a shower and cheeseburger at Camping Headquarters. However, they had taken on a difficult challenge, and emerged from it with exactly what Philmont is designed to instill in young people.

We reminisced about past camping trips and the other thunderstorms that always seemed to greet Troop 21 as it arrived at Horseshoe Scout Reservation for summer camp. This great Philmont experience of which we were near the end would go into a special Scouting memory file. Soon, we were hiking past Staff City, and found our fellows starting to unpack their expedition gear before turning it in at the service building. Will and I made the rounds of the security, welcome center and camping offices to handle the details of our last day at Philmont.

While there had been many changes at the Ranch, the priorities of campers and rangers coming off the trail had not changed. Get clean and get some food. The warm shower cleaned away the accumulated trail dust. It also seemed to melt away some of the fatigue that had set in during the last couple of days. Before starting to shave, I took a good look in the mirror. Yes, it was the same person who had come back to headquarters often as a ranger so long ago. The crows' feet hadn't started to set in, and there was probably more spring in my step then. Maybe a good shave, and some cold water in the face would roll a few of the years back.

Feeling like a new man, I was joined by Will and his friends who had snack bar and trading post on their minds. Normally, I would avoid fast food enclaves, but threw caution to the wind this time and thoroughly enjoyed every morsel of a microwave cheeseburger and pizza. I even considered a second trip to the snack bar, but decided that too much real food too quickly might not be advisable. As it turned out, one of our Scouts did overdose on ice cream and spent the afternoon in some discomfort.

Crew 11 had been the first to return, and was the first to get clean. We must have looked like walking recruiting posters to the rest of the Chester County crews that were starting to arrive.

It was obvious that our itinerary #3 had been an inspired choice. Our friends who headed north were showing obvious signs of recent dampness. Immediately after returning crew equipment, our associates from Troop 55 hogged the washing machines to the extent that I thought maybe they had their priorities misaligned. But then, we had the opportunity of washing clothes at Cyphers, and hadn't suffered any significant rain on the trail since day four.

When we were clean and had read letters from home, we had our final debriefing.

"Would you guys like to come back again?" I asked.

They all answered affirmatively. Several wanted to vary the south country trail again, but most wanted to go north, which was absolutely the right choice for a second time around. There weren't any major regrets, although several of us (myself included) would probably come back with a mega-poncho that could cover the hiker and his pack at the same time. We had suffered no injuries, other than a few minor blisters that had not impeded our progress. We had, of course, been well prepared before coming out, and had enjoyed the services of one of Philmont's top rangers.

All of our Scouts had lost several pounds. I figured it was probably five to seven in my case. When some other advisors drifted in, it was clear that the dads had not weathered the heights as well as the lads. Being the first back, we had cleaned ourselves and our clothes by late morning, and were ready for the Villa Philmonte tour. I was looking forward to this. The closest I had ever come to the "big house" was the time Steve Gregory and I walked around it on our way to a dinner at the Training Center. Our boys were weatherwise by now, and took their ponchos along. Their caution was shortly justified. We took the grand tour, which proved to be quite a treat.

Waite Phillips was one of the great success stories where a young man climbs from modest origins to attain great wealth. What was even greater was his philanthropy. Best of all, he lived to an age where he could see how great the size of his gift really was. After the tour, we headed back to our tents in a light rain that shortly ceased.

I had a couple of important stops to make in Camping Headquarters, and the first, with Will in tow, was to the Ranger Office. It had changed dramatically, and now was a much larger affair. I introduced myself to George Bach, an Assistant Chief Ranger who was in charge that day, and said how much we enjoyed having Todd Johnson as our ranger. Will and I were most graciously received, and before I knew it, an old ranger group picture was placed in my hands. I was shortly mumbling the names from that distant summer as my eyes moved along each of the four rows.

There was Joe Martos, Drew Shebay, Bob Kanaga, Hillbilly Ashby, the Cross brothers, and the Hobbs Brothers, Will and Greg. The name "Hobbs" brought an immediate response, which told me that staffing at Philmont had been passed to another generation. At the center of the picture, inevitably, was Mr. Dunn. Several rangers in the room had heard of Mr. Dunn, but knew little about him. I told them of how Mr. Dunn, in the mid 1950s, was quite literally the founder of modern day rangers. I went on to tell them that Mr. Dunn was the Chief Ranger every year until his retirement in the early 1970s, and that even today's rangers are very much in that man's debt.

We ran into our ranger, of course. In my mind's eye, I knew exactly what would happen. Before our paths would converge, a Scout would see him, and dash over to tell him of our great adventure and how valuable his advice and training had been.

"Hey, Will, you guys have a good time? I'll sure bet you did."

That high point of rangerdom had not changed. They couldn't

wait to tell him about the Phillips climb, the fried trout at P.J., and listening to the coyotes from atop a darkened Tooth. Several of our frisbee tossing crew saw the gathering from a distance, dropped everything to rush over, and breathlessly thanked Todd for his help in getting us started. Todd had heard it all before, but it is something rangers never tire of hearing. I was probably just as pleased to hear it all as Todd was.

The next stop was at the Camping Office where I hoped to renew my acquaintance with Dave Bates. This was a Saturday, and Dave, now Director of Program, was out visiting camps, so I just left word to say hello from an erstwhile, fellow staffer. Our time at Philmont was running out, yet we still had two big events left. There was a rumor of buffalo steaks since Saturday evening was supposed to be the big culinary event of the week.

Somebody said that it was just going to be buffalo burgers. Most of our gang were thrilled at the thought of any kind of quarter pounder. Both rumors were ill-founded since fried chicken was the *piece de resistance* for the evening. If there was any disappointment about having chicken instead of steak, it was not at all apparent. To say we consumed the meal with great gusto would be an understatement.

The evening would be capped off with the closing campfire that, based on what we had heard from across the way at our opening campfire, would be a humdinger. It was. Delivered with precision and enthusiasm, our masters of ceremony treated us to eye-watering, sidesplitting humor and music that kept us rapt for the show's duration. The show was so professionally presented that we were certain that the talent before us could probably write their own tickets in the entertainment world. Humorous references to the summer's fickle weather were punctuated by the real thing as thunder and lightning were all too obvious in the north.

But like all good things, the show ended: in this case, with the awarding of expedition flags by crew chiefs. It was a mighty proud moment when Will turned around in the line, gave me the flag, and said thanks to the Old Scout. The evening closed predictably with the singing of "The Philmont Hymn." What was unexpected was the request for any old staffers to come down front and help lead in the singing. It was a nice gesture. Although I hadn't sung the hymn loudly for what seemed like centuries, the rhythm and lyrics came to me as naturally as they had at those distant Beaubien campfires of my past. Although the campfire was breaking up, we weren't finished with the evening's humor. One crew was singing "The Twelve Days of Philmont" on the way back to our tents. The song, a parody of the Christmas carol, recounts a disaster for each day on the trail. It was so wildly humorous that we hoped it would find its place in the campfire proper.

The coyotes were at it again when I woke up at four A.M. I spent the next hour alternately dozing and thinking about the past ten days and summers past. We were scheduled for an early departure after a continental breakfast. With gear packed and heads counted, we were on our way to Denver and the flight home.

Six hours after leaving the Ranch, we were all sitting at the gate waiting for USAir flight 444 to depart for Philadelphia. But two of us would not be going on that flight. The very airplane that was to take our contingent back to Philadelphia had just arrived from that same city, and among the passengers were Sarah and Holly. We extended our vacation by another eight days, and saw more of the southwest, including the Ranch again.

One week after coming off the trail, we were back in Cimarron after enjoying a leisurely southwestern interlude. Will got to see Wheeler Peak at a closer range as well as Baldy and Touch-Me-Not. We stopped for lunch in Cimarron which had changed in a superficial way. Joey's, Lambert's, and Miss Dee's were all gone, and had been replaced by other retail establishments.

The Ranch was winding down, and, even as we were leaving the week before, we had seen several rangers checking out for the season. Cimarron's service station was busy with more staffers refueling for the trip home. Will was visibly excited as we headed up the road to the Ranch. It was all coming back to Sarah, who remembered her visit many summers before. We were going to spend the night at Nairn Place, now a bed and breakfast known as Casa del Gavilan.

Casa del Gavilan is what Jack Nairn had called his home. Nairn was an eastern industrialist (Congoleum flooring) who retired to the Sangre de Cristos and built his fine place years before Waite Phillips came on the scene. Nairn named his place Casa del Gavilan since it was situated on land where hawks nested. The white adobe-pueblo place, with its eighteen inch thick walls, was bought by Waite Phillips in 1939 after he had made his first gift of land to the Boy Scouts. Waite and Genevieve Phillips lived at "the Nairn" for several years before moving to California. Nairn moved to Santa Fe where he died in 1949.

Dick Fellows Photography, Philadelphia

The Cass family before the Return
Bill and Sarah, Will and Holly

As might be expected, the view from Casa del Gavilan is spectacular, and is dominated by the Tooth. After checking in, we headed back for camping headquarters. It being another Saturday, I missed Dave Bates, but introduced myself to Dean Tooley. I learned that *"apres nous la deluge"* pretty well described conditions at the Ranch in the past week. We had hoped to drive down to Abreu, but learned that it was out of the question. We would never make it due to road conditions. Portions of the Ranch had been flooded. It was nothing like the big flood of 1965, but some camps were cut off. We had only to watch returning campers to see that many looked like river rats. We couldn't make it to Abreu this time, but it was a good reason to return to the Ranch in a year or so.

I knew that I wouldn't be driving out of Scouting this time. I would probably be back in a few short years one way or another—maybe as an advisor on a Baldy-bound trip or possibly to the Training Center. The antelope were playing on the prairie as we drove up to Raton. Somehow I had missed seeing them and the buffalo at the Ranch this trip, but figured that finding them would be a nice objective for the next time. How easy it was now to plan another return.

With the flight home, the shift was complete. Now it was business as usual, but there were two exceptions. This time, I had shot many rolls of film. Seeing the slides, and projecting them for Scout troops, would keep Philmont closer than ever. While I knew that I would be back at the Ranch in a year or two, I had made that important first return to my Summit of Scouting. It was more grand than ever with Young Scout along to share the climb.

Suggested Reading

Over the years, many fine books have been written about Philmont, but some, such as Dave Caffey's *Head for the High Country*, are out of print. Those that are in print include:

High Adventure Among the Magic Mountains, by Minor S. Huffman. Filled with the recollections of Philmont's first general manager, this is indispensable reading for anybody interested in Philmont's history and the personalities who shaped its growth.

Philmont, An Illustrated History, by Steve Zimmer and Larry Walker. To call this a "coffee table book" would be misleading. Illustrated with archival and contemporary photography, its well-researched pages are essential for any Scouting library.

Philmont. Larry Murphy's scholarly work documents the history of Philmont and northeastern New Mexico.

Philmont, Where Spirits Soar. Illustrated with breathtaking photography, this book captures both the letter and spirit of Philmont's trails.

Philmont Country. The Department of the Interior's Geological Survey Professional Paper 505 is a thorough, well-illustrated documentation of Philmont's natural history.